Through the
Broken Glass

Through the Broken Glass

AN AUTOBIOGRAPHY

T.N. SESHAN

RUPA

Published by
Rupa Publications India Pvt. Ltd 2023
7/16, Ansari Road, Daryaganj
New Delhi 110002

Sales centres:
Bengaluru Chennai
Hyderabad Jaipur Kathmandu
Kolkata Mumbai Prayagraj

P-ISBN: 978-93-5702-196-8
E-ISBN: 978-93-5702-214-9

Second impression 2023

10 9 8 7 6 5 4 3 2

The moral right of the author has been asserted.

Printed in India

CONTENTS

Introduction   *vii*

1. Early Days   1

2. Start of the Adult Life   7

3. The Moulding Influences of My Pre-Collector Years   19

4. Collector: A Job That Demanded Mission Mode   47

5. A Productive Run-up to the Central Administrative
   Mainstream   66

6. National Service at the Central Secretariat   74

7. Settling Down into the Role of CEC   95

8. The Largest Electoral Exercise in the World   108

9. Impeachment Blues of 1991   132

10. The Second Year at the Commission   152

11. Fight for Effective Autonomy of the ECI   168

12. Two More Commissioners to Share 15 Minutes of Work   189

13. The Mini General Elections: Tangible Improvement   201

14. A Continuum of Reforms: Pressing Hard for the Advantage   208

15. How the Model Code of Conduct Came to Life   229

16. Consolidating the Reforms   245

17. Voter ID Cards: A Pitched Battle for Its Issuance   259

18. Elections and Public Response of Early 1995   277

19. Intense Battle at the Apex of the Judical Karmabhoomi   285

20. The Two-Commissioners Verdict   299

21. The Private Person–Public Persona Conundrum   318

22. The Final Exam and a Kind Recognition   333

23. I Take A Bow   344

And I Look On   350

Acknowledgements   353

Index   355

INTRODUCTION

After I completed my six-year tenure as Chief Election Commissioner (CEC), many friends wanted me to pen down my memories, especially of my years spent working as the CEC. It took me some time to get round to it. I had my doubts whether people would find interest in as mundane and uninteresting a topic as elections. But some friends kept persuading me. At last, Prof. Vishwanath Karad and his son Rahul, pioneers of the MIT World Peace University, Pune, convinced me and helped me find an assistant, making this book a possibility.

During my time in the Indian Administrative Service (IAS), I occupied various positions in both the state and central governments, but no other position offered me as much public exposure as CEC. I remember one late evening in Mumbai when I was entering the Taj Hotel and encountered a group of Gujarati men and women coming out. The group, especially the women, stopped and said among themselves, 'Oh, it is Mr Seshan!' and shook hands with me. They seemed almost thrilled to run into me. This incident stayed in my memory. That those men and women were so excited to meet a CEC, I took it as evidence that we were doing our job well. The chief election officer of Maharashtra confirmed that the proportion of eligible voters who actually voted in Maharashtra—men as well as women—had increased.

The job of a CEC was not only widely appreciated but also one of the more satisfying posts I was destined to hold. The Election Commission of India (ECI) was able to help the administrative set-up hold better and cleaner elections. During my tenure, people became more aware of the importance of elections. The percentage of the voting population rose substantially, be it in villages, towns or cities, and the elections are now viewed differently than they were earlier. The necessity of fulfilling the onerous duty of casting a vote came to be seen with greater seriousness amid the populace—the young and the old, women and men alike. Media coverage of the election process and the involvement of experts in the process increased. Before I held office, Election Day was viewed as a holiday, when hordes would leave their town and city for an outing. But there is better awareness now among voters and they do not mind the queues at the election booths; they even show the indelible ink mark on their finger with pride.

I was in government service for close to four decades before I became the CEC. Comparing this tenure at the IAS with the one at the commission, it would not be way off the mark to check whether I had suffered a radical internal transformation when I took over as the CEC. No, there was no such transformation, there was no radical change in my style of functioning or my personality. The difference was that earlier, I was answerable to others even though I had reached the top of the ladder in my civil service. But as the CEC, I was answerable to none except Parliament, the laws and the courts. I had to abide by the Constitution and the laws, and pursue the goal of executing free and fair elections.

This memoir is an opportunity to look at my life in retrospect. I have tried to present some good and some not-so-good things that happened in my life, starting with my childhood in Palghat in Kerala near the Tamil Nadu border, more than a thousand full moons ago. I have presented some occurrences as witnessed through my own eyes and through the eyes of those who reported the happenings in the press.

Happy reading!

❦

ONE

EARLY DAYS

I have two birthdays. I was born on 15 May 1933 as the sixth child of my parents, after an elder brother and four sisters. My other birthday is 15 December 1932. Here's the story explaining why.

When I was five, my father took me for admission to a missionary school called Basel Evangelical School, where my brother and sisters were studying. Stephen, the headmaster, gave me an admission test. After assessing the papers, he told my father, 'Your son has answered the test so well that we will admit him directly to the third standard.' But then came a problem: I would only have been 13-years-old when I would have completed secondary school and thus would not have been able to get admitted to the intermediate level, where students had to be at least 13 years and six months of age. The solution suggested by the principal was to advance my date of birth.

From that day on, my official date of birth became 15 December 1932. To this day, I get birthday greetings on both 15 December and 15 May.

BIRTH AND EDUCATION

Our family had the tradition of naming kids after their grandparents. My elder brother was named after my paternal grandfather. I was named after my maternal grandfather, Sesha Shastrigal, who was a sub-magistrate. My complete name is Thirunellai Narayana Seshan. The first name comes from the village to which I belong and the second is my father's name.

My father's name was Thirunellai Samibhattar Narayana Iyer or T.S. Narayana Iyer. He completed his intermediate studies and received his first degree in Palghat. He wanted to study law, but he had to work as a tutor at Palghat first to make money. He went to Madras (now Chennai), studied law and returned to Palghat to practise as an advocate. He rented an old house that stood in a sprawling compound full of mango and coconut trees. That was where my siblings and I grew up. Father had a good law practice, and the civil cases provided a good livelihood. In his later years, he acquired large paddy fields and coconut groves, which he sold off with the coming of the communist administration and the land reforms of 1957. We had a reasonably comfortable living. Palghat is, therefore, my place of origin—in the limited sense that I grew up there.

We were called 'Thalayalies'. People of Palghat know both Tamil and Malayalam. Outsiders find it amusing to hear people of Palghat talk. You could call this language 'Thalayalam', a strange mixture of Tamil and Malayalam, exclusive to Palghat Brahmins.

I can recollect only a few things about my mother, Sitalakshmi. She did not keep good health from the time I was four. She always had some health problem or the other; it had something to do with her liver. My album carries photographs of everyone but her; she did not like having her photograph taken.

My brother, Lakshminarayanan, was older than me by 11 years. In my early years, I did not have much of an opportunity to spend time with him. He cracked the IAS in 1946. This batch was called the war services batch because people who had served in the Second World War were inducted into this batch in 1946. But there were many like my brother who had not fought in the war. After him, came my four sisters—Seshambal, Alamelu, Lakshmi and Janaki.

Our house in Palghat was big. Our neighbour's children would come to our house to play. But I rarely did anything vigorously physical; I was lazy about doing any physical work. The games I played were few, and I hardly did any exercise. But I loved to read books. I also listened to music and the news every day. During the Second World War, listening to the news on the BBC and German radio stations was part of my routine.

Amongst my many experiences at school, I cannot forget a lesson my mother taught me. I was in Class 4 at the time. Neither printed nor cyclostyled question papers used to be given to the students back then. Instead, we would report to school half an hour before the examination, and the teacher would read out the questions, which we would write down.

Sleeping late at night has been my habit since childhood. I would spend my time studying; I used to study late into the night during examinations, too. On one occasion, I studied all through the night for an examination and was happy with the answers I had written. I submitted the answer paper to the class teacher and came home.

My sister or my brother would usually go through the question paper once I would return. As always, I handed over my question paper to my sister that day, and her shrill voice stopped me short, 'What?! You have given me the answer paper. Where is the question paper?'

I still remember the shock I endured that day. 'What do I do...? This is the end! I am done for this year... I will have to sit in the same class for another year,' I thought.

I had taken the Bible exam that day. I rushed to my headmaster's place that very night and knocked on his door, with the answer paper in my hand. I admitted my blunder, and sobbed and pleaded that he should accept the answer paper at that time. The headmaster declined because doing so would have been against school policy. He consoled me saying that failing that day's examination would not impact my annual result. I returned home and told my family about what had happened.

My mother said, 'For God's sake, give up the habit of studying late into the night during exams. Stop reading 48 hours before the exam. Do not keep on studying until the last moment.' My mother's advice stuck in my mind; I religiously followed her advice for every examination, including the IAS entrance test.

School as such was no problem for me. The only teacher who everyone feared was the Sanskrit teacher, as he was known to give harsh punishments. He was physically strong, too. But no teacher, including him, ever touched me; I did not give them the chance. To the best of my memory, I never went to school without having done my homework, I never went late and I never considered going to school as a burden. It was a co-education set-up, but we could not interact with girls back then as students do now. Boys and girls would sit separately. As far as I know and remember, I did not have any competitor and I would score the highest in all subjects.

In that phase of our lives, our mother suffered because of bad health and had to be administered medicines daily. The medicines were not the kind that we use today. They used to be mixtures of around 25 ingredients in liquid form. They could not be stored for even two days, as they would get spoiled. We had to purchase these medicines daily. I was tasked to buy those on the way back from school, and this continued for a long time.

Except for buying medicines for my mother, I did not do any significant household chores. By the time I was 10, my father had become a reputed advocate. If anything was to be bought from a shop, just sending a message was enough and the items would be delivered at home. While servants were available all the time, my sisters did other household chores, such as cooking, taking care of our parents, doing regular pooja, etc. There was barely anything left for me to do. If spotted doing any work, my father would advise me to go and study.

I loved to work in the garden though. I drew water from the well in the garden, which was the only hard manual work I ever did. One skill I learnt was cooking. It is common in our community for males to be good cooks, and I excelled in preparing South Indian vegetarian delicacies.

In a nutshell, childhood was all study, no play and little work for me.

AN UNUSUAL FINAL EXAM

In March 1947, we had our Class 10 board examinations. Around 55,000 students appeared for the examinations in the then Madras state.

That year, something extraordinary happened that is no longer extraordinary today. Some leaked question papers were doing the rounds right before the examinations. One would have guessed that someone must have bought them for a handsome amount and then shared them with others. The question papers eventually reached many students.

My friends discussed the matter amongst themselves and everyone wondered whether these question papers were genuine. As usual, I came well-prepared for the exams. On the first day, the seal of the packet was opened before us and the question papers taken out and distributed to the students. The question paper exactly matched the one that was leaked before the exam.

Some students were very happy. But it caused me some pain to think that even though I had struggled hard, the other students who had got the leaked questions would score better than me.

A short while after the exams concluded, the government announced a repeat exam on account of the leak. After two months, fresh exams were conducted, and we had to study for our subjects a second time. There were rumours of leaks again, but they were false.

I scored 490 out of 600 in all the subjects put together and stood first in my school. It was not as easy then as it is today to score 80 or 90 in English, Geography and History.

One vivid memory from those days is that of Mahatma Gandhi's visit. He had first come to Palghat in 1920 and then in 1947, some months before Independence. I distinctly remember that occasion. I was not even 15 then. Gandhiji alighted at the Palghat railway and there was a huge crowd at the station. There was a meeting in the Fort ground at Palghat. Gandhiji gave a speech in the meeting. I too was part of the crowd and listened with great interest. I can never forget that day.

Then came the day every citizen was waiting for. The country's first Independence Day was an experience I cannot forget. There were celebrations all over Palghat. A flag was hoisted in the college, and sweets were distributed. Many public meetings were held. On the one hand, I and people, in general, were happy that India got her independence, but on the other, there was pain as well.

My brother was in Delhi for his IAS training. He and his fellow trainees were sent to the relief camps as incharge. The Hindus who had come from Pakistan were put up there as refugees. The situation was extremely tense. In one camp, some inmates asked for a facility that was denied by the IAS trainees incharge. The trainees were immediately shot by the inmates. They were of the same batch as my brother.

INTERMEDIATE

After receiving my secondary school leaving certificate, I secured admission for the intermediate course at the Government Victoria College in Palghat. I studied Physics, Maths and Chemistry. It was a co-education college. Ideally, the youngest of my sisters, Janaki, should have joined me there. She had studied with me until Class 10 at school. But unfortunately, she was stopped from going to college.

Most students at the college wore dhoti and half-sleeved shirts. During the rainy season in Kerala, it was difficult to ride a bicycle in a dhoti. I presented my case to my father and soon enough started wearing pants and full-sleeved shirts. That made me the only student in those days to do so. I felt euphoric.

When the intermediate exams were held in 1949, the rare occurrence of question paper leaks reared its ugly head once again. I went to the exam hall praying that the question paper should be different from the one that was leaked. To my dismay, it was not. As before, a fresh exam was held, and I scored 750 out of 950, with a perfect score of 450 out of 450 in Physics, Chemistry and Maths combined.

TWO

START OF THE ADULT LIFE

Having scored an impressive 750 out of 950 in the intermediate exams, I was a picture of confidence, waiting for an admission card from one or the other engineering college. It did not arrive. Unfortunately, I was not admitted to any of the other colleges in Madras either. As a last resort, I met Principal Rev. Dr A.J. Boyd of Madras Christian College (MCC), where my brother had studied and had done well. Although there were no seats even in that college, Principal Boyd gave me a chance and enrolled me because of my brother's reputation.

COLLEGE DAYS

I was fortunate enough to have Physics as a subject. However, just after 15 days at the MCC, I got a letter from Anantpur Engineering College (in Andhra Pradesh), saying that I would be granted admission with specialization in civil engineering—a subject not considered a good career choice in those days. A physics honours course at the MCC was a better choice.

At the college, I was taught modern physics by Dr P.S. Srinivasan. He remained a role model for me—a very good and able teacher indeed. I remember his lectures to this date. The day I met him, I decided that if I were to become a teacher, I should teach just like him. The next professor I liked was V. Narasimhan. From teaching tennis to giving academic lessons, he was a master.

Generally, I love learning new subjects. Though astronomy was not one of the subjects in our curriculum, learning about stars filled me with awe. When the sky was clear, I would join Prof. Walter F. Kibble, one of the respected math and statistics professors at MCC, to see the stars through the telescope and learn about them.

When I left Palghat for Madras, it was the first time in my life that I was venturing away from home for studies. Staying in a hostel was also a first for me. The hostel where I stayed was called Selaiyur Hall, the name based on that of a nearby village.

The hostel food was very good. For breakfast, tasty dishes like idli, dosa, poori and upma were served. The coffee, too, was good. Lunchtime would be from 1.00–to 2.00 p.m. Rice, sambar, rasam, two vegetable dishes and appalam would constitute the normal meal. Once a week, on Fridays, there would be a special meal of pulao and sweets.

Students in the hostel had different study habits. Some woke up as early as four in the morning; I never slept before one o'clock in the night. Even now, I read until late into the night.

I was happy believing that I had escaped ragging, as I had joined late, but alas! It was not for long. I was summoned, in due course, to the side of the water tank in the college garden. All the students who had escaped ragging were queued up there with their shirts off.

One by one, each student was dunked in the water tank. Only after getting in did I realize that they had mixed cow dung, black paint and something else in the water. After taking a dip holding my nose, I came out, took a towel and went straight into the bathroom. I struggled in the bath for an hour to get the dirt off my body, and that was all the ragging there was.

I never felt homesick. Both my maternal uncles lived in Madras and had very good jobs. Both my aunts adored me and made me feel welcome. I spent my weekends at my uncles' homes, going there on Fridays after college and returning on Sunday evenings or Monday mornings.

I did not like to bunk college to go to the movies. The monthly average of my visit to the cinemas was one. There were no theatres near my college. One had to go all the way to the city. On an average, out of every 10 movies that I have watched, five have been English, two Tamil and three Hindi. Staying in Tamil Nadu after retirement, I have heard a lot about Tamil cinema. However, I think present-day cinema is all noise. The purpose of going to the movies is enjoyment, but these days, one feels the need to stuff one's ears with cotton. Besides, there are a lot of double-meaning dialogues, and that is something I don't quite like.

Apart from the movies, the other go-to place for enjoyment during my college days was the Marina Beach. But throughout my stay in Madras, I never had the opportunity to go to Marina Beach with friends, for the visits were only with family.

I had, and still have, great passion for cricket. Though I have not played cricket ever, I was deeply interested in the game. In my college years, whenever there would be a test match, I would go to the stadium on all five days; I have watched almost all the matches played in Madras between 1949 and 1955. I have seen great cricketers like Russi Mody and Vijay Hazare at close quarters, and was thrilled on receiving their autographs. Some days, I would watch the game the entire day, sitting in the crowd and not leaving my place even to go to the toilet. With great pride, I remember two of my college classmates who made it to the national team—N. Kannayiram and C.D. Gopinath.

From time to time, our college would conduct workshops where we would pick up skills like carpentry and glassblowing, among others. I liked the latter—the art of blowing air into molten glass to shape it. The practical classes of glassblowing were an important learning experience for me. After seeing my liking for glassblowing, the workshop trainer taught me the nuances of his art. I went on to make glass toys in the shape of cats, tigers and dogs.

I usually went home to Palghat during vacations, but there were times when instead of going to Palghat, I would stay back in Madras to attend music festivals. I have heard live concerts of Ariyakudi Ramanuja Iyengar and Semmangudi Srinivasa Iyer, amongst others. Early in life, during my school years itself, all my sisters learnt Carnatic music. By studying their notes, I, too, had gained some knowledge of music. A teacher used to come home to give violin lessons to two of my youngest sisters. I had learnt to play the violin along with them and practised on the violin my father bought me. I continued practising the violin from 1942 to 1948 until one day, having seen me practise for a long time, my father said, 'You are wasting time practising the violin. When are you going to study?' I then had to put away my violin, only to never touch it again.

Though I am bad at vocals—my voice is terrible—I have a lot of Carnatic music cassettes. Even today, I listen to M.S. Subbulakshmi, Lalgudi Jayaraman, N. Ramani and M. Balamuralikrishna. Amongst the newcomers, I enjoy listening to Sudha Raghunathan, Bombay Jayashree, S.P. Ram, P. Unnikrishnan, Mandolin U. Srinivas, Hyderabad Sisters and Bombay Sisters. The ones I liked a lot, Veenai S. Balachander and Madurai Mani Iyer, passed away some time back.

Although I never played the violin professionally, I gained a considerable knowledge in music. In fact, many people suggested that being so knowledgeable about music, I could give a discourse on the subject in the music festivals held in December. My critique was also invited by newspapers. But I declined all these offers. I can be a good critic; I am confident of that. But I set aside the idea, not wanting any unnecessary hassle.

In the itinerary of our college's annual programme, there would be eight to nine dance performances. I saw performances by Lalitha, Padmini and Kamala, some of the prominent dancers during those times. Seeing their performances during the college events, my interest in dance was awakened. I also purchased several books on Carnatic music. These books keep company to my detective fiction books and are safe in my library even today.

A TIME OF GREAT PERSONAL TRAGEDY

My brother got married in 1950. Fifteen days after the wedding, my mother contracted smallpox. No medication was available for smallpox at that time. If the government learnt that someone was infected, the patient would be removed to an isolation hospital. There was no case of such patients returning home alive. At that time, I was thankfully in Palghat. We nursed our mother at home. I was constantly at my mother's side, looking after her with my aunt's help. We applied pastes of traditional medications, like neem leaf extracts and whatever else was available, on her skin to soothe her pain. We were fortunate that she recovered. We prayed to God with tears of gratitude. However, she developed pneumonia soon after, and no medication could help her. On 30 April 1950, my mother left for the eternal abode. I cannot forget that grief-stricken day.

The day my mother died, another shock was in store for us. At that time, my sister's children were with us in Palghat. The three kids, my youngest sister and I contracted smallpox. I was in the worst shape of all. Crushed neem leaf paste was applied on my body every day. From 30 April to 15 May, the situation remained critical. Fortunately, we all recovered. But those are some of the most worrisome days of my life.

COLLEGE LIFE AS A TEACHER

I wanted to join the IAS, like my brother did. Another reason to study for the IAS entrance exam was that opportunities for carrying out scientific research were not available to me. In those days, science research laboratories were limited in number in comparison to today, when we have a number of research labs run by bodies like the Council of Scientific and Industrial Research, Department of Atomic energy, Department of Space, the Ministry of Defence and many others. In the research labs back then, the intake was a maximum of 10 people per year. When I completed my honours degree in 1952, I did not have the required money to go to Bombay to pursue research.

After I cleared the final examinations in college in 1952, I got a letter from the college principal, offering me a demonstrator's post. My job as a demonstrator was to help students as they worked on their practicals. I was to be a demonstrator in Physics. Could I miss the opportunity of getting an offer immediately after finishing college, that too in the same college where I studied? I accepted the offer without hesitation. Since I had a lecturer above me, I did not have much work.

A few months after joining as a demonstrator, one of the professors retired. The principal offered me a lecturer's post, and I accepted without thinking even for a second. I was new to the job. The college management wanted to make sure that the students did not cause problems and gave me a small class of 15 honours students. I was supposed to teach the same subjects that I had studied, so it was no issue for me. Later on, I started teaching BSc and intermediate students. I was quite friendly with the students. I would start the class by collectively deciding on what they wanted to be taught that day. There was no need for advance preparations for the lessons to be taught the next day.

The Sri Lankan students of the college did well in athletics, boxing and all sporting events. But they were also known for their rowdy behaviour. Though there were no cinema theatres in Tambaram, tent houses were used as makeshift theatres. A gang of students would visit these tent houses every night. They would usually get back to the hostel at around one o'clock in the night, singing aloud and threatening the watchman at the gate.

When I was put in the Bishop Heber Hall as a lecturer, there was an interesting incident. The History professor, Chandran Devanesan, was the warden of the Hall. One day, he said to me, 'Seshan, you usually sleep by one o'clock. Catch those students who return from the cinema late at night.' I had no choice. There was only one entrance to the hostel. I asked the watchman to lock the gate, and I sat in a dark corner. At one o'clock, the gang was back, singing a vulgar song after having watched a movie in one of the tent houses. They started shouting at the watchman and threatened to beat him up if he did not open the gate. I stepped out of the darkness.

'If you want to come inside, write your names on this paper,' I said. Utterly surprised at seeing me emerge from the darkness, they refused to write their names. I started walking off, telling them, 'Then you will all have to stay outside.'

Only after they wrote their names did I allow the students to enter the hostel. There were 20 of them in all, of whom 10 were from Sri Lanka. I handed over the list to the warden. They were made to pay a fine of 50 paise per head.

The following day, they gathered in front of my room and started chanting, 'A self-appointed sub-warden, Seshan!' However, when I came out of my room, I found no one. They were under the impression that I had caught them and given their names to the office on my own volition.

A week after the incident, I was studying, seated on the verandah attached to my bedroom. Suddenly, the lights went out. There was a splashing sound. As I opened the door, I could feel something sticky under my feet, and there was a foul smell. I opened the main door and turned on the electric supply from the main switchboard. I realized that rotten eggs had been thrown into my room through the open grill above the door to my room, and the eggs had splashed all over. Luckily, there was no damage to my books.

I knew who could have done a thing like this. I went straight to the gang's room and said: 'If you think that I wanted to catch you and inform the warden, you are wrong. It was the warden who asked me to do it. I could not talk him out of it and so I did it… Whether you want to accept it or not is your problem.'

I returned to my room. I cleaned the entire space with the help of a servant and gave the bedcover for cleaning. I did not inform the warden about it, but when he heard of it, he asked me why I did not make a formal complaint. 'Only on your instructions did I catch them that night. I have no personal enmity with them. Kindly do not aggravate this matter,' I requested him.

On his part, Principal Boyd was very gentle. All the students loved him. However, he would draw a line when anyone turned up late to his class. He would say, 'You are fined four annas.' If the student had no money on him, he would say, 'I'll give you a loan,' and transfer a four anna coin from his left pocket to his right pocket. He would then say, 'You have paid the fine. Now you can sit in class.'

After the incident involving the eggs, Boyd sent a message asking me to see him. I went to his room with something else in mind. He asked, 'Those students have given you so much pain. Don't you think they deserve some punishment?'

I said, 'No.'

Boyd found out who had done it and called all the students in that group to his room. He then called me and said, 'I am not punishing them, so that they will always remember you.' One of the miscreants wrote me a letter from Sri Lanka 45 years later, when I completed my tenure as the CEC.

IPS OR IAS?

Even as I worked as a lecturer, I kept up my preparations for the IAS. And while I was preparing for the IAS, I also decided to appear for the Indian Police Service (IPS) exam since the syllabus was more or less the same. In those days, the minimum age to be eligible to sit for the IPS examination was 20 years and for IAS, it was 21. When I completed my degree in 1952, I could appear for neither. The reason was that I was under the eligible age at that time.

I appeared for the IPS exam in 1953. There were no preliminary and main exams in those days—only one consolidated exam was conducted. English language, essay writing and general knowledge were the three compulsory papers, with two optional ones. I opted for Physics and British History. The result was out in 1954, and I stood first in India. I could now join the IPS.

Nowadays, if you join as an IPS officer, you can further try for the IAS. If you clear the IAS exams, you become an IAS officer; if not, you continue in the IPS. But that was not the case in those days. There was a law then that if you joined the IPS, you could not sit for the IAS exam. For me, joining the IPS would have meant a disappointment. On this, my father advised me, 'If you have confidence in yourself, prepare for the IAS exam instead of joining the IPS.' My brother told me the same thing. I decided to not join the IPS and continued with my preparation for the IAS.

Many ask me, 'What should we do to be successful in the IAS exam?' First and foremost, your general knowledge should be more than adequate. You should also be well versed in the topics in the optional paper of your choice. Above all, you should have good proficiency in the English language. In the IAS exam, those having a good command over the English language scored very good marks.

There was only one exam for the IAS, just as it was for the IPS. There were five optional ones. I had opted for two in Physics, two in Indian History and one in British History. Of the maximum score of 1,850, 400 marks were allotted to the personal interview.

The written exam was challenging enough, but there was another danger. Only if you scored a minimum of 140 marks in the interview could you pass the IAS exam, no matter how well you scored in the written exam. A lot of people failed because of low marks in the personal interview.

During those days, the interviewing panel would heartlessly give as little as 10 marks in the personal interview. After joining the IAS, I once asked the Union Public Service Commission (UPSC) chairman, 'Why do you give such low marks? What does it mean?'

He replied, 'You can judge a person from the marks. If you get 10 out of 400 marks, the personality is bad. Through the marks, we tell him: Do not sit for the exam again. Even if you clear the written exam, you will definitely not pass in the interview. If you score 120, your personality is considered to be on the margin and you can groom yourself for the next exam. With 300 marks, of course, you have a good personality.'

Nowadays, it is not necessary to obtain separate minimum marks in the personal interview round.

Since I stayed in the college hostel, I got a lot of time to prepare for the IAS exam. In addition, the hostel had an academic environment, which was conducive to studying. As I gave Physics lessons at the college, I was well versed in everything on the syllabus. I had already studied British History. In Indian and British History, there were compulsory questions based on maps. To prepare for such questions, I used a method, wherein, with a piece of chalk, I drew a map of India on the floor in one corner of my room and that of Europe in another. I marked out the extents of the Ashoka dynasty, the Mughal dynasty and other relevant information. Likewise, on the map of Europe, I marked the important places. I practised and memorized these figure-based questions by scanning the maps in the room whenever I would get the chance.

I bought and read many reference books and studied old IAS question papers. I learnt one thing from this: Year after year, there were stereotyped question papers, only the presentation was different. I moulded myself according to this. I wrote the exam and was pretty much satisfied with the written part. I was confident that I would pass the IAS exam successfully.

I kept on waiting, but received no news regarding the personal interview. When all the other candidates I knew were done with their personal interviews, I was left heartbroken.

'I am doomed,' I thought. 'I could have joined the IPS as my friends and relatives had advised.' Since the opportunity was lost, my spirit was broken. At last, I wrote a letter to the UPSC asking why they did not call me. Was it because I got low marks or because they thought that I had joined the IPS? I wrote that I had not joined the IPS and that they could verify the fact because I was still sitting idle.

After a few days, I got the interview call letter from the UPSC and felt greatly relieved. The last day for personal interviews was 9 February 1955. The interview was held in Delhi, and I knew no one there personally, neither friends nor relatives. I did not know where to stay.

'It will be bitterly cold in Delhi. Take proper clothes,' my friends advised me. Madras people don't need robust winter clothes in Madras, as it is never so cold here. So, wearing the best I had, which was a suit, I went to Delhi by the Grand Trunk Express. Things were bad from the moment I got off at Delhi. Until then, I had not seen such a harsh weather; the suit was utterly inadequate. I managed with some help from A.P. Venkateshwaran, my brother's friend who was working with the Ministry of Foreign Affairs. I stayed with him at the Constitution Club.

I attended the personal interview without any fear. If I remember correctly, there were five persons on the interview panel, which was headed by R.N. Banerjee. Both of Banerjee's wrists were adorned by watches. He took pleasure in attacking people with his questions. It would be the end of a confused person if Banerjee clashed with him. But he did not ask me anything like that. To me, he simply asked, 'You have been working as a lecturer, why did you choose to join the IAS?'

'The lecturer's salary is just ₹150, so I have come here,' I answered.

'Can't you manage on ₹150?' he asked me.

'If I am alone, there is no problem. After marriage, it will be very difficult to manage on that salary,' I replied.

Having given the personal interview, I left for Madras in the evening on the same day. I had effectively stayed in Delhi for just 48 hours. As I was sitting in the Grand Trunk Express, the results were declared. However, I continued to be in the dark about the results as I travelled on the train for close to two days.

I was welcomed by my brother the moment I got off the train at that Madras Central Station. 'Day before yesterday, the result was announced and you have made it.'

The moment I heard this, I felt as if a heavy burden was lifted off my shoulders. Some people had even called me mad for having studied for the IAS after passing the IPS exam. 'I can go to them now and flash it to them that I have passed the IAS exams,' I thought. I was euphoric—dancing with happiness.

Many people think that I stood first in the IAS exams that year, but I didn't. I secured the sixth or seventh rank, I do not remember clearly now. Sanjeev Guhan was the one who stood first. Maths was the subject of his choice, and he scored cent per cent marks in it. In Physics, however, cent per cent marks were never given; as a result, I got only 180 marks out of 200. This is by no means an attempt to belittle Guhan; he was a great intellectual.

Generally, along with the marks obtained in the written exam and personal interview, the marks obtained during training were also taken into account while announcing the final rankings. Getting good marks in the exam but low marks in the training would push the ranking down. Eventually, when the training was over, I had climbed to the second position. But Guhan was always first.

TO JOIN IAS OR IFS?

There is a general impression that people who are ranked high in the IAS and Indian Foreign Service (IFS) entrance exam face a dilemma as to which of the two should they join. The IFS is a more glamourous job. One can travel around the world. But everyone would not be posted to London or Washington. If one is posted in Latin America or in a corner of the African continent, life could be uncomfortable, staying far away from one's family. The children of IFS officers have to change schools and colleges. Then there is the possibility of being separated from one's culture. When it comes to the IAS, one can do good for the masses directly. In my opinion, each job has its advantages and disadvantages.

An analysis of the IAS merit list of today would reveal that a huge percentage of the successful candidates are North Indians. Not many South Indians make it—much unlike my time. We can attribute this to many reasons. Many South Indian job seekers now prefer engineering, medicine or information techology. Some are discouraged by the belief that there is a lot of political interference in the IAS. 'Why face this unnecessary hardship,' they think and cross out the option of joining administrative services. The lower pass percentage of South Indians in the present civil services examination is also an account of their non-proficiency in English. Until two or three decades ago, South Indians took pride in their ability to write and speak good English, but the story is not the same any more today.

THREE

THE MOULDING INFLUENCES OF
MY PRE-COLLECTOR YEARS

With the results of the IAS exam for the year 1955 being announced, it was time to say goodbye to Madras. The academic year had also come to an end. Everyone at the MCC was happy that I had cleared the IAS exam. In April, I bid farewell to the principal and to the professors, and left for Delhi once again, this time for my IAS training.

BASIC TRAINING

The training for our IAS batch commenced on 25 April 1955. In those days, unlike today, it did not take place at Mussoorie but in Delhi. Our training was held at the Metcalfe House situated in the old Civil Lines. This building also housed our hostel, which consisted of 44 rooms in four rows. There were 49 of us in our batch. In addition, there was one person from the previous batch and 10 IFS trainees.

The principal of the IAS Training College had an office in the main building of Metcalfe House. On one side of the office was a discussion hall and on the other, a canteen hall. A proposal was floated at the time for a new building in Delhi. This would also make it convenient to arrange regular speeches of senior officers in Delhi. A new building was constructed in 1960, but even before it was inaugurated, some questioned its need and recommended giving it to a college. Later, this building housed the Jawaharlal Nehru University.

The then Union home minister Govind Ballabh Pant suggested that the IAS training centre be set up in Mussoorie in Uttar Pradesh (now in Uttarakhand): 'It would be good for the IAS trainees and it would be good for that place, too.' Thus, the IAS training shifted from the old building in Delhi to the ones in Mussoorie after 1959.

However, the move to Mussoorie was gradual; my batch trained at Delhi itself, as mentioned earlier. For the first six months, the IAS and IFS trainees underwent training together. Among the IAS trainees, there were two women and one IFS woman trainee.

Physical training was usually conducted on the lawn opposite our hostel at six in the morning. A retired military havaldar major was our trainer. Three days a week, we were taught horse riding. The horses belonged to the Delhi Police and the training was either conducted at the Delhi race course grounds or at the Delhi Police Lines.

It was a dream for me to sit on horseback, and I thoroughly enjoyed it. Training would start on cold winter mornings. In all likelihood, the horses must have been wondering why we disturbed them early on those cold winter mornings. Each horse had its own personality and could be unpredictable.

Equestrian training had its pitfalls; almost all of us fell off the horses during training. Many from my batch were injured in the course of the training. Once, one trainee was violently thrown off a horse and had to spend a long time in bed with a fractured leg. I was not an ace jockey, but by God's grace, I never fell down from a saddle.

Among my classmates, I had great admiration for Vedanarayanan. He would make a dash for the biggest animal around. He would not go through the stages of handling a horse: walk, trot, canter and finally gallop. He would get on to a horse and gallop straight away.

When I entered the service, horses were no longer required in the field. However, horse riding was not dropped from the list of skills an administrative officer had to learn. And, it was rightly so. The reason is that riding inspires the confidence to face every situation. Those without confidence are thrown off by the horse. The horse has an uncanny sense of detecting a rider's nervousness. One thing the horse never tolerates is timidity, and timidity is a quality that can make life miserable for a civil servant. For the civil servant, there is a considerable likeness between riding a horse and tackling a difficult situation. Just as the horse is more powerful than the rider, a politician is much more powerful than the civil servant. But the politician is not necessarily more intelligent. When a civil servant works with powerful and undisciplined politicians, he better be in possession of himself and not reveal even a trace of diffidence. I have always been cautious and firm whether dealing with an animal or a human being. It is not that I distrust people's decision-making process; rather, I do not like being thrown off.

The principal of the IAS Training College in Delhi, K. Radhakrishnan, who hailed from Madras, was an Indian Civil Service (ICS) officer from the Madhya Pradesh cadre. He taught general administration and politics, but did not come to the class very often. The vice-principal was R.B. Vaghaiwala, from the Assam cadre of the ICS. He took classes very often. Pathak, a district and sessions judge from Madhya Pradesh, came to Delhi to teach us civil and criminal law.

Besides classroom lessons, the training included a lot of travel. A month into the training, a group of trainees, including me, was sent to Happy Valley in Shillong for a training attachment with the army, while another group went to Kashmir. As IAS officers, we had to be familiar with the working of the armed forces. We received military training, which entailed going to the rifle range at 5.45 in the morning.

The training in Delhi lasted one year, followed by another year of field training in the state of probable posting. Today, the trainees undergo six months of class training at the academy, followed by one year of training in the state, and another six months of class training. Besides these, they are taught yoga, management and other subjects. It seems to be a better programme.

In the hostel at Metcalfe House, I stayed in room no. 43, right next to a small shop that sold blades, stationery and other such items. It was owned and run by Hari, who also taught driving. Hari had an old Fiat car for this purpose and charged ₹150 from anyone who wanted to learn driving. Just like horseback riding, it was almost mandatory for all trainees to learn how to drive a car. I learnt driving from him. As of now, Hari's son owns a shop at Mussoorie outside the Lal Bahadur Shastri National Academy of Administration premises and to the best of my knowledge, is doing well, as there is no other shop nearby.

As part of the IAS training, it was a norm for the trainees to meet the Prime Minister (PM) once during the training. Jawaharlal Nehru was the PM while I was undergoing training, and I was eagerly waiting to see him. Nehru could barely say hello to everyone, as there were 50 of us who met him; he did not have the time to speak to each of us individually. I was very disappointed that I could not interact with him.

Our training in Delhi ended in March 1956, and I returned to Madras after the exams. K. Kamaraj was the chief minister (CM) of Tamil Nadu. It was usual for IAS officers appointed to Madras to meet the CM. I could speak to him only for two minutes during which he asked about my place of origin and posting. When I took charge as assistant collector (training) in the last week of April 1956 in Coimbatore, the Madras government ministry was a small one. In all, there were eight ministers. In those times, Kamaraj visited Coimbatore very often. He would ask me with great affection, 'What did you learn, my dear man? What are you doing now?'

Assistant collectors under training would be attached to a village officer and were expected to work with that official. One had to eventually pass a written examination on revenue matters. The syllabus comprised the process of revenue collection in a village, how accounts were maintained and other related matters. Only on passing the exam could we get our next posting.

I was to train with a village officer in Ikkaraibooluvampatti, 20 km from Coimbatore. There was no means of transport easily available in the area. Though I was authorized government transportation to visit villages, my father bought me a brand new car. I rented a house near the race course, got minimal furniture and was fortunate to get Narayanan, my brother's cook. During my posting in Ikkaraibooluvampatti, I would begin each day by having breakfast, packing my lunch and leaving home by car or bicycle, depending on the condition of the roads.

The villagers would gather on seeing my car coming from a distance.

An assistant collector, besides being trained in revenue matters, also received training on how to handle criminal cases. One learnt about all the aspects of handling a case: sending a warrant, collecting documents, recording witness statements and then writing the order. The judge would supervise how the cases were conducted and how they were disposed of. Except one or two theft cases, I mostly got prohibition cases. There was a ban on liquor at that time, and so there were plenty of prohibition violation cases.

An unusual case was a firecracker accident. During Diwali festivities, a person had set off a firecracker while covering it with a tin box. He went ahead despite being warned by bystanders. When the cracker burst, the tin broke into pieces and one of the pieces cut the veins in the neck of a child standing nearby. Owing to the grievous nature of the injury, the child unfortunately died. As a result, I gave a year's imprisonment to the accused.

As part of the training, we were also sent for short attachments with other officers in administration—for instance, 15 days with the superintendent of police (SP), 15 days with the executive engineer, some days with the block development officers. In the process, we got practical experience through on-the-job training. As one learnt the ropes, one learnt how to deal with the people, too.

There is always a rivalry between the IAS and IPS officers as to who is superior. But when I was attached at Coimbatore, the then SP treated me as a son and taught me all about police work.

People say that Tamil is the only language used in the conduct of government business in Tamil Nadu. But even now, in some villages, the revenue records use only Urdu and Persian words. I came across these words when I went to Ikkaraibooluvampatti. Emperor Sher Shah Suri had brought about many reforms in revenue management, all of which are reflected in the records. The words used in his time continue to be used to this day. Surveying of the land goes by the term 'azmoish', which is an Urdu term meaning assessment. The village pond is annually desilted or cleared of algae by the people of the village. This practice is called *khudi-maramath* in Urdu, meaning self-refurbishing. The term has been altered to *kudimaramath* in Tamil. The annual discussions to settle the revenue dues pertaining to each village are called *jamabandhi*, which is also an Urdu–Persian word. As mentioned in the revenue records, a well with no water is known by the Persian term *'nadurust'* (out of order, indicating need of repair).

Usually, the assistant collectors who were on training were not authorized to write anything in the official files. My collector, Joseph, permitted me to go through the files, so that I would know what was happening. Sometimes, he would ask me, 'You know a file came in yesterday. What was important in it?' I applied this same method of teaching when I taught my trainees once I became a collector. The trainees had my permission to come to my house at any time. They could walk into my dining room and dine with me, too.

My training as assistant collector was completed in March 1957. General elections were due at that time. Both Parliament and assembly elections were to be held simultaneously. Apprehensive that the new assistant collectors might make mistakes during the elections, our training period was extended by a month and a half.

Joseph decided that my time would be put to best use if I assisted him in election work. He had a condition: 'All files connected with the elections should come to me only after you have gone through them.' As we got busy, Joseph told me grimly, 'Get started. I will hold you responsible if anything goes wrong with the election work.'

I barely had any interest in elections in those days. The clash of ideologies that competed for power hardly thrilled me. However, I had no doubt about Joseph's seriousness and knew that he would hold me responsible if anything was to go wrong. I tried to learn all that was possible to learn about elections in six weeks.

In six weeks, I read and internalized all the rules pertaining to elections applicable at that time. This became the foundation for my later work as the CEC. Most of the rules and regulations of those days, 90 per cent or more, are followed to this day. From the announcement of elections to the announcement of the results, the work today is more or less the same as in those days.

Coimbatore district has three parliamentary seats. I still remember that C. Subramaniam contested from the Pollachi area. On the day of polling, there was a huge storm. I received a word that a school building where balloting was to take place had collapsed. When I reached the spot, there was panic among the voting staff. But luckily, the rains had abated. I asked the villagers to provide a number of charpoys and sheets. In a short while, we were able to erect an enclosed space that served as the polling station.

Some 35 years on, when I would become the CEC, these learnings would matter to me.

MY FIRST ASSIGNMENT

After completing our training as an assistant collector, we had to appear for two exams, on successful completion of which we would be appointed as sub-collector. I cleared both the exams before I finished my training and was given the designation of sub-collector (training). This post had not been given to anyone before me; I was the first to get this special designation with the term 'training' inserted in it. Once elections got over, I was appointed as sub-collector in Dindigul. I joined in the first week of May 1957. This was my first job with an independent charge. My brother had also served in Dindigul between 1950 and 1952 as sub-collector.

Madurai was one big district then; it has been divided now. Almost half of Madurai district came under Dindigul division. Dindigul town was big in terms of both geographical area and population. In those days, Dindigul had a notorious reputation for water storage—so much so that a recalcitrant young girl would be 'threatened' with marriage to a Dindigul groom.

My first encounter with a minister in an official capacity happened shortly after I joined as a sub-collector in 1957. Some time prior to that, there was a complaint about a village headman who had been putting his hand in the till. One evening, when I was standing outside my house, Narayana Pillai, the 53-year-old tehsildar of Palani taluk and a man of much experience, walked up to me and handed me a paper. It read: 'The revenue of ₹3,000, collected against "thakkavi loan"[1], which had to be deposited in the government account, has been misappropriated by the village officer.'

Without wasting a moment, I wrote in the margin of the same paper: 'Suspend, charge sheet and begin criminal proceedings.' This was the correct response as recommended in the books that I had studied. Handing the paper back to the tehsildar, I said, 'Hand it over in my office and take appropriate orders from there.'

The office was a short walk from my house. It was the height of summer, and there was not a single tree in that compound. Pillai showed remarkable reluctance to walk the distance to lodge the official papers and start proceedings against the wrongdoer. When he remained standing before me, I got impatient and asked, 'Why don't you take the paper to the office?'

He replied, 'Sir, there might be problems. The sub-collector should not act in haste like this. Please do think over the order.'

'Why would there be a problem if I order action against a village officer who has mishandled government money?' I asked, expressing my ire to the tehsildar.

'Is the sub-collector aware that the village officer's wife is the head of the Palani taluk Congress committee? So, if we were able to take action against him, the higher political echelons might not like it; they would get angry,' he told me with great hesitation.

'Don't worry, just do what I have asked you to do,' I told the tehsildar emphatically.

That night, the village officer was suspended and arrested by the police. The problem started 48 hours after the suspension. A senior leader came from Madurai to meet me at my office. He was a close friend of Kamaraj and was the Madurai district party head.

He started with a threat of hounding me and implored me to take the case back, as it would tarnish the image of the party, but I firmly stood my ground, refusing to take back the case.

---

[1]Thakkavi loans were short-term loans given to peasants by governing authorities for crisis management or developmental activities. Such loans even existed during the Delhi Sultanate times. A variant of this was in vogue when the author was a sub-collector.

'Oh, I know what is to be done with you. I will treat you the way you should be treated,' he threatened me before leaving.

He went straight to see the Madurai collector, Balasubramaniam. He told the collector what happened and requested him to direct me to have the police case withdrawn. The collector answered in a plain simple word: 'No.'

Vexed, the leader then appealed to the revenue board. After reading the appeal, the board dismissed it. A week after this incident, ministers P. Kakkan and V. Ramaiah were to visit Dindigul. Kakkan hailed from Melur of Madurai district. Home, police, revenue, public works, social welfare and welfare of scheduled castes departments were under him. Ramaiah was from Trichy. He had Electricity and several other departments under his control.

The ministers were to arrive by the Trivandrum Express at seven in the morning, and arrangements were made for their reception. It had only been a month since elections, and they were on a tour to thank the voters who had voted the party back to power, though the pretext was that they were monitoring the development work.

After having breakfast, the ministers proceeded to the nearby villages by car. In the back of the car, the ministers were seated on either side and I sat between them.

About 15 minutes had passed when Kakkan looked at me and asked, 'Mr Sub-Collector, why are you working against the Congress?'

'No, Sir. I have not done anything against the Congress or for the Congress,' I answered.

'If that is so, would it not have been enough for you to take departmental action against the village officer of Kalayamputhur? Why did you register a police case? I am the minister incharge of police and revenue. I instruct you to withdraw the case.'

'It is true that you are the minister. But to take back the police case, you need to send me a written order after you go back to Madras. I will definitely take back the case then,' I told him quietly.

'What I say is not enough?' he shouted.

'Not enough, Sir,' I replied.

Kakkan asked the driver to stop the car and asked me to get out.

Without a murmur or protest, I got out of the car. I was stranded in the middle of nowhere and was standing under a tree on a hot sunny day, all suited and booted, until I could figure out my next course of action.

I eventually reached my office in my old departmental transport. I borrowed a spanking new jeep from the executive engineer there and went ahead of the politicians to reach the villages to ensure that their programmes went off without a hitch. I saw to it that the mics were working and that the police were around for crowd control.

The last programme was to be held in Vedasandur. It was a communist stronghold, with a staunch communist as the local Member of the Legislative Assembly (MLA). The ministers' address was scheduled for 8.00 p.m. I realized that a Congress minister saying anything objectionable in the communist area could cause trouble. Therefore, I called the tehsildar.

'This is the Opposition's place. If the ministers speak in an offensive manner or criticize people for not voting for their party, there would definitely be some reaction, or more likely a disruption, which we should be ready to tackle,' I said. The disruption I was referring to was a common tactic. Those who came from the villages carried rats with them. They would ensure that the fuse is suddenly blown off. Once it got dark, they would let out the rats close to where the women were seated and would shout 'snake, snake'. People would run helter-skelter and leave the venue out of fear.

Having warned the tehsildar of the possibility of such an occurrence, I asked him to connect the minister's mic to a car battery: 'Even if the electricity is cut off, the mike would continue to work. Thus, the minister can speak without hindrance. Similarly, keep all our jeeps parked opposite to the meeting place and ask the drivers to be seated inside. If electricity goes off, tell them to switch on the jeep lights immediately.'

Even though the assembly was regarding an official purpose, Kakkan spoke of politics: 'You did not vote for the Congress; you have cast your vote in favour of the Opposition. You will not benefit from this; Congress is the big party in India. In spite of this, you have given your votes to a small party.'

As the minister was thus taking the voters to task, there was a loud bang and the electricity went off. There was darkness everywhere, and sure enough, someone yelled, 'Snake... snake...'

But as already arranged, the jeep lights came on and the mic continued to function with the help of the battery. After the meeting was over and the gathering had dispersed, Kakkan went straight to the tehsildar and commended him on all the pre-arrangements made.

'Even my mic was functioning. And I got light from the jeeps. You have acted intelligently,' he said.

'Whatever arrangements you have seen were not done by me. They were arranged by the sub-collector who is sitting there in the jeep,' the tehsildar replied.

Kakkan was surprised. He came to the jeep and asked me, 'Why didn't you come to the dais?'

I replied, 'You had asked me to leave the car. After that, why would I come to the dais?'

'If that is how you felt, why did you follow me?' he asked.

'That's my duty,' I said.

'I asked you to get out of the car because I was upset. However, it was not necessary to stay away from the dais,' he said in a subdued tone.

That very night, he went to Dindigul and then returned to Madras. Three days after this incident, CM Kamaraj came to Dindigul. I accompanied the collector and the SP to the station to receive the CM. He was accompanied by his cabinet minister Kakkan and Mrs Lourdhammal Simon, minister for local administration. He was welcomed with a garland by the collector, and I was standing behind the latter.

Moving ahead, Kamaraj called for me, 'Seshan, come here.' I complied.

'I heard Kakkan treated you badly?' asked Kamaraj.

'Nothing like that happened, Sir,' I said.

'What happened that day has come to me in a police report,' he said.

The ministers standing nearby were watching all this. Kamaraj advised Kakkan loudly, 'It is not good either for you or for me to ill-treat the officers in this manner. If the officers do any wrong, call them individually and tell them. Do not humiliate them before others.' He went on, 'You are the minister for revenue. Ask the aggrieved party to place their appeal with the government. For this, why did you have to offload the sub-collector from the car? You must learn the basics of politics. If government officers are humiliated, the government is humiliated. If he made a mistake, you should have informed me.' Having said this, Kamaraj got into the car and left.

SOME MEMORABLE EXPERIENCES

Another event that proved to be a major learning experience took place around the same time as the aforementioned incident. It instilled in me a strong belief that negotiations can solve many problems.

In 1957, the monsoon rains had failed. There was very little water in the Vaigai, and so water was rationed. It was released on alternate days from the reservoir. I got an SOS message from the office one day: 'In Nilakottai village, a mob has gathered and is trying to break the iron gate to open the canal. Please come immediately.'

Since I started off immediately, I did not take along a sufficiently strong police force. I had only four policemen and some revenue officers with me. It occurred to me that noticing the police might enrage the villagers and worsen the situation. So, I left the police personnel at a distance and reached the scene with just the revenue officials. I found around a thousand people assembled at the site. It was the first time in my life that I had confronted such a huge and hostile crowd.

'We don't want to talk. Open the canal,' they shouted.

Somehow, I convinced them to come to a nearby tree, under which some sat and some stood. I started to explain the official position, 'I can only open the sluice if water is available in sufficient quantity. How can I open it when there is not enough water? Moreover, the water has to go further down to Melur and Nattam, too. Please understand this.'

Talks went on in this fashion for three hours under the shade of the tree. Finally, they accepted what I was trying to convince them for.

'Can you assure us of supply a water on alternate days at least and that too continuously without any stoppage?' they asked me again and again. Only after having received assurance to that effect did they disperse and return to their homes. And I heaved a sigh of relief.

Another incident I remember is the then PM Nehru's visit to Gandhigram, which is 7 km from Dindigul towards Madurai. This flourishing village had been established on either side of the national highway by Dr Soundaram Ramachandran and her husband Dr G. Ramachandran. It was a relatively new establishment, just over a year old. Towards the end of 1957, there was a proposal that the the PM should visit the village.

At that time, there was unrest in the neighbouring Ramanathapuram district because Pasumpon Muthuramalinga Thevar, the leader of the Thevar community, had been arrested, the reason being a confrontation between Hindus and Harijans.[2] Though this had happened in Ramanathapuram district, people belonging to the same groups lived in Madurai, and some areas under my charge were also in a state of unrest.

There were many events scheduled for Nehru at Gandhigram on the day of his visit, and it was to be a day-long engagement. After the day's programme, he was supposed to go back to Madurai. Collector Balasubramanian, SP Lakshmi Narayanan and I went to Gandhigram to discuss the arrangements with Dr G. Ramachandran.

Ramachandran was a strict Gandhian. He described the plan, 'In the morning, Nehru will speak in a meeting here. After that, he will rest in the room opposite the meeting place. From there, he will walk down and cross the highway to reach the part of the village on the other side.' He wanted to take Nehru across the highway on foot.

'Making the Prime Minister walk in the present state of unrest is an avoidable headache,' I said.

Ramachandran instantly flew into rage. 'This person is saying that the Prime Minister is a headache. I will not speak to him anymore,' he shouted.

Balasubramanian immediately intervened and said, 'Sir, he did not

---

[2]Rajasekaran, Ilangovan, 'Memories of Mudukulathur', *Frontline*, 14 February 2018, https://bit.ly/3QfdZzt. Accessed on 28 February 2023.

call the Prime Minister a headache. He only said that taking the Prime Minister on foot is a headache. There is communal tension in this area, and we have to be careful.'

Ramachandran was not pacified. But when the visit happened, the PM crossed the highway by jeep at Gandhigram. Ramachandran continued to be a nuisance during the entire visit, but the SP, Col. P.S. Viswanathan, managed to run things smoothly. For me, it was a memorable visit by a PM who inquired about the progress of various government programmes and listened to all responses very patiently.

MARRIAGE: THAT HOROSCOPE AGAIN!

While I was posted at Dindigul, my father started searching for a bride for me. He knew how to read horoscopes, and I would help him match the ones he would bring, whether it was for me or my sisters. I was introduced to the basics of astrology by my father. After I would be done with the basic matching, he would further check the horoscopes. The shortlisted ones would then be taken to a 'professional astrologer'.

As a youngster, I learnt a lot about astrology while matching horoscope for my sisters. The learning did not stop there—my fascination for the subject kept me at it at every opportunity I got. More than a decade later, when I became an IAS trainee, I had an opportunity to visit an old library in Tanjavur, which housed a treasure trove of rare Sanskrit texts on astrology. My reading until then was limited to what was available in a small bookstall near my home in Palghat. Reading was required to strengthen the foundation I had already built. As I pored over all those horoscopes, I started trying to decipher the language of the stars.

There was one horoscope that I avoided analysing—my own.

Coming back to the topic of my marriage, when I took independent charge in my first assignment, I had, kind of, 'arrived' and was ready for marriage. My father started searching for a bride for me and, being an expert at matching horoscopes, became deeply absorbed in it.

I was still a sub-collector at Dindigul when my father sent me a horoscope proposing a possible alliance. It was of Jayalakshmi, a girl from Bangalore (now Bengaluru). It came with a caution from my father that she might not bear children if her horoscope was right. It was discarded after a cursory look. Then another horoscope came with the same caution, and this happened again and again.

Then I took a look at my own horoscope. It had all the indications that I would rise high in stature, that I would have mastery over speech, that my word of command would find instant compliance, that I would have many enemies but they would not vanquish me. But there was one unpleasant indication—I might not have children.

When I thought it over, one thing became clear. If it was not in my stars to have children, what was the point of looking for a bride who was destined to have children? By astrological logic, my wife could bear children. But by rational interference, that would happen only if she was unfaithful. My father admonished me when I said this to him in a remark.

One day, my father gave me a horoscope of a girl from Bangalore along with her photograph. That was the photograph of my future wife, Jaya. What was great about it was that it was the same horoscope I had seen the year before in Dindigul.

On 30 December 1958, my father and I went to Bangalore to meet her. I told my father that going to see the girl was only a formality. At that time, my brother was a collector at Coimbatore. He and his wife, too, came to Bangalore.

I was told that Jaya had completed BSc at that time, and she played the veena very well. They told me I can ask the girl any question, but I refrained from doing so. When we left, we did not tell them whether we liked the girl. My father told them that we would inform them after we returned home.

We were scheduled to go to Coimbatore from Bangalore. On the way, we stayed in Mysore. There I told my father, 'I like the girl. You can take care of what is to be done next.' Immediately, my father called Jaya's family and informed them of our acceptance.

My wedding took place on 9 February 1959. The betrothal was a day earlier. The wedding ceremony was arranged at my father-in-law's house in Bangalore. It was a quiet ceremony. After completing all the related rituals, we went to visit the temples of Guruvayur, Palani and many other places.

HEAT AT THE TAMIL NADU SECRETARIAT

My posting as a sub-collector did not last long. A new assignment awaited me. I had been at Dindigul for 15 months. My next posting was as undersecretary in the rural development department.

Long before Rajiv Gandhi and Mani Shankar Ayer spoke about the Panchayati Raj, Nehru and Balwantrai Mehta had a scheme for this in 1955–56. They spoke about giving more powers to village panchayats. In this connection, training was organized for the IAS officers in Mussoorie. For this, I was the only one nominated from Tamil Nadu and sent to Mussoorie in 1958. I took charge after coming back from the one-month training.

My work at the Madras secretariat was hectic. In the central government, S.K. Dey was the minister for rural development. He introduced many schemes for rural development and the Panchayati Raj. In Tamil Nadu, the rural development department implemented these schemes, where I was the undersecretary. R.A. Gopalaswamy, ICS, was the development commissioner. Later, he became Tamil Nadu's chief secretary. He formulated many rules and regulations as to how the panchayat schemes were to be run in Tami Nadu, what steps had to be taken to run the schemes smoothly, and so on. After briefing me over the phone at five in the morning, he would ask, 'When will you finish writing the minutes of the meeting?' And he would not have the patience to wait for my answer. He would immediately say, 'Come to my room at eleven o'clock.'

The minister responsible for my department was the CM himself, and all the files went to him. However, Kamaraj did not answer questions pertaining to our department in the Assembly. Instead, it was C. Subramaniam who answered them, being the leader of the party in the Assembly. Kamaraj answered only once, when a question was raised about Subramaniam himself.

FIGHTING OFFICE POLITICS

Every year, there would be a collectors' conference in Ooty at the Tamil Nadu government bungalow named Tamilagam. During one such meeting in 1962, Kamaraj's close confidant, Venkatachalapathy, was unwell and advised by doctors to not go to Ooty. As he had to miss the conference, the responsibility of overseeing all the work was handed over to me.

Krishnaswami Pillai was working with me at that time. He was on par with me in rank and was to participate in the Ooty meeting. He sent me a note: 'It is your duty to send a car to Mettupalayam railway station to take me to Ooty. Make the necessary arrangements.'

I was angry when I read the note, as it was written by Pillai without proper courtesies that were due from one officer to another. He was senior to me in age. But respect, courtesy and protocol are the things that matter. Had he asked for the same in a polite manner, I would have definitely made the arrangements. Having arranged cars for many others, it was no burden to manage one for him, too. Because his note was hurtful, I wrote my reply on that note and sent it back to him.

I completely forgot about the note until the end of the meeting, which had concluded successfully. But apparently, without taking up the matter with me, Pillai had complained to the seniors. And on his part, Venkatachalapathy had passed some remarks about me to a junior of mine.

'You could have told me if I was wrong. That being said, why did you have to complain to a junior about me?' I asked Venkatachalapathy.

Venkatachalapathy retorted angrily, 'What, Seshan, are you holding a darbar?'

'I am not holding any darbar,' I said.

'It seems you did not send a car for Krishnaswami Pillai,' Venkatachalapathy's face was turning red and hot.

Even as he was boiling with anger, I replied with patience: 'Krishnaswami Pillai had sent a note addressing to me as if I was a servant working under him. Only for that reason did I not send him a car.'

'What you did was wrong,' said Venkatachalapathy.

'You have the right to say so. In fact, you can say more. But you are wrong in speaking about me conducting any darbar. You should take back that comment and apologize,' I replied, knowing well that Venkatachalapathy was my superior.

'If I do not apologize, what will you do?' he asked me angrily.

'I have worked in this department for four long years. Please get me transferred to any other department. I am going to tell the chief secretary about my decision now,' I answered and returned to my office.

At that time, Gopalaswami was the chief secretary. His room was nearby. Within a few minutes of my talk with Venkatachalapathy, I got a message that the chief secretary would like to meet me. I went to his room. He looked angry.

'Why are you so offensive with Venkatachalapathy?' asked Gopalaswami. I apprised him of what had happened.

'For four years, I have worked in this department. You know how I work,' I said, 'Now, kindly move me to some other department. If you don't transfer me, I will go on a leave.' Gopalaswami looked at me in surprise and anger.

All this happened on 1 June 1962. I was given an order after one hour of this incident. It was mentioned that I had been transferred to the finance department, which was in the same building. It was added that the room meant for me was not yet vacant.

I returned to my old office and waited. In the next one hour, there was a new order transferring me to the small savings department. While I was amused and wondering at what was happening, another order reached me. This time, they had transferred me to the agriculture department. As I was getting ready to leave for the day, there was a phone call from the Chief Secretary.

'Do not dream that I will keep you in the secretariat. I will transfer you out of Madras,' he said.

'It is all the same to me,' I said and proceeded home.

On the same evening at 6.30, I got a call at home. It was the Chief Secretary calling!

'Seshan, I am going to transfer you to Krishnagiri. Your responsibility is to divide the district into two,' he said.

'Yes, Sir,' I replied.

'Work will be difficult there,' the Chief Secretary warned me.

'No problem. I will look into it.'

'Who do you know in Krishnagiri? Where will you stay?'

'I do not know anyone. I will stay in the tourist house.'

'What about your wife? Where will she stay?'

'Sir, the government should not worry about my wife.'

He did not ask any more questions and put down the phone. Gopalaswami was senior to me by 30 years. He had joined the ICS before I was even born.

At the office, the next day, the Chief Secretary called for me, and I readied myself for the next order.

'How do you know R. Venkataraman?' Gopalaswami asked me angrily.

'I know him as a minister for industries, transport and labour,' I answered.

'I did not ask that. As an individual, how well do you know him?'

'I know him as an important minister. Other than that, I do not know him personally.'

'When did you meet RV last?'

'There was a meeting two months back. To help my secretary, I accompanied him to the meeting carrying some files. At that time, RV was sitting in the first row and I was sitting in the third row. I saw him there. But I did not get any opportunity to meet him after that.'

'Did you meet RV yesterday night?'

'No. Why are you asking all these questions?'

'He has requested your service for the post of director in the transport department. How is it that he knows you personally?'

After a few minutes, Gopalaswami handed me an order transferring me to the transport department as director. I took charge of the Tamil Nadu transport department as director on 2 June 1962. To this day, neither do I know why RV made a request to appoint me to this post nor did I ask him about it.

TRANSPORT DEPARTMENT DIRECTOR WITH A BUS DRIVER'S LICENCE

The transport department had its head office at Pallavan House, which was opposite the Island Grounds in Madras. My brother, Lakshmi Narayanan, was the secretary incharge of this department. But the issues related to the transport department were looked after by R. Thirumalai, who was the additional secretary. The files would not go to my brother.

Today, the Metropolitan Transport Corporation (Madras) Limited has replaced the transport department. In those days, city buses also came under the control of the transport department, which was named as Madras State Transport Department, or MSTD for short. Kanyakumari district also had government buses in operation. In other districts, only private buses ran. However, long-distance interstate bus routes were run by the MSTD. They operated on the Madras–Bangalore and Madras–Trichy routes.

Prior to my taking charge, there were only a few bus stands and workshops in Madras. I set up the Mandaveli bus stand, T. Nagar bus stand, Adayar workshop, the transport workshops in Kodambakkam, Vadapalani and in other such places. When I took charge there in 1962, there were only 1,400 city buses. In one and a half year, the number increased to 1,800.

In those days, the Tamil Nadu government's transport service was exemplary. Only 35 people were allowed to be seated in a bus. 'Not more than 35 people' was the order given to the conductor. We could sit comfortably stretching out our legs. The department enforced strict discipline and timely plying of the buses. In fact, we had published an advertisement in the newspaper saying, 'Set your watch by the State Transport Bus'.

There was little work for the conductor in these buses because all the seats were booked well in advance. These long-distance buses were operated only during the day and not at night. I suggested to RV that we should run the night service, so that we could earn more profits.

'The railways are there for the convenience of the masses who wish to travel by night. It is not right to compete with the railways.

Besides, accidents could occur because of night driving. So, let us not take any risk, Seshan,' answered RV.

The situation has drastically changed now. Today, there are buses plying in the night. Many more transport corporations have also come into existence.

In this new posting as well, there were many notable incidents that stayed with me till the end. Among them was a one-day strike called by the labour unions, when I had called up for a file connected with the dismissal of employees who were sleeping during duty hours. M. Bhaktavatsalam was then the CM and home minister. There was every possibility that the strike would not be confined only to the transport service. I decided to inform the CM about the situation.

At 5.30 a.m., on the day of the strike, Bhaktavatsalam alighted at the railway station. F.V. Arul, inspector general (IG) of police, and I had gone to the station to receive him. As the minister walked to the car, we relayed the news about the strike to him. He listened carefully and said, 'With the policemen at your disposal, control the strike.'

We then met with the union leaders and said, 'Please do not go on a strike. People will be put to inconvenience. Your demands can be addressed through negotiations.'

However, they were not in a mood to listen and went ahead to stop the buses.

I went to the main bus depot. About 40 per cent of the employees were on strike. Some had reported for work and were on duty, not being too keen to go on strike. A few were hanging around with guilty expressions, unsure of what they should do. I drove the first bus to break the strike. The bus windows were covered with wire mesh. As we went out of the depot, a hail of stones smashed into the vehicle. The police had to do a lathi charge. More than 40 other buses were subsequently driven out. The strike collapsed by around noon. All city buses started plying thereafter.

There were also some instances where I had to take some firm administrative actions. Some of the actions I took against erring workers drew the ire of my seniors, including my brother. I was accused of being heartless. Later, I saw the particular file in which my brother himself had made that remark about me being heartless. To that, RV had responded with, 'Director knows his job.'

In the transport department, drivers and conductors came under the transport section, and mechanics and engineers came under the engineering section. Some problem or the other often arose between the two groups. For instance, a driver would take a bus from the workshop in the morning and later complain that the brake was not functioning properly, the clutch was not in perfect working order, the bus could not be driven due to the pressure of the brake, the steering could not be moved, and so on. He would station the bus on the road, hang a breakdown board on it and sit quietly—and that too during peak hours. Whenever a bus would break down, commuters used to experience great inconvenience.

The mechanic would inspect the bus and find everything to be working fine, adding that the driver was just making unnecessary complaints. In the hullabaloo, one would be at a loss to take a decision as to who was correct. The reason was that I did not have the requisite technical knowledge about the bus. If I learnt how to drive a bus, I would be able to find a solution to such problems and also be able to identify the culprit and punish him, I realized.

I wrote to Thirumalai saying that I was going to learn how to drive a bus and sought his approval. He wondered why I wanted to do the unnecessary work. He finally gave his approval when I explained the reason. I went through the motions and learnt how to drive a bus. When someone passed the driving test and got his licence, a separate badge number would be allotted to him. They gave me a badge bearing no. 2956.

Was it enough to merely learn how to drive a bus? To know the practical problems faced by drivers on crowded roads, I went to the workshop one morning at 5.30 and took a bus shuttling between Mylapore and Parry's Corner. All the conductors and drivers at the workshop were surprised as no director before me had ever done such a thing. Taking the conductor along, I worked the full shift from 5.30 a.m. to 1.30 p.m. on that route.

I also went to Madurai, Trichy and other places to supervise long-distance operations. I was given a big Plymouth station wagon. I would start my tour at seven every morning, along with Mathew, the driver. On the way, if I came across the department's bus, we would flag the bus down with a hand signal and I would go into the bus. After checking that the tickets had been issued properly and that there was no issue with the number of passengers, I would return to my station wagon.

On one such official trip, near Viluppuram, I came across one of our buses heading towards Trichy and boarded it. My station wagon was following the bus. I approached the bus driver and asked him to step aside; I would drive the bus. Since the driver knew who I was, he was respectful, but he declined and said that he would continue driving. When he did not accept my request even after I repeated it two or three times, I shouted at him to get up. The passengers had been watching me and were shocked. One passenger thought that an officer was throwing around his weight.

A few passengers asked me, 'You have a plan to bang this bus?'

I replied that I was a trained driver.

'How can we trust you?' asked one of them.

Only after I showed them my licence and the badge did the passengers relent. With the driver seated behind me, I drove the bus from Viluppuram to Perambalur.

I did not stop at working as a driver. I decided to do the conductor's job as well, so that I would learn about the practical difficulties a conductor faced at his job. Again at 5.30 a.m., I went to the workshop, took the conductor's leather bag, tickets, change for five rupees and did a full first shift from 5.30 a.m. to 1.30 p.m. Incidentally, I did not wear a uniform.

There was criticism from my colleagues. They asked why I had studied for the IAS if it was only to carry a conductor's bag. They said I was mad, but I paid no heed. I got hands-on experience and a better understanding of the difficulties faced by the conductors during peak hours. This would not have been possible had I not stood in their shoes.

What was now left was the technical side. I asked the government for permission to repair bus engines. I pointed out to my senior officers, who were surprised to hear this, that only if we learnt the intricacies of the maintenance of a bus could we criticize the complaints of a mechanic. I got the permission immediately.

In due course, I did all kinds of work—taking the bus to the ramp and getting it washed and greased, changing tyres and batteries, opening gear boxes and cleaning them.

AN ADDITIONAL JOB AND AN ADDITIONAL DESIGNATION

While I was still at the transport department, I was tasked with another job. September 1964 was a testing time for the entire Tamil Nadu. There was scanty rainfall, and drought conditions prevailed all over the state. There was scarcity everywhere. The secretary of the finance department, T.A. Varghese, called me over the phone one day.

'Seshan, you have a very good van! Let's use it to go on a tour to all the districts in Tamil Nadu. We will conduct a survey to find out which districts have had a good harvest and which districts are under drought.'

'Sir, I am the director of the transport department. What is my connection to this tour?' I asked.

'Though there is no connection between food grains and transport, you should still help me. The deputy director working under you will look after all your work. If there is something important, you could go to the office once a week and see the files.'

Varghese and I proceeded on the tour in my van. The harvest was good in the districts of Thanjavur and Trichy. There was a drought in Ramanathapuram district. Though the harvest was good in Nagercoil, there was a problem: rice was illegally being transported to neighbouring Kerala.

Finally, at the end of the tour, Varghese realized that there was no granary to stock grains in the places where the harvest was good. It was a big problem. To solve this, warehouses had to be built. These were to be located close to the place of harvest or of usage. That was his conclusion.

After discussing the matter with the chief of civil supplies, Varghese proposed a plan to construct warehouses at four different places: Aduthurai, Thanjavur, Trichy and Chromepet near Madras. Usually, the Public Works Department (PWD) is entrusted with the responsibility for such constructions. However, Varghese gave me the responsibility because the PWD was already loaded with other works. With this, I got an additional designation as deputy commissioner of civil supplies (godown construction), or DCCS (GC).

R. Balasubramaniam was the civil supplies chief. He had been the collector when I was posted in Madurai. In the transport department, there was a chief engineer named Vaz. I took him on my team. Not wanting to lose any time, meetings were promptly organized. A decision was taken to construct warehouses to stock 50,000 tonnes of grains at each place. Soon, the work started. To construct these four warehouses, we arrived at an estimated expenditure of ₹2.6 crore. I sent a file asking for permission for the required expenditure; there was no elaboration, just a one-line request. After my senior officers signed, eight ministers signed the file in the next 10 minutes. Cabinet approval was thus obtained. It was decided that the four warehouses must be ready to store the grains of the January 1965 harvest. So, we got a target of constructing the four warehouses within 120 days from the date of approval.

For this, I went to Hyderabad and purchased asbestos. T.A.S. Balakrishnan was the director of industries for Tamil Nadu, and was responsible for cement control. For all the four warehouses, the requirement of cement was 4,000 tonnes. On seeing my requirement, he exclaimed, 'Seshan, are you crazy? How will you transport these cement bags to four different places? Do you know how many lorries will be required? Is it feasible at such short notice?'

'Sir, please don't worry about these things. Kindly sanction the required cement,' I told him.

'Let me see how you are going to transport it,' Balakrishnan challenged with a laugh.

We arranged for 700 lorries on SOS basis. Balakrishnan was exasperated to see the speed with which all the 4,000 tonnes of cement was transported to the four sites.

Once a week, Vaz and I would visit the construction sites. Work was progressing fast, and 15 January was the deadline. I was quite sure that it would be a major achievement to construct these four warehouses in a matter of 120 days. But something came up in the last week of December.

On 24 December 1964, glancing through the newspaper, I saw the news headline that there was a severe storm in Rameshwaram. A bridge had collapsed due to the flood. In another instance, an express train had crashed near Dindigul, and flights in the area were cancelled or delayed.

I had planned an inspection tour and was keen on making it happen. Since even the rail tracks had been disrupted, I decided to drive. That day, in office, we spent time planning the route and getting the station wagon ready for all eventualities. I had to cancel the inspection tour for the time being.

I returned home and went to bed only to be awakened by the telephone at two in the morning.

It was Varghese again: 'Seshan, you are going to Madurai. As the Madurai collector is on leave, go there and help the collector of Ramanathapuram. Reach Madurai as quickly as possible.'

I explained that it was not feasible to travel and that I already tried the previous day.

His answer was: 'What I am asking is not whether you tried to go yesterday. What I am saying is that you are going today. Now.'

When I tried to plead that there was no way to go, with roads breached at several places and airlines services suspended, he pretended to be surprised.

'There is no need for a senior officer to be told how he should go to Madurai,' he said and disconnected the phone.

I rang up the Trichy collector and asked him the status of the roads leading to Madurai.

'No roads going to Madurai are open. The national highway is strewn with uprooted trees,' said the collector. Nonetheless, I was all set to head for Trichy and Madurai. At 10.00 a.m., I was sitting in my van. A jeep followed our van with four staff members of my department.

Along with them, there were four labourers with all kinds of tools. I started my journey.

Up to Ulundurpettai, on the way to Trichy, the road was clear. The problem started only after that. We travelled as quickly as we could and reached Madurai at two in the morning the following day. I stayed in the circuit house at Madurai, which was then the headquarters of both Madurai and Ramanathapuram districts. M.M. Rajendran was the collector of Ramanathapuram. He was supervising work at a relief camp.

Because of the heavy storm, Rameshwaram had become an island. We dropped packets of upma in Rameshwaram by plane to help with the relief work, but it did not reach the people. The packets could not withstand the impact of landing and would split open, spilling all the contents. To tackle the problem, I had the packets and plantains stuffed with paddy straws in gunny bags, which were then stitched tightly. When these bags were thrown from the plane, the straws cushioned the impact. We could at last help in distributing food.

Chief Minister M. Bhaktavatsalam, and the then finance minister, T.T. Krishnamachari, came to Madurai to assess the extent of damage. After three days, I was planning to go to Madras, when I received a long telegram. My head was in a swirl when I tried to read it. The telegram consisted of English words placed in a haphazard order. I realized that it was cypher. Immediately, I rang up Diaz deputy inspector general (DIG) of police. He had received a similar telegram and it was being deciphered by specialists. I immediately went to his office. I learnt how to decipher the code and we were at it until two in the morning.

'Some party workers are going on a strike. So, there may be a need to use force to arrest them,' was the message. It also contained the names of those who were to be arrested.

Finally, after finishing all the work at Madurai, I returned to Madras and met Varghese. 'You are appointed as collector of Madurai. Go and take charge immediately,' he said.

After handing over the charge of the transport department and the work related to the warehouse construction to my deputy

T.V. Venkataraman, I took charge as the collector of Madurai on 11 January 1965.

The warehouses that we had started building were ready by the time of the harvest. It was, by all standards, a remarkable feat that the construction of four warehouses was completed within a record time of 120 days.

FOUR

COLLECTOR: A JOB THAT DEMANDED MISSION MODE

Madurai was an extraordinarily large district in the mid-1960s. It had an area of 11,654 sq. km and a population of four million. Though Madras was Tamil Nadu's capital and South India's prime metropolis, it was Madurai that was its political nerve centre.

What thrilled me the most about Madurai was not its political tradition or cultural heritage. The greatest thing about it, for me, was and still remains the Meenakshi Temple and the grandeur of South India's temple architecture as could be witnessed there. I visited the temples almost every day.

The collector's post is an awkward job because of it being an administrative nightmare. There is virtually no fixed responsibility for this post. The fundamentals of the system, created by the British 150 years earlier, for the collectors of those times, remain the same for those in the present.

Be it a plane crash, train derailments, floods, an industrial strike or just about anything, it is the collector who is expected to be the first person to take responsibility and visit the site. The collector needs to be leading from the front.

I have worked at different types of government posts in my 36 years with the IAS—as secretary as well as cabinet secretary. I have also worked as the CEC, which is incidentally not part of the government. Of all these posts, working as a collector brought me far greater happiness than any other post I ever held. An individual in need can be directly and immediately helped by a collector.

THE TURBULENCE OF THE ANTI-HINDI PROTEST

On taking charge as the collector of Madurai, I started learning the written and unwritten rules relevant to the collector's post. But I never anticipated the calamity that was waiting to strike me within 15 days of my joining.

On 23 January 1965, a letter was issued by the Tamil Nadu government. An approximation of the letter is produced below:

> When India became a republic in 1950, it was declared that in the next 15 years, Hindi would become the official language... An agitation denouncing the announcement is likely. The collector has to see to it that no untoward incidents take place. Not only that, the collector has to take pre-emptive action to stop agitating people from disturbing the Republic Day function. At the same time, clamping of prohibitory orders within the city is forbidden; if clamped, the public functions held in connection with the Republic Day celebrations would get affected.

There seemed to have been an utter lack of compassion when it came to dealing with the local people's feeling of pride in their culture and language that dated back several thousand years. And the requirement to handle the backlash without prohibitory orders would only make things difficult. I found it strange that such an order could be passed.

In any case, PM Nehru had declared that Hindi would not be thrust upon non-Hindi-speaking people and that English would continue as India's official language as long as people wanted it. But this did not allay fears enough, and for some reason, there was a widespread agitation decrying the imposition of Hindi.

I checked with the SP over the phone. He said that students in Madurai were planning a showdown against the announcement. As there were many colleges in Madurai, I asked him to make careful arrangements. He said a procession was planned for 25 January and confirmed that necessary precautions had been taken regarding the same.

When I received the salute at the Republic Day parade in Madurai's police lines, there was no disruption of the event. The parade ground was effectively barricaded. A small crowd had gathered outside but dispersed after a while, after shouting slogans against the imposition of Hindi and against CM Bhaktavatsalam.[3] But the calm did not last long.

The trouble started when a small group of protesters took to a procession along a narrow street passing near a shrine of Goddess Meenakshi. The local Congress office was housed in a building at the end of that street. The procession reportedly halted for a moment in front of the office. There are different versions of what happened that day.

According to one version, as the procession passed by the Congress office, some people in the procession raised slogans against the government and the imposition of Hindi, and that was why the fighting started. Another version mentions that some people charged out of the Congress office and attacked the peaceful protesters with weapons and blood was spilled.

I was in my office when the incident happened. I left it to my officers in the field to deal with the situation as they saw proper. Reports of violent demonstrations from various parts of Madurai were pouring in as the hours passed by. No area of the district remained unaffected. If action was completely avoided or delayed, Madurai could burn. And there was fear amidst the officialdom.

The situation took a turn for the worse the next day when both the pro- and the anti-government parties asked for permission to hold processions. I asked for the SP's advice. He said that if given permission, they would fight on the Vaigai bridge, and the government order did not allow prohibitory orders. I asked what could be done without clamping a ban, and the answer was 'nothing.'

---

[3]Kutty, K. Govindan, *Seshan: An Intimate Story*, Konark Publications Pvt Ltd, New Delhi, 1994, p. 87.

'It's my duty to uphold peace in my district. So, I will issue the ban order. Whatever has to happen, let it happen,' I said and signed the order.

The SP informed the IG about the order. From the IG, the news spread to the secretariat. Within minutes of my signing the order, I got a telephone call from Chennai. It was P.M. Belliappa, the deputy secretary. He was appalled at what I had done and a duel of words followed.

'If you have any problems with my signing the ban order, tell me now. I will hand over the charge. If you want to administer Madurai district sitting in Madras, you may do so,' I said bluntly.

'No! No! If the ban is clamped despite the government's order against it, the Chief Minister will get angry. I am trying to impress that on you,' Belliappa said.

The CM had not asked me anything regarding my clamping of the ban order. But apparently, he was under pressure from all kinds of organizations that were accusing him of human rights violations. Varghese, who was the chief secretary, called me up. He told me that the government did not want a blanket ban on the assembling of people in Madurai. It could take action against the collector and undo his order if he was not willing to toe the line.

'Nothing doing, Sir. It is the district magistrate who has to decide where and whether prohibitory orders should be imposed. And I am the district magistrate. The government can do nothing about it, except, of course, remove me from my post. Please do so, Sir, I will be thankful,' I said.

I think being firm paid off. All over the state of Tamil Nadu, the Republic Day festivities were carried out peacefully and without much trouble. However, the very next day, protests occurred in Dindigul, Kambam, Theni and other places. School and college students participated in the strike. For the next three months, until April, cases of arson and violence were reported from everywhere in Tamil Nadu. Such a thing had never happened in the history of the state. The military was called in all areas of strife. News about strikes continued to pour in: 'five dead in clashes', 'ten died in police shooting', and so on. Though Madurai was a volatile district, there were no fatalities on account of the strike in Madurai district, until an unfortunate incident took place.

DEALING WITH PROTESTS AND VIOLENCE

In some cases, lathi charge had to be ordered, some of which I had personally led, albeit reluctantly, for the sake of the larger good. One such incident took place in the vicinity of the National College where one of my old Physics professors from the MCC, Varadachari, was the vice-principal.[4] There was a time-honoured tradition that policemen did not enter any academic campus unless summoned by the principal. The students of National College had by then become as restive as students elsewhere and were impatient to hold a demonstration.

I spoke to the students and laid down the law: 'As long as you remain within the campus, even if you are shouting slogans, there is no problem. But don't come out on the roads. The road is mine. If you want to go home, please go in ones, twos or threes. If you are in groups of five or more, I will disperse you.'

However, the defiant students did not listen and began to march out of the college campus. I had personnel from the Malabar Special Police[5] at my disposal. They were especially raised during the Malabar rebellion. They wielded lathis naturally and could bring down every target with a single blow, elegantly executed. They were ordered to disperse the students. And I gave an order to the SP: 'Suvarna, see that they do a clean job.'

I had told my old professor that he should not try to protect his students when they were heading for a collision with the policemen who had been ordered to disperse the crowd. He ignored the warning and moved forward along with the crowd of students. And he paid the price for it. He took a blow and went down with blood flowing from

---

[4]Kutty, K. Govindan, *Seshan: An Intimate Story*, Konark Publishers Pvt ltd, 1994, p. 90.
[5]Malabar Special Police or MSP was a paramilitary unit of the state police of Kerala.

his forehead. Even Principal Srinivasan was hurt. I felt no remorse doing my duty. I was only thankful to Madurai Meenakshi that no one was killed.

When everyone was resting in the lull that had set in after the lathi charge, thinking it was all over, we got the news of an unfortunate incident. A foreign tourist had come to Tamil Nadu from Kerala through the Theni district border. He had arrived in the midst of the conflict and had gone straight to the police station. He had asked for police protection to go to Madurai during the disturbance. A police officer had obliged and taken him in a jeep.

When the jeep had entered Kambam, agitators threw stones at it. Not stopping at that, they had scratched 'Hindi down, down', using a nail on the jeep. Sitting inside the jeep, the police officer had pulled out his service revolver and shot at the crowd several rounds. But only a donkey had died. The frightened foreigner had then decided he no longer wanted to tour Tamil Nadu and wanted to return to Kerala instead. The police officer had dropped him back at the Kerala border. However, on the way back, he was stopped by the crowd, which again started pelting stones. The police officer once again resorted to shooting. This time, a boy died. The police officer had then fled the scene for his life.

Enraged at the boy's death, the people attacked the Kambam police station. The constables went through hell that day. The mob entered the police station and took whatever they got their hands on. All the records of cases kept inside the police station were burnt. They took away all the guns. The frenzied mob also stripped two police constables of their uniforms and took them away in a vehicle and set fire to it; a sad and unforgettable incident it was.

This killing of the policemen happened on 10 March 1965. I was in Madurai at the time and received the news at night. I went to the village, which was 70 km away, taking along the reserve police force and the army units. Aware that I was coming, the agitators put up barricades on the roads. When we removed the barricades and reached the village, it was empty.

We could not do much. A case was filed. It took two years for the case to be brought to a conclusion. No one was convicted. The morale of the Tamil Nadu police hit a new low.

An incident at Nagercoil that took place some weeks earlier was already weighing heavy on the minds of the policemen. An SP was sitting in his vehicle parked in front of Scott Christian College. A college student had approached the SP and said something, which had escalated into a heated exchange of words. The student had then spat on the SP and ran away. Standing there with his dirtied face, the enraged SP had shouted, 'Don't spare the college students... Shoot them.' Immediately, the constables standing outside the college had climbed over the compound wall and started shooting at the students, as a result of which one student lost his life. Within the next few days, the SP had been suspended. It was all over the papers and the news also reached us through confidential official circles. At that time, I was the director of transport, Madras. I met the chief secretary and requested him to reconsider: 'I am not saying that what the SP did was right. He may be wrong in his action. But in the present situation, suspending him will have a bearing on the morale of the police.' But the request did not have any effect.

After this, when there was a riot in Madurai and an officer ordered a lathi charge, the constables replied, 'Sir, in Nagercoil, too, the police took action. But when the matter was taken up and objections were raised, they were not supported.' So saying, they declined to carry out his order. The anti-Hindi protestors had to be tackled.

Problems kept cropping up one after the other, and they kept me on my feet. When I thought with relief that the riots were over at last, there was an announcement with regard to the elections to the panchayat unions.

There were 375 panchayat unions in Tamil Nadu at that time, with 27 in Madurai district. Traditionally, violence was common during panchayat union elections.

The panchayat union election was slated to take place in Tirumangalam, 40 km from Madurai. It was the responsibility of the local deputy collector to conduct the election. G.V.G. Krishnamurty was occupying the post at the time. He had reached his post on promotion and was a very fair-minded person. Four days before the elections were about to begin, Krishnamurty spoke to me over the phone and expressed his deep worry, 'A group of voters has been taken to Bangalore and another group of voters has been taken to Pondicherry. On the day of voting, when the groups meet, violence is bound to erupt.'

Elections were scheduled at 5.30 in the evening. Krishnamurty called me around 4.00 p.m. to say that the situation was very grim.

'How long will you postpone the election? Even if there will be a fight, action has to be taken as per the law,' I said.

I called the SP and gave the orders, 'Speak firmly to the mob. If they do not respond, use force.'

An announcement was made that elections would be held as scheduled. When the group from Bangalore entered the village, fighting and riots started. The police opened fire and seven members of the public died.

When I reached Thirumangalam, it was 8.00 p.m. Around 400 people were standing in groups. On seeing us, they started shouting that they would beat up the police. 'As in Kambam, burn them,' they shouted. We held a meeting and brought the situation under control. We took all the steps to complete the government formalities arising from the situation, especially in respect of the deceased.

The villagers asked for the bodies of those killed to take them in a procession for the last rites. If permissions were granted, further riots were certain to happen and I was sure of it.

'According to the religious practices of the deceased, we are ready to make arrangements for their last rites. But I will not give permission for taking all the bodies together in procession,' I said firmly.

'Not acceptable,' they shouted.

'If that is so, on our own initiative, the government will conduct the last rites according to the religious practices of the deceased and the bodies will be appropriately disposed of,' I walked away after saying this. We then set up camps under a tree till the bodies were disposed and the situation dissolved.

After 10 days of this incident, I got a letter from the chief secretary, which turned out to be a surprise, and a pleasant surprise it was. The letter read: 'Owing to the manner in which you handled the confrontation at Tirumangalam, no problem cropped up. The government appreciates you for the efficient handling of the case.' This letter was a big boost to my confidence, considering that I had my bag packed and was rather expecting to be transferred or face some enquiry.

THE KASHMIRI MAPPILLAI

While I savoured the thought that my difficulties were over, a new problem cropped up in April 1965. Around that time, a news item appeared in a local daily that Sheikh Abdullah was charged with acting against the interest of the nation. As a result, the central government had arrested him in Kashmir and sent him to Ooty.[6] No one was allowed to meet the Sheikh or talk to him.

Harmohinder Singh was the collector for Ooty at that time. He was one year junior to me in the IAS. Under security arrangements, the Sheikh was brought to Coimbatore by flight and from there taken to Ooty by car. I pitied Harmohinder that he had such a big headache to handle, without knowing that the headache would be mine very soon.

An interview of the Sheikh in the local daily surprised me. When there was an order that he could not meet anyone, how did the correspondent meet him? That same night, at around 10, I received a call from the chief secretary. This is the gist of what he said:

> We sent Sheikh Abdullah to Ooty. But the Ooty collector could not give proper protection. A foreign correspondent met Sheikh and an article about him was published. The government is in a fix. We have taken a decision to shift Abdullah from Ooty to Kodaikanal. I will give you 48 hours. Meanwhile, look for a place to keep Abdullah and make necessary arrangements.

---

[6]Ramakrishnan, T., 'When the "Lion of Kashmir" Landed in Kodaikanal', *The Hindu*, 31 March 2022, https://bit.ly/3ZQKt8q. Accessed on 27 December 2022.

Kodaikanal is in Madurai district, so the detainee was now my responsibility. There were no good buildings under the government's charge in Kodaikanal. All were in a dilapidated condition. One exception was Kohinoor, a mansion built by Nawab Ali Yavar Jung who had migrated to Pakistan. Kohinoor became a refugee asset of the government. If that building was to be used to accommodate the Sheikh, the government officers who came to Kodaikanal would not have any good place to stay. For this reason, I gave up the plan of housing him at Kohinoor.

In Kodaikanal, there was a travellers' house, under government control, meant for long-distance travellers. I decided to accommodate the Sheikh in that place. We started the repair works, had it whitewashed, demolished the old bathroom and built a new one. The Sheikh travelled from Ooty through Coimbatore, Pollachi, Palani and Dindigul and arrived at Kodaikanal. I welcomed him. He was tall and fair, with a pink tint to the skin. I took him to the house. When he saw the room, his faced turned deep red. He asked: 'Do I have to stay in this room?'

I said, 'Yes.'

'You got me wrong. How can any human being stay here? Only horses will stay in a room like this. How dare you keep me in this place?' he glared like a wounded lion.

'Please do not make a decision in haste,' I said, but he did not pay attention to the advice.

'I will not stay here,' he said emphatically.

I asked for two days to make arrangements and meanwhile somehow managed to get him to stay there.

On the second day, I had to shift the Sheikh to Kohinoor. On seeing the building, his face lit up with happiness. He was placed on the second floor, and I was only too happy that we could have guards on the lower floors to keep the security tight.

As I was stationed in Madurai, I visited Kodaikanal once a week. I would personally supervise the security and other arrangements and gather feedback. Having reassured myself that all was well, I would return to Madurai. The Sheikh was under my protection for two years from May 1965.

Though he was ill-tempered and disapproved of things in the beginning, the Sheikh's nature towards us changed for the better eventually. We affectionately called him *mappillai*, which means son-in-law. His behaviour was unpredictable as that of a son-in-law.

There was an order from the government that whatever Sheikh Abdullah asked for should be provided to him. Once, he asked me for a radio. I obliged. During our conversation, he disparagingly called me an 'ordinary collector.' I agreed with the description but did not miss the unmentioned undertones; I waited for an opportunity to give him a fitting reply. That opportunity came in the next two days, when he asked for an umbrella.

Immediately I said, 'I will write a letter today itself and obtain sanction. After getting permission, I will get you the umbrella.'

My answer angered him and he said, 'Even for purchasing an umbrella, you need to write and get permission from Madras?'

'Yes, Sir,' I am only an ordinary collector. So, I need to get permission from Madras,' I said quietly.

He burst out laughing, 'Oh! You are paying back for what I said two days ago?'

'Yes, Sir,' I said, smiling. But, of course, I immediately purchased an umbrella and gave it to him.

While buying fruits for the Sheikh, there would be times when we would not be able to find some he wanted. For such fruits, like apples, we would go to Batlagundu. The apples available at that time were very small in size. Once, he called me over and showed me an apple I had bought for him.

'Is this an apple?' he asked.

'Yes Sir, that is what we call it,' I said.

'In my land, such apples are given to donkeys and pigs. No human will eat it,' he said and threw away the apple.

'Sir, this is the best fruit we could manage to get. We bought these especially for you. There is no fruit available around which is better than this,' I told him with respect. That did not mollify him, and then I too got angry.

With some impatience, I said, 'Don't tell me "I get this or that in my land," "you are an ordinary official" and such other things. We did not invite you to Kodaikanal. I do not know why you have come here. And it is not necessary for me to know that.' It was only after this plain-speaking that he stopped complaining.

Sheikh Abdullah walked on the banks of the Kodaikanal Lake daily. We would see to it that nothing untoward happened or no unauthorized people passed by him. On the way, if someone would say 'Hello', the Sheikh would reply with a 'Hello', too.

One day, he happened to pass by a cloth shop on his way back. The shopkeeper greeted him and said, 'Please come in, Sir. We have a lot of suit material befitting one such as you.' With these sweet words, he welcomed the Sheikh inside his shop.

The shopkeeper, thinking it the perfect opportunity to make a sale, pushed all his old clothes, which no one else would buy, on to the Sheikh. After the clothes were purchased, he sent me a bill. I was shocked to see that the shopkeeper had billed him ₹7,000 for those useless clothes.

I called the shopkeeper to my office and told him: 'You have charged exorbitant rates for clothes that are not even worth a few rupees. Tell me the real cost and take the correct amount. Or else, we will see to it that your shop disappears before Sheikh Abdullah comes out for a stroll the next time.' The threat did the trick—he charged the correct price for the clothes.

On the bank of the Kodaikanal Lake, there was a hotel run by Mrs X, an aging Anglo-Indian woman who was an English army officer's widow. She had the reputation of having sued a previous collector and his SP in a defamation case in which she had won one rupee as damages. Apparently, she did not think much of the IAS and ICS officers.

Mrs X thought it was her right to invite the Sheikh to her hotel when he went for a stroll around the lake. And the Sheikh would even agree. Many who visited Kodaikanal were more than willing to spend some time with the Sheikh. Among them were businessmen and film stars. The policemen accompanying the Sheikh would be uneasy with such socializing. But they did not dare tell the man, who was once Kashmir's PM, that he could not associate or correspond with anyone without my approval. Eventually, I learnt about all of this.

I sent a word to Mrs X that she should not entertain the Sheikh without the district magistrate's permission. Apparently, she was livid with rage. She insisted that she would continue to do what she liked. I decided that the best response would be to persuade her. The municipal engineers of Kodaikanal were very helpful in my cause and also very ingenious. As a result, Mrs X, much to her dismay, found that the water pipes in her hotel would burst due to high pressure or the fuse in the electrical system would be blown due to high voltage. This happened rather regularly. Each time, though, when she reported the problem, the engineers would respond quickly to sort out the problem, so she had nothing to complain about. It was the ingenuity of the engineers that they pumped water at pressure high enough to burst the pipes or fixed the fuse in such a manner that it would need to be fixed soon. The woman eventually mended her ways.

Back then, for correspondence, the rule was that I would read all the letters to and from the Sheikh before forwarding them with my seal. One day, he spoke in a honeyed tone and asked for a favour, 'I will give you a letter. You should send it across without reading it.'

'When there is an order that all your letters can be sent only after me having read them, how can I send this letter without reading it?' I asked him.

'You will not ask this question if you see the address,' he said and showed me an envelope addressed to Dr Radhakrishnan, President of India, New Delhi.

I told him with a hint of laugh, 'You may write a letter to the President or to the Prime Minister or anyone. But it's my duty to send it only after I have read it.'

'Why don't you speak to Delhi? They will also agree to it,' said Abdullah, not ready to give up.

I could have opened the letter despite lying to him that I would not. But I did not have any interest in doing so. 'Why should I talk to Delhi when there is an order from them on this matter? I will not speak to them,' I said.

The Sheikh kept offering one reason after another. The discussion started at 10 in the morning and ended at three in the afternoon.

'Okay, if that is your decision, I am going on a fast, that too, fast unto death,' he said decisively.

I did not give up either and said, 'I will arrange all the necessary facilities for your fast.' He glared at me for a moment and then went inside.

Though I showed Abdullah a tough face, I had a fear that something untoward may happen. I immediately went to the rest house and reported the matter to the Madras secretariat over the phone. An officer asked me to send the letter without reading it. 'We will handle it. How does it matter?'

'It's you who passed this order in the first place. And now you are asking me to overlook it? If that be so, please send me an order in writing,' I said.

At this, the officer withdrew his words.

In a short time, there was another phone call, 'Unwanted problems may arise. Send the letter without reading,' said an officer from Chennai over the call.

'Send your orders in writing, and I will immediately send the letter without reading,' I replied. But no new orders came.

The Sheikh refused to eat anything. In approximately an hour's time, I received a call from Delhi. This time, it was a high-rank officer from the central government.

'Mr Collector, why are you creating problems?' he asked.

'I will dispatch the letter only after I read it,' I repeated myself.

Within five minutes of the call, Abdullah called for me. I went inside, apprehensive of yet another problem. He gave me the letter he had written. I looked at him in surprise.

'I am giving this letter in protest. I do not know whether you will read this letter before sending. But I am not worried,' he said.

I read the letter in front of him. It was written in English. In it, he had conveyed that India and Pakistan should become friendly with one another.

'Everyone in the world knows your viewpoint as regards to India and Pakistan. When it is so, why did you create a problem by asking me not to read this letter and threatening to go on a fast unto death?'

He replied in anger, 'It is a matter of principle. You are a servant of the President.'

'I am not a private servant of the Prime Minister or the President. I am a government employee. So, it is my duty to follow the orders laid down by the government,' I countered.

'Okay, get me food,' he ordered. With that, his fast came to an end.

After this incident, no major problem cropped up during his remaining two-year stay in Kodaikanal.

One of the Sheikh's closest friends was Mridula Sarabhai, daughter of the great industrialist Ambalal Sarabhai. She complained that he was not being looked after properly under Seshan's protection. She wrote a letter to this effect to CM Bhaktavatsalam. I do not know whether Bhaktavatsalam took any action. However, my name came to be known, even among central ministers, on account of Sheikh Abdullah's detention.

In 1967, general and state legislative assembly elections were due. In Tamil Nadu, Dravida Munnetra Kazhagam (DMK) won and formed a government; C.N. Annadurai became the CM. Annadurai requested Indira Gandhi to take the Sheikh anywhere outside Tamil Nadu, following which he was taken to Delhi. He was not keeping good health and had to be admitted to a hospital in Delhi.

THE REAL CAUSE FOR THE FALL OF THE CONGRESS IN TAMIL NADU

There was yet another unfortunate incident during my tenure as the collector. It concerned rice, the staple food of the state. Rice in the public distribution system was not reaching the fair price shops. Large crowds would assemble outside the shops, and long queues would get out of control.

I felt responsible for the situation. Though I wrote several letters to Madras, no supply arrived. And when it did arrive, it was inadequate. Instead of 10 kg, only 2 kg was available per family. And what was available was not even of average quality. Worms and insects would be found crawling in it. Having no alternative, the poor were forced to purchase the poor quality rice.

Ahead of the elections, in March 1967, Indira Gandhi came to Tamil Nadu to address public gatherings. Kamaraj said, 'I will win even if I sleep.' It was not that the dismal state of the fair price shops was not known to him, he just did not grasp the extent of the dissatisfaction among the people owing to the non-availability of rice. He was confident that he would win the election.

A catchy Tamil slogan raised by the Opposition (DMK) went: '*Virudhunagar annachi, arisi vilai ennachi* (Elder brother from Virudhunagar, what happened to the price of rice?)' The DMK won with a thumping majority. Annadurai became the CM. Ever since then, the Dravidian parties have been running the government in Tamil Nadu. This ordinary failure to provide rice to fair price shops has kept a national party out of power in the state for nearly 50 years now.

After Annadurai became the CM, he came to Madurai in May. I met him and asked for leave, as I was due for a transfer and getting leave would be impossible soon after taking charge in a new place. Annadurai accepted the proposal and sanctioned my leave. Incidentally, one of the Tamil dailies reported that the relationship between Annadurai and Seshan was badly strained: 'It is because of this that when Seshan asked for leave, Annadurai immediately sanctioned it.'

My wife and I decided to visit important places in Tamil Nadu. We hired a car and travelled to religious destinations in the state, worshipping at the temples there. When I was at Kutralam, I received intimation that I had been selected in the preliminary rounds to attend a one-year training at Harvard University in United States of America (USA). Apparently, when Bhaktavatsalam was the CM, he had recommended my name for this programme.

THE ONE-YEAR ACADEMIC BREAK AT HARVARD

Every year, about 12 government officials from countries in Asia, Africa and Latin America are invited to Harvard University to be trained in modern economics. It is a programme conducted in memory of Prof. Edward Mason, and the duration is approximately one year. From India, there were three of us that year; besides me, a candidate from Maharashtra named Kanga, an IAS officer, and K.N. Rao from the audit and accounts department. From Pakistan, too, there were three.

If our wives went along, we had to buy their air tickets out of our pockets. We were given an additional $85 per month for personal expenses.

I went along with my wife. This was my first trip abroad. She took along many of her silk saris. There was a flight for London and another from London to New York, 48 hours later. My brother's friend Venkataraman was in London at that time. As we were coming to London for the first time, he came to the airport to receive us. We were happy in anticipation of touring London till the time we discovered to our shock that my wife's baggage had not arrived. All her silk saris and other clothes were in that baggage. There was not even a single change of clothes. We spent those 48 hours in London enquiring about the status of our baggage with the airport authorities.

We finally reached Boston, where temporary arrangements for a stay of four to five days had been made in the house of a senior professor at Harvard University. The aged couple took excellent care of us. They were quite surprised to learn that we were vegetarians and asked: 'How are you healthy without eating meat?'

Within a week, we got a small rented apartment inside the university campus. The rent was $140. Gas, fridge and such other necessary household amenities came with the house. We purchased only a few vessels. After meeting the household expenses on vegetables, milk, fruits, rice, dal and the like, we could save $50–100 every month.

My wife got a job in the university—arranging books in the library. She was paid $2.35 dollars per hour. By the time I finished my training, I had managed to save $1,500.

Of the several courses needed for me to graduate, one course I took at the university was mathematics for economists. The associate professor for the course happened to be Subramanian Swamy. His appearance was always calm. Once, at mealtime, when we all sat together and chatted in the room adjacent to the dining room, Swamy joined us. Looking at the Pakistani students, he jokingly said, 'We in India will develop a bomb and drop it on your head.' Swamy and I soon became friends.[7]

Swamy only spoke to us in colloquial Tamil. As he was married, he usually came to our house with his wife, asking, 'What's special today?' He would have dosa and then go back. Both he and his spouse liked my wife's cooking. Whenever they took an outstation trip, we went along in their car. They were very friendly.

Generally, getting a PhD at Harvard University is difficult. There is an examination that lasts six hours. Then a thesis has to be written and defended. Writing down everything, finishing it and then getting a PhD was a major task. While some would make it in two years, others would take longer. But Swamy finished everything successfully in six months and got his PhD in less than a year, surpassing and surprising all. Moreover, his subject—index number problem—was a tough one. For this achievement, he was highly regarded in the university. Everyone praised him as an intellectual. That high intellectual Swamy returned to India. After searching for a suitable work, he settled down for teaching subsidiary economics at IIT, Delhi. But even there, he did not get his due and was eventually removed. The matter was resolved in the courts in his favour finally.

Swamy often said, 'It was because of Indira Gandhi that I, who got all recognition at an American university, have been sidelined here in India.'

Later, he entered politics. After that, I could not stay in touch with him for a very long time. We would meet at airports occasionally.

After I finished my training course at Harvard, we decided to go on a trip around America. There was not much money for travelling luxuriously or for renting fancy hotel rooms. Thus, we chose a bus service for travelling and that too at night. The bus journeys were exhilarating. It was a one-month non-stop trip in which we covered

---

[7]Seshan, T.N., *En Kathai*, Tirunelveli Thennindia Saiva Sithantha Noorpathippu Kazhagam Ltd, 2002.

many parts of America. The only problem, of course, was the lack of vegetarian food.

Finally, it was time to return. With the collector's post behind me now, I was looking forward to my new assignment. It was not with the state government. But I seemingly became an object of pity with the next one.

FIVE

A PRODUCTIVE RUN-UP TO THE CENTRAL ADMINISTRATIVE MAINSTREAM

On my return from America in August 1968, I was posted to the Department of Atomic Energy. Apparently, the chairman of the Atomic Energy Commission of India, Dr Vikram Sarabhai, wished to appoint an IAS officer as a deputy secretary in the department. He expressed his wish to L.P. Singh, the home secretary in the central government, and asked if there was anyone who would fit the bill. At Harvard, as part of the exam papers, I had written a major paper on atomic power. In it, I had given a detailed description of the advantages of using atomic power and how it could be effectively used to benefit the masses. The professors at Harvard had appreciated my work. This had come to Singh's notice, who recommended my name, taking my paper on atomic power in due consideration.

The head office of the department was in Mumbai, and this was where Dr Sarabhai was stationed. In this department, there were many scientists but very few IAS officers. I thought that it was a good posting but was cautioned that there would be confrontations aplenty. Scientists and IAS officers are always at loggerheads. It troubled me to hear that all the IAS officers who had served there until then had left before the end of their terms.

When my posting order was published, all my friends took pity on me as if I would be trapped in the department. When I asked for the reason, they told me that atomic energy scientists had scant regard for the IAS officers. I met a revenue board member at Madras, who said, 'My condolences on your appointment.' Anyway, I decided to join.

The one condition that I had laid down was that I would join only on allotment of a flat, as getting one in Mumbai was extremely difficult. 'House will be allotted; start immediately,' was the reply. I joined the department in August 1968. My office was near the Gateway of India at the Old Yacht Club.

Dr Homi Sethna was the director at the Bhabha Atomic Research Centre (BARC), which was under the atomic energy department. He was an engineer by training. He had hoped that he would become the head of the department after the death of Dr Homi Bhabha, the father of Indian nuclear programme. The government instead appointed Vikram Sarabhai, who was then at Ahmedabad, as the head of the department. As his dream was shattered, Sethna had become bitter. The animosity between Sarabhai and Sethna was akin to that of a snake and mongoose. They quarrelled daily. Even over a trivial matter, they would have verbal duels in front of officers.

There was not much of an official connection between Sethna and myself. I had to assist only Sarabhai. Sethna thought that I favoured Sarabhai. If any official file was sent to Sethna, he would get angry and say, 'What does Sarabhai think of himself? I will not allow this.' And he would not sign the file, throwing a spanner in the works.

Even though these conflicts continued, all facilities for scientific work were available in the atomic energy department. I worked there from 1968 to 1972. It was a good time, as I learnt a great deal in those four years.

WORKING WITH A PRODUCTIVE AND WORKAHOLIC GENIUS

Vikram Sarabhai did not have any sense of superiority when it came to professional hierarchies. Though there were many conflicts between Sethna and himself, he did not talk ill of him.

He was never the one to waste his time. When he would not be able to find time to look into official matters in the normal course, he would honk his car horn exactly at 5.30 a.m. in front of my house and would ask me to brief him on the way to catching a flight at the airport. I would thus accompany him till the airport and discuss official matters on the way.

On one such occasion when he picked me up in his car, we could not speak much. He asked the secretary to purchase a ticket for me. I protested saying that I had brought no clothes, to which he replied that I could return the same day. Patiently, he discussed all official matters with me in the flight and I returned to Mumbai by the evening flight. These in-flight discussions happened several times after that.

But this wonderful man had a sad end. At that time, the atomic energy activities and the space activities came under a single department, which was under him. When the Bangladesh War erupted in 1971, our department was requested to extend some aid, and we obliged. In due course, the war came to an end.

An idea was floated that atomic energy and space activities should be put under two separate heads. Sethna played this card in such a manner that even Indira Gandhi was taken up with this idea. Sethna had good rapport with many in the government. He worked against Sarabhai with the help of his close political friends. It was a matter of great sorrow for Sarabhai when he learnt of Sethna's plan. Indira Gandhi called Sarabhai and told him about her decision. In the next 15 days, the atomic energy and space departments were separated. Sarabhai was heartbroken. He died on 30 December that year.

Vikram Sarabhai's death was a mystery. Whenever he went to Thiruvananthapuram, he stayed at Kovalam. Just when the space activities were being taken away and segregated from the atomic energy department, he was at Kovalam. He had spoken to his secretary until two the previous night. Sarabhai usually drank coconut water in the morning and did not touch coffee. The peon brought Sarabhai plain water and coconut water early the next day and knocked on his door. For a long time, he did not receive any response. He went to Sarabhai's secretary who was staying in the next room. When the secretary peeped through the window at the top of the latched entrance door, he was shocked to see that Sarabhai was lying lifeless.

Though doctors said that cerebral haemorrhage caused Sarabhai's death, mystery shrouds his death. But having known him personally and having seen the circumstances first hand, I have no doubts... The real reason behind his death was that he was heartbroken due to Indira Gandhi's decision to divide the atomic energy and space departments into two.

UNJUST ADVERSE REMARKS ON MY CONFIDENTIAL REPORT

In early 1972, PM Indira Gandhi wanted to transfer me from the atomic energy department to the space department in Bangalore. But Sethna would not let me go. After waiting for two months, the PM issued orders transferring me to the space department.

In an IAS officer's career, becoming joint secretary on promotion was (and still is) important. If the confidential reports (CR) recorded annually by senior officers do not note one's performance up to the mark, one would not get a promotion. But then, if there are adverse remarks in the report, the rule is that the concerned employee has to be informed about it.

When I was working in the atomic energy department, Sarabhai did not write my CR. The reason was that, as a scientist, he did not take these administrative matters seriously and so did not bother about it. Sethna, who came after him, did write my CR, even though I had not completed the mandatory minimum period of three months of service under him.

When I was in Bangalore on my next posting, Satish Dhawan, who was the secretary to the space department in Bangalore, called me to his office one day to show a letter from Delhi. What Sethna wrote in my CR was communicated in that letter. His initial remarks were favourable, but at the end, he wrote: 'He is aggressive, abrasive and is a bully to those under him.'

I was pained to see the report as, among other things, it could prove to be an impediment to my promotion as joint secretary. I wrote a letter to the cabinet secretary T. Swaminathan and it ran up to 10 pages. In it, I requested for the remarks to be expunged. I had worked well and there were no problems with my performance during that time. If Sethna wished to know more, he could read the files that were duly maintained. I asked that, after considering my application, Sethna's remark be expunged or I would resign from the IAS.

After three months, I got a call from the Prime Minister's Office (PMO) saying that the PM would like to meet me. I went to her office in South Block, Delhi. She was busy writing in a file. After a while, she raised her head and asked: 'Oh... are you Seshan? Why are you misbehaving like this? Why is Sethna angry with you?' Only then did I understand that the meeting was about the CR written by Sethna.

I politely replied, 'Madam, I have not spoken to anyone about this till date; now I will tell you. Sethna and I do not have any problems between us. Sarabhai and Sethna had serious differences. As I was with Sarabhai, Sethna turned against me. That's why Sethna has written those adverse comments. Moreover, I have not spoken against Sethna at any given point of time.'

'Are you aggressive?' she asked.

'If any work is given to me, I usually work aggressively. But I have not hurt anyone,' I said.

'Are you abrasive?' was her next question.

'If some work is to be done within a certain time and is not completed, I will be abrasive,' I said.

'Are you a bully?' she asked.

'No, Madam. He who tortures a powerless man is called a bully. I am not that kind of a person,' I said and waited fearfully for her next question.

She then summoned her peon and said, 'Call him.' Sethna entered Indira Gandhi's room.

'Homi, why have you written this in the CR of this young man? When Sarabhai and Dhawan have appreciated Seshan, why did you write this?' she asked Sethna while I was still standing there.

She looked at me and almost angrily asked me to leave. I left the office. Having seen her anger, I thought my promotion would not come through. But after some 10 days, I got a letter stating that Sethna's remarks had been expunged by the government. After two months,

I got promoted to the joint secretary's post. I served at the position in Bangalore till 1976.

A BRIEF TENURE IN TAMIL NADU

After the dismissal of the Karunanidhi government in 1976, Governor's Rule was imposed in Tamil Nadu. I was appointed secretary in the industries department in Tamil Nadu and took charge in April 1976. In the assembly election that followed, M.G. Ramachandran, popularly known as MGR, won and became the CM. The industries department was directly under him, and I was to report to him. But the relation between us soured. A few months later, I was transferred to the agriculture department. The reason was that we had a difference of opinion and could not work well together.

I will narrate the facts of the incident that preceded the transfer without drawing any inferences.

One morning at 8.30, I received a call from the CM wherein I was curtly asked to send a particular file with an 'appropriate' note. The documents in the file were related to a small company which had been set up to make a chemical named furfural.[8] Apparently, the company had not been able to make progress with the project as planned. It was not able to pay back the loan taken from the Tamil Nadu Industrial Development Corporation (TIDCO). The loan could not be written off for it would reflect adversely on the exchequer. It was proposed that the TIDCO could run the company.

I had detailed discussions with S. Guhan, who was the then finance secretary. We decided against the deal as proposed by the firm. MGR closely questioned me as to why the company's proposal could not be accepted. Keeping the exchequer in mind, he asked whether it would not be better to close the chapter after all that had happened. I could not see eye-to-eye with him on the idea.

So, when I was asked to send the file, I promptly did so, without a moment's delay, sans any note. How it was finally disposed of was not my concern then, and I don't know what happened to the company. But

---

[8] A colourless liquid organic compound

shortly afterwards, Chief Secretary V. Karthikeyan summoned me to convey that I was being 'brought down'. My only expressed wish to the Chief Secretary was that the transfer should take place then and there. So I was 'brought down', literally; I was moved several floors down to the first floor in the same building to take charge as agriculture secretary.

Eventually, I took the initiative to ask for a posting outside Tamil Nadu. The post that came my way was that of member (personnel) in the Oil and Natural Gas Commission (ONGC) in Dehradun. I was happy to shift to the cool climate of Dehradun, away from the heat of Tamil Nadu politics. I joined ONGC in December 1978. I was a member incharge of the personnel in the commission, looking after more than 50,000 personnel working in Assam, Gujarat, Maharashtra and other states. I served in the ONGC for one and a half year.

At that time, Hemvati Nandan Bahuguna, from Uttar Pradesh, was the minister incharge. If an order was issued to transfer someone to Assam, I would receive a phone call in the next few minutes from Delhi. Bahuguna would be on the line: 'Seshan! Have you transferred this person to Assam? He has children...cancel the order.'

Having no alternative, I would cancel the order. I ended up cancelling many orders like this due to the intervention of the minister. One day, I called the minister and said, 'Whenever I issue an order to transfer any person to Assam, either you or your PA call me to have the order cancelled. I would rather you relieve me of the post of member incharge personnel. Why should I get a salary?'

Bahuguna's expression changed, 'Seshan, this will be the last time I will interfere with your work. Hereafter, neither I nor my PA will interfere in transfers. But see to it that no problems arise.'

Therefore, there was no phone call from Bahuguna regarding transfers as long as I worked there.

The work in ONGC was not demanding. It offered me little challenge. I had no problems dealing with the large workforce of the organization. Once the workers' problems were settled, there was nothing more to do in my office than to read the Ramayana or tune in to the radio for an occasional veena recital.

When I had enough of my stay in Dehradun, I approached the

cabinet secretary, N.K. Mukherjee, for any suitable posting in the administrative mainstream, but nothing came of it. I was sent back to Space Commission in Bangalore in 1980. It was also the year Indira Gandhi returned to power.

Bangalore always felt like home to me. The issue of space research involved me in a satisfying endeavour.

Indira Gandhi had the Space Commission directly under her, but I had very little interaction with her during this period. My meetings with her were limited to briefing her on the subjects of space whenever she faced a question in Parliament. I tried to be as thorough with the topic as possible.

One morning, when I was in Canada on some official work, I was getting dressed in an eighteenth floor room of Ottawa's Radisson Hotel and listening to music cassettes I had brought from home. I was getting ready to attend a meeting in connection with procuring things for the space centre in Bangalore. I suddenly received a telephone call from Venkatesan, my private secretary, and he said: 'Your next appointment has been announced. It's in Delhi.' I was thrilled.

It is a matter of pride for any IAS officer to be posted as secretary. The reason is that Delhi is India's power hub and political centre. A lot of work can be accomplished there, ranging from the department work to contributing to Parliament work. There would be opportunities to interact with ministers, right up to the PM. Delighted on hearing of my Delhi appointment, I asked as to which department I had been posted. Venkatesan said it was the newly created department of forests and wildlife, which came directly under Rajiv Gandhi. I was happy that I would be working under the young Rajiv Gandhi but had a slight apprehension as to how Rajiv would treat me.

SIX

NATIONAL SERVICE
AT THE CENTRAL SECRETARIAT

Secretary, department of forests and wildlife, was my first appointment in New Delhi. Staying in Delhi was not without difficulties, accommodation being one of the many problems. Fortunately, the space department had a guest house, and I found temporary shelter there. Normally, it should not have been all that tough. When an officer is posted to Delhi as a secretary, the juniors usually arrange a car, house, telephone and such facilities. But my situation was different; I had no assistants, not even a peon.

PLAYING MIDWIFE TO A NEW MINISTRY

One of the most important decisions taken by Rajiv Gandhi after winning the elections in 1984–85 was to create a new department of forests and wildlife. It was carved out of the agriculture ministry. There was increasing concern for the disappearing forest cover and its subsequent impact on the environment, including wildlife. Flora and fauna conservation needed concerted action and Rajiv Gandhi created a separate department towards this goal. To back up this decision, he took a couple of other initiatives too. One was that he upgraded the post of the inspector general of forests to special secretary to the Government of India. Up to that time, the inspector general of forests, under the agriculture ministry, was equivalent in rank to an additional secretary in the said department. The person occupying the post then was Rego.

Rajiv Gandhi was the cabinet minister, and there was a minister of state. The latter did not know English, and I did not know much Hindi. Naturally, I had a lot of problems interacting with him.

So, I had communication problems with the minister, an inspector general of forests who was no longer the top bureaucrat in forestry, with no cabin to do my official work, no phone and no car. I was setting up the entirely new department of forest and wildlife, and all I had with me were three or four people. Though the new department was hived off of the ministry of agriculture, we received little 'co-operation' from that ministry. In those initial months, the ministry showed a high degree of pettiness. I was denied even the most basic facilities and had to struggle for everything. It took me three months to establish the bare bones of the fledgling department.

Needless to say, I had a very rough time in those early days. For a while, I regretted accepting the promotion. I wished I could have continued in the calm environs of Bangalore.

On assuming office, Rajiv announced a very ambitious project. He said to me, 'The forests in our country are being degraded and destroyed. There is the danger of change in climate and temperature. I am going to promulgate a scheme to plant trees in an area of 50 lakh hectares every year.'

By all standards, this was an extraordinarily ambitious initiative. To plant one hectare, we need 2,000 saplings. You can calculate the enormous number of saplings needed for 50 lakh hectares. In order for them to grow, it was necessary to plant, safeguard and nurture them. The target was unbelievably difficult, but with Rajiv having made the remark with his first speech on television as PM, there was no going back on the commitment.

When questions are raised in Parliament, the concerned ministers must answer them, with inputs from the respective secretaries. Such inputs are usually discussed in meetings between the ministers and the respective secretaries. After I assumed office as secretary, the first such meeting that took place almost set the tone for much of what was to follow.

A Member of Parliament (MP) had asked the PM a question with regard to the forest department. The question was: 'You have said that you are going to plant trees in 50 lakh hectares! How are you going to achieve it?' Rajiv had to answer this question in Parliament.

In the meeting, he asked me: 'Mr Seshan, how are you going to plant trees in 50 lakh hectares in a year?'

I had earlier asked my department officers whether a plan had been chalked out but learnt that they had not proposed any such plans.

I bluntly told the PM, 'The undertaking for planting trees in 50 lakh hectares was given by you. We know nothing of the scheme.' There was pin-drop silence. I continued, 'One hectare is two and a half acres. To achieve the target, we need wasteland area amounting to 125 lakh acres. Where would we find that much land for the purpose? We can plant 2,000 trees in a hectare. At this rate, for 50 lakh hectares, we would require 1,000 crore saplings per year. How are we going to produce these many saplings? The cost of one plant is ₹2.50 and hence, we require ₹2,500 crore to produce the saplings. But we have allocated no budget for this. Other than this, we will need money for watering the plants, to pay for the labourers' wages and other expenses.'

While I was saying all this, the officer sitting beside me tugged at my shirt, taking care that Rajiv would not see it. Another secretary whispered, 'Seshan, keep quiet.'

I told the secretary loud and clear, 'Why keep quiet? I am not saying what is not correct. I am stating facts.'

Having heard this exchange, Rajiv said, 'Seshan, you are quiet candid.'

'Sir, I would like to speak the truth. I am not deriding your scheme. I only detailed what a Herculean task it would be in practice,' I said.

After the meeting, my colleagues took me to task.

One said, 'Is this the way to speak to a prime minister?'

Another said, 'Seshan, your goose is cooked. Wait for your transfer order.'

Contrary to what my colleagues expected, I did not get any transfer order. I heaved a sigh of relief when, instead, Rajiv appreciated me for having spoken frankly. He did not like a person who did not know about a particular issue but acted as if he knew everything. He would be angry if he caught anyone pretending that he knew more than he actually did.

It was decided that the afforestation project would be initiated anyway. There were many patches of wasteland all around the country, which were not fit for cultivation. It was proposed to plant trees in five lakh hectares in such areas. Rajiv created a separate board called the National Wasteland Development Board (NWDB) and appointed his advisor Arun Singh's close friend, Dr Kamala Choudhary, a management expert, as its chairperson. It was announced that she would look after the scheme of planting trees. And I, the secretary incharge of forests and wildlife, was made the executive secretary of the NWDB.

Seven or eight months after I became the secretary, Rajiv decided to merge the Department of Forests and Wildlife with the Department of Environment to make the new Ministry of Environment and Forests and Wildlife. A separate full-time secretary was appointed to the NWDB.

WHEN THE LEADERSHIP IS ENVIRONMENTALLY FAR-SIGHTED

Before Rajiv Gandhi, his mother Indira Gandhi's approach to protecting forests is worth mentioning here. As a PM, the diminishing population of tigers in the country worried her. She had started Project Tiger in 1973. The reason for the fall in the population of the tigers was that they were hunted ruthlessly in those days.

To support one tiger in the wild, 30 sq. km of forest area is needed. The area goes up depending on the number of tigers. Keeping this in view, Indira Gandhi came up with Project Tiger. But most politicians failed to grasp the significance of the idea.

One of the initial successes I found as secretary of the new ministry was that I managed to nudge the central government to take a small step towards protecting our forests. There are tens of thousands of kilometres of railway track in our country. If there is a sleeper for every 1.5 metre track, you can estimate how many millions of cubic feet of wood would be needed for the railways alone. The forest that would be cut down to meet the requirement would take decades to regenerate—or might not at all. Only those aware of the cumulative impact of such activities can feel alarmed. The Railways have now changed their preferences. These days, most sleepers are made of cement and steel, as they last longer and cost less. Usage of wooden sleepers has been limited to slopes and bridges.

Apart from innovations, there was quite a lot of routine work in the ministry. The big headache was that many cases would be forwarded to me from different states, seeking clearance of forest areas for development works. Such applications should ideally carry specific details. However, the cases I received would not have the complete details. Hence, such files had to be kept as pending, without sanction, awaiting the required details. The applicants would be the cause of the delay, but very often fingers would be pointed at me. I have had to make efforts to defend myself on such occasions.

Before the Department of Environmental Protection was added to my charge, environmental protection existed as an ordinary science department. On its upgrading, Rajiv asked me to draft the Environment (Protection) Act, in order to deal with environment-related problems. The Act was brought in 1986. It was my task to look after all the work related to this Act. When the Act finally came out, countries across the world appreciated it and spoke highly of it.

There were some significant water project-related challenges that came my way when I was holding office as secretary of the ministry: the Narmada Dam case, for instance. While there were benefits associated with the project, it would affect the livelihood of many. My political bosses took a call that the project should go ahead and so it did. But, while giving permission, I added a condition in my order: 'Work on the dam should not proceed faster than the rehabilitation work needed to compensate those who lose their homes and money because of the project.' Unfortunately, even today, the tribal people have not been compensated properly.

Another similar case was that of Tehri Dam. The project was not advisable, considering its potential adverse environmental impact. But considering other factors, including a loan received from Russia, the government eventually gave a go-ahead to the project.

A project across the Mahanadi had a different consequence though. The study showed adverse environmental impact. Even though a lot of money had already been spent on the project, I stood firm on it and it was eventually abandoned. Though I did feel a sense of disappointment that we were stopping developmental work, there was no alternative.

THE LOOPHOLES USED FOR CORRUPTION IN FORESTRY

Things have come to such a pass that there is no department in India that has not witnessed corruption. Wherever you go, you see it. If the market price of a teak tree is ₹50,000, forest officials would sell it for a much lower price to a forest contractor. The contractor would sell it at market rates and cut a commission for the officials from the profits. The commission received on this would be shared up to the top. Politicians are hand in glove with these elements on both sides.

Some politicians and officers would come up with a proposal for laying roads for tribal people. Citing this reason, they would cut thousands of trees and sell them for a good price. Forest officials have another way to cut trees. After selling all the useful trees, which are then cut down, they present a proposal to plant trees in its place. They then start planting eucalyptus. Though it does not require much water, there is no advantage in planting eucalyptus trees. Usually, the fallen dry leaves of trees are eventually converted into fertilizer. But the leaves of eucalyptus trees are not useful in this way. Moreover, we plant trees to prevent soil erosion. In this aspect too, eucalyptus tree is not much of a use, as the roots don't go deep and it does not help with holding the soil. The net result is that the forest does not regenerate and the land becomes more or less useless. As if doing so is not enough, the corrupt go on to grab and occupy the forest land. In this way, lakhs of acres of forest department land are now in the possession of India's rich people.

Corruption is a nexus. In one of my earlier books[9], I have narrated a story of frogs' legs. There is tremendous cruelty meted out to frogs, all for harvesting their legs that are eventually served as delicacies abroad. So, we had a law against exporting frogs. However, somebody had already done the damage and was trying to get the consignment out of the country. The consignment was stopped at Chennai harbour and then again at Calcutta. The trader used all the influence he had, including ministers, to get the job done. Till the very end, he could not get permission. The argument he offered was that the frogs have suffered already, so why not benefit from the export. He was turned down for obvious reasons.

One of the other challenges taken up by Rajiv during the time I was in the ministry was cleaning of the Ganga. We did our best to complete the project, but the challenges were aplenty: there were factories, money-starved municipalities, traditional professionals who rendered services of catering to the dead bodies. Then it was found that electric crematoriums set up on the banks were not being put to use for a reason as simple as lack of electricity. Infrastructure for cleaning the polluted water, before it reaches the river, was built, but the local governments were not able to run it for lack of funds. The efforts were on when I left the ministry, but even three decades later, cleaning the Ganga still remains a challenge.

HOW I ENDED UP WITH THE RESPONSIBILITY OF THE PM'S SECURITY

Even while I was the secretary in the Ministry of Environment and Forests and Wildlife, the responsibility of protecting the PM was given to me.

It is not unusual for an IAS officer to gain experience in fields like revenue, industry, labour and agriculture. In my career until then, I had also gathered experience in the atomic energy department and in the space research department; in these two departments, I had

---

[9]Seshan, T.N, *En Kathai*, Tirunelveli Thennindia Saiva Sithantha Noorpathippu Kazhagam Ltd, 2002.

Through the Broken Glass

spent nearly 15 years. Owing to my tenure as collector in Madurai, I had some knowledge of law and order. I, however, did not have much understanding about dealing with security.

When I was in the forests and environment ministry as secretary, I had the habit of going to office on holidays, too. Though it was a holiday on 2 October 1986, I was at the office taking care of some pending work. There was a cricket match going on somewhere, so I had switched on the television and was keeping an eye on the score as I went through the files. Suddenly, the telecast stopped and a news flash appeared: 'Rajiv Gandhi was shot at by an unidentified person. But he was unhurt. The person who shot the Prime Minister was later caught. Rajiv proceeded with his programme and did not cancel his other appointments.' I was shocked.

The very next day, I was summoned by the PM. When I went to see him, the place was naturally swarming with policemen.

'Seshan, I would like you to make a full inquiry into yesterday's incident at Rajghat and submit the report to me,' Rajiv said.

Thinking that the responsibility was rather unusual and heavy, I said that I had never handled any job pertaining to security and someone else may be more suited to the task.

'You speak frankly. You do not fear anyone. Because of these qualities, I am giving you this job,' Rajiv said.

As Rajiv instructed, I met B.G. Deshmukh, the cabinet secretary. A four-member committee was formed. Deshmukh, one Mr Gupta from the home department, an officer of the intelligence department and I were on the committee. I was to do the leg work and had strictly been allotted four weeks to complete the job.

Sitting in the committee room of the Cabinet Secretary, I called in everyone related to the case. As I had no prior experience in handling such matters, the work seemed difficult at first. Soon, I got the hang of it. I wrote a 150-page report about the deficiency in the security arrangements and the precautions to be taken in future. I wrote the report myself because if it were to be given to a stenographer, it could have been leaked. So, I prepared only one copy. After a committee meeting on 26 October, I gave the report to Rajiv. I do not know what he did with it. As my job was done after submitting the report, I went back to my regular work.

A little less than two months later, on 15 December, I received a phone call from the PMO asking me to meet the PM at the airport. He was returning from a trip to Jaipur. I was surprised because he had never called me to the airport before. I hastened to the Delhi airport. Rajiv arrived and told me that he had some important work for me.

Rajiv had an imported, red, bulletproof jeep. He would drive it himself. He sat at the driver's seat, Chidambaram sat next to him and I sat behind. As he drove, Rajiv told me that he wanted to implement the security precautions I had recommended in my report. I asked how I could help.

'By taking security under your charge,' Rajiv said nonchalantly.

Chidambaram agreed that it was a good suggestion, 'And we can replace him with another secretary in the forests and environment ministry.'

But Rajiv did not want that. He wanted me to look after both security and environment.

I replied: 'Let it be as you wish.'

A week later, I got an order from the cabinet secretary's office in this regard.

SO WHAT IF I GOT EVEN UNDER RAJIV'S SKIN?

I was allotted a room in the North Block and was given support staff as well. The office of the minister of state for home, Chidambaram, was situated in the same block. Chidambaram would hold meetings daily. How security was to be given, what to do when Rajiv is in Delhi, how to make security arrangements when he went outside Delhi or abroad, how to appoint or select the candidates required for this job—he gave advice and suggestions on all such matters. I implemented all of them.

Following the assassination of Indira Gandhi, the Special Protection Group (SPG) was formed on the initiative of Rajiv and Arun Singh, the minister of communications at that time, to protect the PM and his family. The SPG and I worked very closely together. An imported bulletproof car for Rajiv's security would cost too much. So, we turned the Ambassador cars into bulletproof ones. I had to take care of all aspects of Rajiv's security. Often, I would go to his home to check on his food for security reasons and to check whether all was well. As I went to his residence very often, I grew very close to him. The SPG would ask me to convey things to Rajiv which they were hesitant to say directly to him.

Rajiv never took his personal security lightly. But there were times when he overruled us. He overturned my strong opposition to his visit to Colombo to sign the Indo–Sri Lanka Accord. Despite Chidambaram backing me, Rajiv would still not listen. And despite our best efforts, Rajiv was attacked by a Sri Lankan sailor who swung his rifle butt at him. He narrowly escaped serious injuries.

I had a job to do and the job was to keep India's PM alive. I became strongly aware that if my methods brought me unpopularity, so be it. Some of my methods even embarrassed Rajiv. There were occasions when I snatched a biscuit almost out of his mouth. I went on to remind a startled Rajiv that the PM should eat nothing that was not tested beforehand.

Rajiv had a great wish to be with the people, and the people wanted to see their PM. At such occasions, it was often necessary for me to physically interpose myself between the crowds and the PM. Once in Kolkata, when Rajiv had gone on an election tour, I had to run with the PM's car for several miles to be present when he got off, in the anticipation of an excited crowd mobbing him. On these occasions, I had to be close on the heels of those providing physical security.

On Independence Day, in 1987, a freedom run was organized. Rajiv was to run from Vijay Chowk to India Gate in the capital, and was to be accompanied by many people, including some of his cabinet ministers. He had arrived in his tracksuit while I was dressed in black trousers and a closed collar coat. While waiting for the freedom run to be flagged off, he found an opportunity to tease me, 'Why do you stand suited and booted? Why not run with us, Seshan? It would help you cut down your avoidable fat.'

I replied, 'Sir, some of us have to stand upright, so that you can sit, stand or run.'

The path marked for the run was a security nightmare. We had no problems securing a small stretch of the route. However, further ahead, crowds were to join in, and there was no way we could ensure security. As soon as the PM had run a few yards, the security cordon closed in around him, forming a tight ring and soon bundled him into a car and sped him away to his home. The PM was furious when he reached his residence. He showered all permissible epithets on me, since I had wrecked the run. But it was my job to supervise the PM's security. I was happy that I had done my job and did not take his words to heart.

A CRITICAL PIECE OF ADVICE THAT RAJIV DID NOT TAKE

The PM's security is an extraordinarily sensitive issue. Let us trace it historically. Indira Gandhi was assassinated in October 1984. Elections took place soon after, and Rajiv Gandhi came to power in January 1985. As said before, the SPG was set up to take care of the PM's security.

There was no legal basis for the SPG. Every police force requires a legal basis. For example, if the police sub-inspector draws a gun on you in the police station or in a crowd or when there is some violence, he is backed by the authority of the Code of Criminal Procedure. As the station house officer, he has certain powers. Similarly, each of the special police forces, whether Central Bureau of Investigation, Central Reserve Police Force (CRPF) or Border Security Force, has a law governing its functioning. The SPG had no law governing it. If in the course of protecting the PM, the SPG personnel were compelled to draw their guns and shoot, they had nothing to protect themselves with, except for claiming the right of self-defence—not the defence of the PM but their own defence.

There were discussions that we needed a law to govern the SPG. I was given the job, and I drafted the legislation for the SPG Act. Even today, it is in the statute book for anyone to read.

One particular section of the Act said that the SPG shall provide proximate protection to the PM and his immediate family. I went up to Rajiv and suggested that we needed to include past PMs and their families too in the Act. Another question was whether it should only be about protecting the PM or the President, too? It was decided that the SPG Act would only cover the PM and nobody else.

In 1988–89, I told Rajiv, 'Today you are the PM, tomorrow you might no be. But the danger to you, because of whatever you did or did not do as the PM, will remain.'

I quoted the example of USA, from which we borrow many things. There, the Federal Bureau of Investigation looks after the president's family even long after he is dead and gone. Citing this practice, I argued that Rajiv and his immediate family would need protection even after he gave up the job due to election loss or any other reason. The laws should protect the PM and his immediate family, along with the former PMs and their immediate families. But Rajiv did not agree. He thought that people would believe he was doing it out of pure self-interest. He said no for the former PMs; it was enough to include the present one. I tried to convince him but in vain.

The Act that was passed read: 'PM in office and his immediate family.' These were the only people to be covered by the SPG. Those who were responsible for dealing with security later seem to have subsequently amended the law. That is how, for example, Sonia and Rajiv Gandhi's family are protected even today.

I remained incharge of the PM's security even though my other portfolio was shifted from the forests and environment ministry to defence. The latter was all together a different ball game.

When I was in the defence ministry, the issue pertaining to the Indian Peace Keeping Force in Sri Lanka cropped up. In my view, it was a mishap. As the events unfolded, the armed forces were constrained to act as a police force, which put severe restrictions on their freedom to use the skills they were trained for. The force was eventually withdrawn and though we acted firmly as a nation, we endured heavy losses.

Then, there was the incident in Maldives where some people tried to take control over the government there. India responded to their government's request and the armed forces did a clean job—and a quick one at that. In two days, order was restored and it took the relationship between the two nations to another level.

One personal milestone I achieved in this period in the defence ministry is that I lost 21 kg in a matter of months. But a lighter Seshan was still a fat man.

WHEN THE BOFORS ISSUE WAS RAGING

When I was appointed secretary in the defence ministry, the appointment was criticized from different quarters. While some commented that a person who had never worked in defence had been appointed as the secretary, newspapers wrote that I had been appointed to guard the Bofors deal[10]. It was true that I had no connection whatsoever with the defence ministry and the criticism was justified, but as far as Bofors was concerned, I played a peripheral role in it.

When I became defence secretary on 2 June 1988, much had already happened on the Bofors deal. The joint parliamentary committee had sat and had given its report. But in every session of Parliament, the Bofors deal used to be raked up and there would be discussions on it. At times, I used to prepare answers in connection with the deal for the defence minister, K.C. Pant.

I handled the issue as any civil servant would—with reference to available papers. When I came to the defence ministry, there were no papers there with regard to Bofors. I never saw one scrap of the original paper on Bofors, even though I was the defence secretary from June 1988 to February–March 1989. The papers, in custody somewhere, were definitely not in the defence ministry. There were photocopies of some documents in files, but not of the whole set. N.N. Vohra and T.K. Banerjee worked in the defence ministry at that time. As these

---

[10]An allegation of kickbacks being paid to Indian citizens by the Bofors company were made in the Swedish radio station based on a whistle-blower's account on 16 April 1987. The amount paid was supposedly the 2020 equivalent of ₹690 crore for a deal signed in the year 1986 for Bofors guns worth ₹17,000 crore. Rajiv Gandhi was the PM at that time, and so the Opposition and media took him to task over it.

two had handled the Bofors case already, I prepared answers for Pant with their help. Other than this, I had no connections with the Bofors deal. And I have no personal position on the deal either.

Then there was the signing of the deal for the purchase of HDW (Howaldtswerke-Deutsche Werft) submarines from Germany. This had happened before I had joined the ministry. The machines offered by the French were reported to be the best. Many newspapers had, therefore, criticized the purchase of the submarine from Germany instead of France. Some wrote that crores of rupees had changed hands in the deal. The comptroller and auditor general (CAG), who investigated this case, too, had recorded an objection to the decision of the government.[11]

Being the secretary, I had to defend the government before the CAG. But since the incident was something that happened before I came to the office, it made things very difficult for me. Since the CAG had written the adverse paragraph on the HDW submarine deal, it came up before the Public Accounts Committee for discussion. Jaipal Reddy and Jaswant Singh, who were members of the committee, put me in a corner.

The government's position was that the alternative French offer of the submarine was rejected because its self-noise was greater than that of the German HDW submarine. This meant that the HDW submarine had greater stealth. This was the technical advice of the naval headquarters. As the defence secretary, I defended the government's position. Being the civil servant incharge, I had to support the position taken by the government. That is all I did—nothing more, nothing less.

Unfortunately, the Public Accounts Committee was split down the middle between the members from the ruling party and the Opposition parties, who were part of the committee. I never saw the Public Accounts Committee's report on this CAG audit paragraph relating to the HDW submarine.

But it is common sense. The whole point of a submarine is stealth.

---

[11]Kutty, K. Govindan, *Seshan: An Intimate Story*, Konark Publishers Pvt Ltd, 1994.

What is the point of hiding underwater and travelling in a submarine if it made a racket?

WOULD I SERVE AS THE CABINET SECRETARY?

At a time when there was much speculation about the next cabinet secretary, I received a phone call from Rajiv summoning me to his office. He asked me, 'Seshan, what is our opinion on the appointment of the next cabinet secretary?'

At that time, there were four senior officers on the list of probable candidates, but all were due to retire in the following two to three months. On the other hand, I had close to 22 months before retirement.

'I would not mind if you were to appoint any of my seniors as the cabinet secretary. I will continue to work, telling myself that my time has not come. But, if any of my juniors, however outstanding, is appointed, instead of going to court and filing cases, I will resign.'

While I was saying this, Rajiv listened intently. After this conversation, he did not speak to me at all regarding the appointment of the cabinet secretary.

On 15 February 1989, after lunch at the Naval Mess at Colaba in Mumbai, Rajiv called me aside and in his characteristic mischievous way said, 'I am going to move you to the Cabinet.' These were his exact words.

I said, 'That is fine, thank you very much,' and moved away to take care of lunch.

He called me back and asked, 'Don't you want to know why and in what capacity.'

I said, 'No, I don't want to know. If you had wanted to tell me, you would have done so. I am not going to bombard you with questions. If you don't want to tell me, you won't change your mind even if I ask.'

At my reply, Rajiv went away laughing.

Back in Delhi, on the fifth day after this conversation, Rajiv called me to his office. 'I wish to appoint you as the cabinet secretary. Doing so, I would make you supersede four of your seniors. I am not worried about that. But there is a hindrance,' he said, smiling and pausing for effect. 'My ministers do not like the fact that I am appointing you as the cabinet secretary. They harbour fear about you.'

I suggested that the only way to allay the fear was to make someone else the cabinet secretary.

Just then, the minister of state for parliamentary affairs, Sheila Dikshit, walked into Rajiv's room, 'What is your opinion about making Seshan the cabinet secretary?' Rajiv asked her.

She looked at me for a second, 'Seshan is tough, so we are all apprehensive.'

'So, Seshan, did you hear Sheila's words?' Rajiv asked.

'Sir, I cannot change myself at this age. Every IAS officer would wish to attain the cabinet secretary's post. Having taken me to the threshold of the cabinet secretary's post, you now say that the ministers harbour fear about me,' I said.

Rajiv just smiled.

Two days after that conversation in Rajiv's office, I got the order, and after due procedure in March that year, I became the cabinet secretary. I continued in that post until the end of 1989 when I was shifted out rather unceremoniously. My tenure had lasted less than a year. It was a rewarding experience, and it was not without its unique moments.

RAJIV'S RUN-IN WITH THE ELECTION COMMISSION

One morning, Rajiv called me to discuss some important issues. I hurried to his office. He said, 'I have decided to expand the Election Commission of India. Two additional election commissioners will be appointed.'

'The Election Commission started functioning in 1952 and has been working for the last 37 years without any problem. One person is enough. Why do you unnecessarily want to add more members?' I asked him.

'The panchayat elections have to be conducted. The work will be heavy. So, I am going to appoint two additional members,' Rajiv explained.

In October 1989, Rajiv introduced the Panchayati Raj Bill. But it was defeated in the Rajya Sabha.

'The Panchayati Raj Bill has not been passed in the Rajya Sabha. How will the panchayat elections be held? Why add two members? I do not understand,' I said once again.

Rajiv was adamant, 'I am going to appoint two additional members to the Election Commission.'

'When it is the wish of the Prime Minister, so be it!' I said and returned to my office.

They were eventually appointed.

I have been accused of being instrumental in the appointment of those two additional commissioners. In truth, the cabinet secretary has nothing to do with the appointment of election commissioners. Only the law ministry and the PMO are involved. So, as the cabinet secretary, I did not have any role in it.

Peri Shastri, who was a good friend of mine, was the CEC at that time. The rumours were that Rajiv wished to appoint two additional members because he did not have any faith in Shastri. The day after they were appointed, I received a call from an angry Shastri, asking me, 'Who does the Prime Minister think he is?'

'I think he thinks he is the Prime Minister,' I told him.

He wanted me to tell this to Rajiv, among other things.

I replied, 'If you don't have his phone number, I can give it to you. You please tell him yourself because I am not a postman.'

On 17 October 1989, the government announced the general elections. I was called to the PMO one morning and we discussed many cases. At the very end, Rajiv said that he was going to call for elections in November.

'We should have elections on 21, 22 and 25,' he said.

'We should not decide the dates for the elections. Only the Election Commission has the right to do that,' I said.

Rajiv did not pay any heed to my words, 'Elections have to be conducted on the dates I have given. Tell that to Peri Shastri,' he ordered.

'I am sorry,' I said. 'My understanding of the law is that under the Representation of the People Act, 1951, the President shall sign the notification on the date which may be specified by the Election Commission. So, for me to go and tell the CEC the exact date is inappropriate. We can only inform the Election Commission of our wish to have the election in November, but we do not have any right to order the Election Commission to conduct the election on particular dates. In this situation, how can I inform Peri Shastri about the exact election dates?'

Rajiv became angry and said with an air of finality, 'Okay! If you cannot inform him, I will send Deshmukh.' Deshmukh was the principal secretary to the PM.

After this incident, I went back to my room. Deshmukh apparently went and, I believe, a meeting took place between Deshmukh and Shastri that was not cordial.

Shastri rang me up again and asked the same question, 'Who does the Prime Minister think he is?'

I replied, 'He still thinks he is the Prime Minister.'

'Let him be the Prime Minister. But who is he to order me? Does he not know that the Prime Minister has no right to order the Election Commission?' an angry Shastri asked.

'Why don't you speak to Rajiv Gandhi directly,' I said.

'I do not like to talk to him. You ask him on my behalf,' said Shastri.

'I am sorry! The law is with you,' I said. 'Do what you can do according to the law.'

'No, no! I do not like to fight with Rajiv Gandhi,' said Shastri.

'What can I do about that?' I asked. Even as I was speaking, Shastri put down the phone without answering.

Finally, elections did take place on those particular days. But Rajiv was defeated. A new government was formed, under the prime ministership of V.P. Singh, with external support.

A BRIEF TURBULENT TENURE UNDER V.P. SINGH

The very first issue that the new government led by V.P. Singh, after he took charge on 2 December 1989, was confronted with was that of the alleged abduction and recovery of the daughter of Mufti Mohammed

Sayeed, the then home minister in a coalition government.

During this crisis, the Government of India and that of Kashmir were on high alert for nearly 100 hours. As the cabinet secretary, I was on my feet for most of this time in the central control room, helping to deal with the crisis. I came away with the feeling that many of those involved knew far more than what they were willing to admit.

Another concern at that time was regarding the fact that Rajiv had limited the SPG cover to only the serving PM and his immediate family. The very next day after V.P. Singh became the PM, that is, on 3 December, there was a meeting called under my chairmanship to discuss whether or not to continue to give security cover to Rajiv.

'The security threat to Rajiv Gandhi has still not diminished. So, the security provided to him should not be disturbed. SPG security should be given. But the government has to take a decision on it,' I said in the meeting and wrote the same in the official file. I indicated that the statutes could easily be amended through presidential assent. But the V.P. Singh government did not agree to it. As long as I remained cabinet secretary, until the third week of December, no decision was taken in connection with Rajiv's security. After I was moved out of the cabinet secretary's post, the SPG security given to Rajiv was withdrawn. Who took that decision and how it was taken was brought out in the Verma Commission report[12].

I had been in the cabinet secretary's post under Rajiv for just eight months when V.P. Singh took charge as the PM. It was well known that the two did not get along well and that I was close to Rajiv. When we add it up, it is easy to draw conclusions. So, when V.P. Singh became the PM, I knew that my days as the cabinet secretary were numbered. Sure enough, it became evident that he had made up his mind.

On 22 December, a despatch rider came to my home with an envelope. The time was 11.30 p.m. I guessed it was about my transfer, and so it was. I was appointed a member of the Planning Commission.

---

[12]'Rajya Sabha, Unstarred Question No. 1959', Ministry of Home Affairs, Government of India, https://bit.ly/3ZTK7Ox. Accessed on 17 March 2023.

The ouster did not upset me. But I was disappointed that the PM did not feel the need to have a word with me before doing what he did. Even the PM's principal secretary, B.G. Deshmukh, with whom I had served as an intern, did not find it appropriate to give me a hint. Then there was Vinod Pande, my batchmate, who was to take over from me. I did not call him directly, for it could have been embarrassing in the situation.

The next day, I asked an officer of the cabinet secretariat a suitable time for Pande to take charge. Pande preferred 11.05 a.m. Anything earlier or later would be inauspicious. I reached there two minutes before time, and he came on the dot.

For two hours that day, we sat together and exchanged personal and official notes. The only difference was that he was sitting in the cabinet secretary's chair and I was sitting in the visitor's chair. Having handed over the charge to him, I walked out and headed for the Planning Commission.

There were 11 members in the Planning Commission, including me, under Ramakrishna Hegde. People would jocularly call us 'Hegde's eleven'.

Though Hegde gave me due respect, the other members of the team avoided me since I was not well-liked by V.P. Singh. We could divide the members of the team into four groups. J.D. Sethi, L.C. Jain and Rajni Kothari were close to Singh and were in the 'first class' category. I was a 'fourth class' member; they would not call me for any important functions or for meeting the PM.

From time to time, Jain would brief me on what was discussed with the PM, and I was grateful for the small mercies, more for the mercies than out of interest in what was discussed.

In the Indian government, there are many useless institutions, and the highest of them was the Planning Commission. I worked for nearly a year as member of the Planning Commission, and what I did there is not worth talking about.

The pace of work in Yojana Bhawan was also hopelessly slow, and I would get worked up. No meeting scheduled there ever took place at the notified time. When I found meeting after meeting taking place an hour or more after the schedule time, I removed the clock in my room and sent it to the commission's secretary with a note attached to it: 'There is no need of a clock in Yojana Bhavan where nothing is done on time.' Sometime later, I sent him a calendar for similar reasons.

None of these protests made any impression though.

During this time, some clerical genius suddenly decided to drastically reduce my salary, so that I may receive only what a Planning Commission member would normally get. They did not so much as apply their minds to consider that I was still in service with the rank of cabinet secretary to the government. When I side-stepped into the Planning Commission, I was not demoted. I continued as an IAS officer who was due to retire in the end of 1990. So, according to service rules, only my role had changed, not my conditions of service. I had to present a case for the restoration of deducted pay to people who had great difficulty in getting the point. I struggled till the matter was settled, much to my satisfaction.

I was grateful for the conjunction of events that brought V.P. Singh down and helped Chandra Shekhar rise. But that gratefulness was more on the account of my farewell to Yojana Bhavan and the thought of moving to a place new.

SEVEN

SETTLING DOWN INTO THE ROLE OF CEC

The V.P. Singh-led government fell and a new government under Chandra Shekhar was formed. When the latter became the PM in November 1990, he informed me of his intention to return the cabinet secretary's post to me.

However, I was due for retirement on 31 December that year, and I informed him about the same. I also told him that the IAS cadre was not happy with a retired person acting as the cabinet secretary. He then proposed, 'Why don't I make you the principal secretary to the PM?' I told him that I was not a good choice, that I was a very difficult person to work with, and that he would be better off finding somebody else. This discussion went on for three to four days in the last week of November 1990.

Meanwhile, the then CEC, Peri Shastri, passed away owing to ill health. The government did something that was very unwise. It went ahead to process the appointment of Rama Devi, secretary, law, as the acting CEC. On the fourth day after Devi took over, I got a phone call from the cabinet secretary, Vinod Pande.

'We are planning to appoint you as the CEC. Are you interested?' asked Pande.

I was surprised on knowing that someone would think of me as the CEC. So, my immediate reaction was to say no because when did I ever have anything to do with elections? I had come into contact with elections as the assistant collector (training), at Coimbatore in 1956. The next time I ever had contact with elections was in 1967, when the Congress was soundly defeated and the DMK came to power. But from 1967 until 1989–90, for 20 years or more, I had served in scientific departments. I knew nothing about elections. I, anyway, did not think very highly of the CEC's post. I did not know much about it at that time.

And so, I said, 'No. I do not want it. I am not fit for that role.'

SUBRAMANIAN SWAMY'S SUSPENSE OFFER

The ECI is dealt with, in the government, by the law and justice ministry. Subramanian Swamy, my friend, was the minister incharge. As he was also holding the portfolio of the Ministry of Commerce and Industry, Swamy had led the Indian delegation to world trade meetings in Brussels. From Brussels, he rang me up several times to assure me that the PM had excellent intentions towards me and would accommodate me in a suitable post. Nothing came of this until 7 or 8 December, when Swamy returned from Brussels.

Swamy came straight to my house, 'Seshan! You have a very good job on hand. I won't tell you now. I will tell you at night.' So saying this, he went off, leaving me puzzled.

Swamy and his wife came to my house at midnight, and we spoke until two in the morning.

'I told you that you have a fine offer. It is the CEC's post,' Swamy said.

'Vinod Pande already asked me about it,' I said.

He replied, 'I want an answer from you, so that I can process the papers to make you the CEC.'

I asked him to give me a day's time to make up my mind.

'I will give you until 6.00 p.m. to think over it. Get back to me with a good decision,' he said and went off.

It was Swamy's responsibility to find a CEC. But Swamy had later said that I had begged him to get this job. What led him to say that is not clear to me even today. Was it because Swamy and I were no longer on friendly terms or was there some other reason, I do not know. I don't want to get involved in a controversy with him. But I did not seek the CEC's post. In fact, before accepting it, I spent several hours agonizing over it.

THE MIRACULOUS INPUT FROM KANCHI NAILED IT

After Swamy left that day, I pondered over the decision for some time, trying to think whose advice I could seek. It was two in the morning. I knew the number for the telephone by Rajiv's bedside. I dialled. Rajiv picked up the phone and said, 'What is it? You, and calling at this hour?'

'Can I meet you tomorrow morning?' I asked.

'There is a lot of work in the morning. We can meet at night,' he said.

'It will be too late,' I said.

'*Acchha*,' he said, 'Okay, can you come now?'

'I do not have a car. If you kindly send me a car, I can come,' I said.

The car arrived at my home in a short while. I went to Rajiv's place. It was 2.30 a.m.

I told Rajiv about the CEC post offered and asked his opinion whether I should take it.

'What? Is he going to give you the CEC's post? He will repent later,' Rajiv said. 'This job is neither good for you nor will appointing you as the CEC be good for Chandra Shekhar. Take this job only if no other job is available.'

I spoke to Rajiv until 5.30 a.m. and then went back home. Later, I asked for an appointment with R. Venkataraman, the president, so that I could meet him at eight in the morning.

Within a short time, RV called me on phone, 'Why the formalities? Come and see me directly.'

I went to the Rashtrapati Bhavan and gave him the news and asked, 'Should I take this job or not? You should direct me.'

'The CEC's job will not suit you. You can't get any other job?' he asked me.

'Whom can I ask for any other job?' I said.

'If there is no alternative, take this job,' RV's advice was in sync with that given by Rajiv.

After that, I rang my brother in Chennai and asked for his advice. 'You are going to be 58. Why do you wish to be stuck in Delhi? Come here. It would be supporting for me too,' he said.

After my brother, I asked my father-in-law for advice. 'I cannot even distinguish between a municipal commissioner and an election commissioner. Let me do one thing. I will ask for an advice from the astrologer Krishnamurthy Shastri of the Malleswaram Shiva Temple,' he said. He called me back after an hour, 'However much you may deny, you will take up this job. You will be in this job for six years. And for those six years, it will be like sitting on a bed of thorns. But nothing bad will happen.' This is what Krishnamurthy Shastri had predicted.

I was confused. I could not decide whether to take up the job or not. As a last resort, I decided to consult one last person.

Until the fifty-sixth year of my life, I never had a darshan of the Kanchi seer. I had never been to Kanchipuram. My father used to go there very often. After the Rajiv Gandhi-led government was defeated, I had met the Kanchi seer once.

Asking the seer's advice about taking the job of a CEC would be right, I thought, and so I rang up the Kanchi mutt and put the query across to a friend there. He agreed to ask the seer. He called back in 20 minutes, 'There was a great surprise. Before I could even ask the seer, he himself said, "It is a respectable job, ask him to take it", and gave his approval.'

Immediately, I rang up Subramanian Swamy, 'You gave me time until six, but there is no need to wait. I am ready to take charge of the post of the CEC.'

On 10 December 1990, the order was released. On 12, I took charge as the ninth CEC of India.

So, did I want to become the CEC? No, that is untrue. Did I dislike becoming the CEC? No, that is also untrue. I am not a hypocrite to say I did not at all want to become the CEC. I had serious reservations as to whether I would function well as the CEC. The rest is history.

DID I USURP A WOMAN'S OPPORTUNITY?

Controversy started the day I took over as the CEC. The daily newspapers tried to imply that I had usurped Rama Devi's chances. It was understandable if she was unhappy. But such appointments are not made according to some pre-fixed pattern of succession. Every bureaucrat knows this, and she was a very senior officer.

Based on a Press Trust of India report, *The Indian Express* quoted a Janata Dal spokesman saying: 'Irreparable damage has been caused to the independence of this important and sensitive constitutional institution.'[13]

Several women's organizations too took exception to the government's decision not to appoint Mrs Rama Devi as the country's CEC. And they questioned the government's commitment to women's equality and laws for their protection.

The CEC's post had alternated between a civil servant—an ICS or IAS officer—and a person with legal know-how. Peri Shastri was a legal person, and prior to him, the CEC was a retired IAS officer.

That Rama Devi was not happy that she was not regularized in the post of the CEC was natural. Some might say that the CEC's job was full of legal work, and therefore only a lawyer should be appointed, but that is not true. Others might say that the CEC has a lot of administrative executive work, and so only an IAS officer should be appointed, but that is not true either. The post calls for a combination of experience in both areas. So, the post could have gone to either of us, and more appropriately to me, going by the pattern of alternation. Rama Devi and I had no problems between us and subsequently even got on very well with one another. Differences at the official level are healthy and essential, so that the exchange of ideas brings out the best in everyone.

---

[13]'JD Criticizes Criticizes Seshan's Posting', *The Indian Express*, 13 December 1990, https://bit.ly/3kotKt6, p. 9. Accessed on 16 January 2023.

TUNING UP THE WORKSPACE

When I took charge as the CEC, I probably did not realize the magnitude of the task ahead of me, but my goals were clear. The very next day, on 13 December, while speaking to the press, I said, 'And a lot more needs to be done in almost every sphere of the electoral process, including the electoral rolls, polling stations, code of conduct and the role of the civil servants and the polling personnel to make the elections foolproof.'

When I visited the ECI office for the first time, I realized that I had work cut out for me: the easy-going atmosphere, the stinking toilets, and the broken furniture told me that a lot needed to be done there.

I started with the CEC's room. There were pictures of all kinds of gods hanging on the walls, probably for decades together. I had them promptly removed from the walls, making them look neat and free of clutter. A cosy old chair, with bugs crawling all over it, stood in a corner. That too was removed.

The next thing I took on was the housekeeping. When it became clear to my staff that I would not tolerate even a single piece of furniture or fitting not functioning properly, the environment of Nirvachan Sadan began to take a shape that was to my liking.

I was more than certain that the amount of work done in the ECI did not require so much time that the staff would need to do overtime. The overtime bill of the commission dropped drastically from ₹7 lakh to less than ₹1 lakh per month after I took over. Similarly, the surprise checks helped in improving the general discipline. The housekeeping helped in sprucing up the work environment.

A major bank had a branch in the premises of the commission, and it had accounts of all kinds of people not associated with the commission. The fact that many people not connected with the commission were visiting the body's premises was not acceptable, as it undermined the office's discipline. Soon, in place of that bank, another major bank set up a branch to serve the commission and its employees exclusively.

Next on my agenda was clearing the backlog of election-related work. Among things that could be immediately tackled were the cases related to election returns to be submitted in the prescribed format. The verification of such returns was not much of a question before I stepped in. But even this exercise seemed too much of a bother for thousands of leaders who had set out to lead the people. A cut-off date was fixed for verification of the expense accounts of any candidate who had figured in the elections since 1987. I reviewed 40,000 cases. The exercise was easy, though no one had ever thought it as a necessary task. As many as 14,000 people who had contested in elections had not even bothered to submit returns of expenses. The law was enforced and the whole lot of them were disqualified.

ADJUDICATION ON THE SYMBOL CASES

For the political parties, their election symbols are very important because it is something they are recognized by. But the election symbols are a property of the ECI. The commission allocates them and manages them according to the applicable laws. Very often, the symbols come under dispute. Two or more factions of a party may stake claim to one symbol, and in such a case, it is the role of the commission to adjudicate. The first such case that I had to handle was the lotus case. Arjun Singh, leader of the Congress party and former CM of Madhya Pradesh, had filed a petition in October 1990 before the commission— this was a few months before I joined office as the CEC.

The backdrop to this case was that the Bharatiya Janata Party (BJP) president L.K. Advani had undertaken a rath yatra in which the BJP's lotus symbol was extensively used. Arjun Singh claimed that, after the incorporation of Section 29A in the Representation of the People Act, 1951, (which covers all election-related issues), it was incumbent upon every political party to amend its constitution, so as to reflect faith in the secularism, unity and integrity of the country. He claimed that it was only after such an amendment to the party's constitution was made that any political party could be registered with the ECI and allotted a reserved symbol to contest the elections.

According to Arjun Singh, since the BJP had undertaken a campaign for building a temple at the Ram Janmabhoomi—which was a religious issue—the party ceased to be secular in nature. Therefore, even if it were to amend its constitution, it had to be deregistered as a political party, with its lotus symbol being frozen as a result.

The BJP fielded a reply in which it raised two primary objections: one, that the ECI did not have the right to entertain such a petition; and two, that once the party had been registered by the commission, it did not have the authority to deregister it.

The day I joined my new post on 12 December, Arjun Singh filed a fresh application seeking interim orders for freezing the lotus as the BJP symbol. Now the urgency of it was that the panchayat elections were imminent in Madhya Pradesh, and contrary to general belief, all local body elections are fought all over the country on party lines and with party symbols. Hence, Arjun Singh's insisted that the lotus symbol be frozen and taken away from the BJP for them having, in his words, 'misused' it for the rath yatra.

At the first hearing on 24 December, the BJP asked for time, and the hearing took place after two weeks. On that occasion, the BJP pointed out the fact that while I had accepted Arjun Singh's petition, I had not called up for hearing a similar case that the BJP had filed a year ago. In that particular case, a vice president of the BJP, Ved Prakash Goel, had petitioned that the Congress (I) should not be registered as a political party, since it had given assurances to voters in Mizoram that the state would be made a Christian state. So, besides accusing me of making haste in taking up the case, there was the implicit accusation that I was partial in my approach, as I had not taken up an 'identical' case brought up by the BJP much earlier.

The two cases being compared were different in nature. While in the case against the Congress, Goel was objecting to the process of registration of a party, in the BJP symbol case, it was an appeal for deregistration. During the process of registration, it is very clear that no third party has any role. So, the commission only gave an acknowledgement for the appeal by Goel. This was communicated to the BJP, but they were not satisfied and kept saying that I was partial.

Through the Broken Glass

There was nothing partial or pro-Congress about this case. I was doing my duty. I had no personal feelings regarding it—none whatsoever. What personal feelings can one have? Though I had been the Congress government's cabinet secretary during Rajiv's tenure, I was not going to show any particular favour for or against them. Nevertheless, as happened in many other cases in my subsequent tenure in the commission, anything I did was looked at from the party angle. My actions would be labelled pro-Congress and anti-BJP.

As for the lotus case, the issue shifted to the primary objection as to whether a third party had any right to bring the matter before the commission. Therefore, on 10 January that year, the arguments were restricted to the preliminary objections raised by the BJP. After hearing the arguments for an entire day, the matter still remained inconclusive. I asked both sides to present their arguments in writing. This matter could not be taken up until around April when elections were imminent and decisions had to be made keeping in mind the fact that parties' symbols would play a major role in the upcoming general elections.

The case was finally heard on 5 April and the final order was issued on 12 April. Upholding the right of Arjun Singh, it was ordered:

12. The constitution vests in the commission the sacred responsibility of conducting elections to, inter alia, parliament and state legislatures. Article 324 of the constitution confers on it plenary powers of superintendence, direction and control of such elections. The Supreme Court has held in the case of *Mohinder Singh Gill vs. Chief Election Commissioner and others* (AIR 1978 SC851) that the said Article 324 is a 'reservoir of power' for the commission and where the law enacted by the parliament is silent or makes insufficient provision it can act in its own right as a creature of the constitution, in such vacuous are, to meet any contingency which could not be foreseen or anticipated with precision. In the words of Goswami J. in that case, 'where these (provisions in the enacted laws) area absent and yet a situation has to be tackled, the Chief Election Commissioner has not to fold his hands and pray to God for divine inspiration to enable

him to exercise his functions and to perform his duties or to look to any external authorities for the grant of powers to deal with the situation.'

13. Therefore, even if there is no express provision in the law conferring locus standi on third parties to be heard in the matters relating to the registration, deregistration, recognition or derecognition of political parties, the Commission, in the absence of a specific provision in the law, can hear them if they have something relevant and worthwhile to say, which would enable the commission to discharge its sacred responsibility of conducting elections in a free and fair manner and advance that object.[14]

Though the reasons were clearly stated and the appropriate laws quoted, the BJP was not at all happy with the decision. With elections coming up in the near future, they took to the streets and accused me and the Congress of collusion. Three days later, on 15 April, a rally led by L.K. Advani and M.M. Joshi protested my decision and agitators courted arrest. They came up with one-liners like 'Save EC from Seshan'. Advani, president of the BJP, was reported as saying, 'It was a command performance; the orders were blatantly partisan and thoroughly mala fide.'[15]

The BJP was reported to have started building a contingency plan to use a new symbol, just in case. But that was not needed. On 16 April, based on a consensus with all political parties, the hearings in all the party symbol cases were postponed until after the general elections. Thus, status quo prevailed.

During this period, the Shetkari Sanghatna, an organization for farmers founded by Sharad Joshi, sought derecognition and deregistration of the Shiv Sena, alleging that it was inciting communal passions. This case was similar to the Arjun Singh vs BJP case. As in the case of the BJP, I had reserved my decision, postponing it for a

---

[14]The author has a copy of the order in his private collections.
[15]'BJP Plans Nation-Wide Agitation', *The Times of India*, 13 April 1991.

later time due to the impending elections. Both the BJP and Shiv Sena participated in the general elections with their own symbols. The case could be taken up only after the general elections of 1991.

A FIGHT FOR THE TWO LEAVES SYMBOL

Two months before polling was to happen in Tamil Nadu, Subburaman Thirunavukkarasar filed a petition claiming a split in the All India Anna Dravida Munnetra Kazhagam (AIADMK) and claimed to be representing the party in place of J. Jayalalithaa, who he said had been expelled from the party. In support of his claims, he submitted a set of affidavits and asked for time up to 30 April to present more. Since there was less than two months to go before the polls, he asked to be allowed to use the AIADMK's symbol (two leaves) or to freeze it.

The counsel for Jayalalithaa pointed out that the doctrine of latches was applicable in the situation since the case was filed over six months after the supposed split was said to have taken place. Similarly, according to the provisions of the Representation of the People Act, it was the duty of the concerned party to inform the ECI about changes in the office bearers of the party well in time. Thirunavukkarasar could not explain why the changes were not intimated to the commission within the mandatory period of six months.

Thirunavukkarasar's other point of contention was that the number of MLAs supporting either groups should not be taken as the criterion to decide the symbol case. Rather, the strength of party members in the organization should be the deciding factor, especially since the Assembly was already dissolved by then. This also did not go in Thirunavukkarasar's favour, since the established precedent was that strength of the organization as well as Assembly would be considered. Incidentally, it was in a case dealing with the AIADMK that it was decided that the strength in the Assembly did matter.

Finally, the defendant also pointed out that the petitioner, by asking for time, was making it difficult for the commission to take a decision in time, forcing it to issue an interim order and freezing the symbol.

On examining all the angles of the case, it became clear that the petitioner had not come clean on the issue, and there was no reason for the ECI to entertain his claims. So, the commission issued an order dated 22 April 1991:

15. In view of the foregoing, I am of the considered view that the petitioner is not entitled to any relief, interim or otherwise, under paragraph 15 of the Symbols Order. I might have considered the prayer of the petition for ad hoc recognition as a state party, as a special case, for the purpose of the current general election, if the petitioner had shown that he enjoyed the support of such recognition as a state party under any of the criteria laid down in paragraph 6(2) of the Symbols Order. But no such things has been done or even attempted to be done by the petitioner. Accordingly, the petition dated 26 March 1991 of the petitioner Shree S Thirunavukkarasar is hereby dismissed.

IF JANATA PARTY + LOK DAL = JANATA DAL, THEN HOW MANY PARTIES REMAIN?

A case relating to the origin of the Janata Dal came up to the commission. This party came into existence in September 1988 at the time of the general elections. As a new party, it had members from the Janata Party and the Lok Dal. The problem was that, when the members got together to form a new party, there were dissensions within the original parties.

In mid-1988, Hemwati Nandan Bahuguna was the president of the Lok Dal and Devi Lal belonged to the same party. Ajit Singh was the president of the Janata Party and Indubhai Patel was its vice president. The two parties resolved to merge under the name of Janata Dal, with V.P. Singh as the president. Four days later, the Lok Dal removed Bahuguna from the presidentship and elected Devi Lal in his place. On 4 January 1989, a petition was filed by V.P. Singh, Ajit Singh and Devi Lal, seeking recognition of Janata Dal; and they wanted the ECI to allot them the symbol of the ploughman within wheel (*chakra haldhar*). A number of representations and caveats were filed in the case.

The final order in this case, which I signed as the CEC, was influenced by the Supreme Court verdict in a case that involved in the split and the merger of a part of the All Party Hill Leaders Conference in the Congress Party. I observed in the verdict: 'The merger of a political party with another political party amounts to effacing or wiping off its existence and for taking a decision of such a momentous nature, the wishes of the general members have to be necessarily ascertained, as such decisions may be tantamount to signing the death warrant of the party.'

In the case of the factions of the Janata Party, according to the counsel, only 113 persons were present on the day the parties were claimed to have merged. Considering everything, I concluded that no general body meeting took place and that the Janata Party and the Lok Dal continued to exist as two parties. This verdict went in favour of Subramanian Swamy, who was one of those responsible for placing me in the CEC role. But facts were on his side, and this was the only legal decision possible. Needless to say, accusing fingers were pointed in my direction, saying that I had favoured him.

Though this seemed to be much ado over a symbol, it became necessary to have a fresh look at party symbols. Several symbols were removed from the commission's list after discussions with the concerned groups, except in the case of the swastika, which was taken down for obvious reasons.

Small birds and animals were taken off when a party in South India decided to wring the neck of birds in their rallies because the symbol of the party in opposition was a pair of doves.

EIGHT

THE LARGEST ELECTORAL EXERCISE IN THE WORLD

Subsequent to the fall of the Chandra Shekhar government in March 1991, the President declared that a new Lok Sabha should be constituted by 5 June in the same year.

The ECI was already in a state of preparedness. On 14 March, after I met the President, I announced that somewhere by the end of May, elections would be held. At that time, I also expressed that, drawing upon the experiences of the commission in the 1989 Lok Sabha Elections, I was keen to make additional security arrangements for 'sensitive' states like UP, Bihar, Haryana and others where, in the words of my predecessor, (Late) Peri Shastri, he had witnessed the 'bloodiest-ever elections'.

The general election was expected to be a huge exercise. There were an estimated 512 million voters in the country, up from 498 million in the previous general elections. There were 579,810 polling booths in the previous Lok Sabha elections, and the number was likely to go up. The revision of electoral rolls had been completed throughout the country, with the exception of Kerala and Kargil in Jammu and Kashmir (J&K).

In due course, the model code of conduct came into effect. State governments were asked not to transfer officials concerned with elections after 25 March. No ministerial pronouncements of developmental programmes would be made after 2 April 1991, as the actual dates for the elections were to be announced somewhere in the first or second week of April.

Meanwhile, there was a debate in the press whether the model code of conduct could be enforced. However, I had assured that if governments resorted to transfers after 25 March, there would be 'corrective steps' wherever a 'colourable exercise' of authority would be noticed.

I knew very well that I would possibly not be able to prevent malpractices from happening, but I was sure wrongdoers would not get away with it. At a press conference in Patna on 30 March, I said: 'I do not claim that the polls would be 100 per cent fair, but I can certainly assure you that if I cannot prevent a misdemeanour, I would see to it that nobody would be permitted to reap the benefits of their misdemeanour.'

On 10 April, I held a briefing of the poll observers (government officials appointed to act as eyes and ears of the ECI during elections). This time round, they were going to visit their beats thrice in contrast to the earlier practice of one visit. I had asked for 300 observers in all, and on that day, 200 officers attended. They were to visit their respective states from 20–30 April to supervise the arrangements. Then they would visit again from 1–10 May to ensure that the campaigning had been peaceful. The third visit would be a few days before the polling date, and they would stay in the respective constituencies until the votes were counted and the results announced.

There was special focus on sensitive constituencies. In all, 800 central and state observers were to be deployed by the commission itself in view of the demand from the public, political parties and candidates. The number of central observers of the rank of joint secretary had increased fourfold this time, as compared to 70 in the 1989 Lok Sabha Elections. The central observers were finally appointed to sensitive constituencies on 22 April.

GOVERNMENT VS REFEREE

Early in April, the Government of India had violated the model code by sanctioning out-of-turn telephone and cooking gas connections. I wrote to the government about it. Subsequently, it was reported in the press that Satya Prakash Malaviya and Kamal Morarka, the minister for petroleum and the minister of state in the PMO, respectively, had accused the ECI of overstepping its limits in ordering a halt to these connections. It was reported that the ministers had stated that the communication from the commission would be treated with the contempt it deserved. When the reporters asked me about this, I replied, 'The honourable ministers' remark would be dealt with the respect it deserves.'

As a counter move, Morarka accused the commission of doing nothing when a secretary to the government (Sam Pitroda) was working for the Congress (I) campaign.

In a press briefing, when asked about my role as the CEC, I likened it to that of a football referee and said that various levels of caution would be issued to those concerned as the situation developed: '...yellow cards, green cards, red cards and ultimately the long whistle...' would be used.

As the month went by, I persisted in raising objections about those out-of-turn connections of cooking gas and telephone lines by the government. The government began to resent it. On 25 April, Morarka reportedly spoke critically of me while interacting with the press. He defended the connections by saying that objections could be raised only if the government misuses its power to influence voters and added that the government could not sit on urgent and justified applications for these facilities.

A see-saw battle continued for the next few days, and the PM himself had to intervene on 4 May and asked his ministers to end the duel with me.

THE NEED TO PULL BACK FROM IMPENDING ANARCHY

The ECI had become wiser after witnessing violence in the previous general elections. But electoral violence was not a universal phenomenon; only some constituencies, clustered in particular states, had this problem. Some states had a rather severe problem: the right of franchise of many was literally being taken away by goons and mafias, thus ensuring that an individual chosen by thugs was projected as elected to the august houses by the people of the constituency. Five states were particularly under the scanner: Bihar, West Bengal, Uttar Pradesh, Haryana and Andhra Pradesh, with cases from Bihar being most severe. To get an idea of how bad the situation got, let's pick up two examples, rather notorious ones—West Bengal and Bihar.

The reports received by the ECI from West Bengal showed that the conditions on ground were far from acceptable. The ECI gets its information from multiple sources—the press, home ministry, Intelligence Bureau, state governments, the commission's own officials being some of the major ones. Decisions were taken based on the totality of evidence available with the commission using all these inputs.

Of the total 42 constituencies, 10 parliamentary constituencies were declared as affected, 13 badly affected and a further 13 very badly affected. The reports cited that communal, extremist, criminal and mafia-related problems could occur in these constituencies. While communal and group clashes and kidnapping were variously predicted to take place most probably before the polls, there were expected to be instances of booth capturing, jamming and rigging during the polls.

Because of many such reports from West Bengal, it took its place in the list of 'sensitive' states. The CM's reaction to this classification was rather aggressive. Jyoti Basu took it as an insult to the people of the state. He thought I was out to 'terrorize the people' of the state. Speaking at a rally on 2 May, he said: 'Peaceful polling is the hallmark of Left Front rule, and people have died. Hindus, as well as Muslims, have died. But there was no communal riot. Goondas, both Hindu and Muslims, are murdering people.' Basu continued his tirade in subsequent rallies.

Reports about Bihar were far more worrying. All the 54 parliamentary constituencies in the state were shown as highly vulnerable to the kind of forces that could affect the conduct of free and fair elections. Fifteen of these constituencies were said to be 'very badly' affected.

As the date of the elections drew near, prepoll violence was already nine to 10 times higher than prior to the 1989 elections. The state administration had not taken adequate measures. It was reported that there was vicious caste-based campaigning against certain classes and that the CM himself was leading this campaign. A number of candidates with criminal background were in the fray, and there was widespread belief that musclemen and criminals would be employed extensively by the ruling party. In one incident, in the presence of the district magistrate, a senior superintendent of police was pushed down to the ground by the supporters of a candidate and a jeep was driven over him, fracturing his leg. This was reported as an 'accident'.

There were attacks on prominent leaders like Mulayam Singh Yadav and Advani when they were campaigning and addressing gatherings. The police remained mute spectators to the mob violence.

The CM had won over the general secretary of the dominant labour union of the home guards who were to man the polling booths. On 22 April, more than 8,000 home guards and ex-home guards effectively blocked the streets of Patna city. Some 60 to 70 per cent of the 58,000 home guards in the state belonged to the backward communities. The state government had proposed to raise their strength to 120,000. Private militias, senas and criminal gangs were active all over the state. Added to this concern were the 15 to 20 identified gun factories.

A report in *The Times of India* of 9 May 1991 said that the high-powered committee headed by the union home secretary Raj Kumar Bhargava, deputed by the central government to assess the situation in Bihar, was understood to have favoured postponement of the election in the state. However, the CM had reportedly said that it would be the state government that will issue the certificates to the winning candidates.[16]

---

[16]Banyal, S.S., 'Govt Panel for Postponement of Polls in Bihar', *The Times of India*, 9 May 1991.

The central committee report only described the 'alarming and shocking' situation in the state and cast doubts on the ability of the state government to ensure a free and fair poll.

By 11 May, the ECI had a more or less complete picture of the situation in Bihar, with most of the central observers having sent their reports. A final decision on holding polls in the state would be taken only after studying the home ministry's assessment on 12 May.

The next day, in a brief to the press, PM Chandra Shekhar reiterated that he was not in favour of dismissing Bihar or any other state government at that time.

Though this is how it appeared in the two states, in totality, it became evident that the run up to the 1991 Lok Sabha Elections was significantly less violent than during the corresponding period in the previous polls. The actual polling followed. Necessary arrangements were also made for this phase. Central security units were asked to conduct mobile patrolling at six lakh polling booths. The sensitive constituencies were categorized and paramilitary forces comprising over 55,000 personnel were deployed throughout the country to check election malpractices. In Bihar, nearly 145 companies had been deployed, and each company was to patrol four to five booths during the days of polling. Six constituencies of Bihar were marked for special monitoring, as they were hypersensitive.

As expected, there were episodes of violence and booth capturing, and I did my job paying no heed to the consequences. With the first phase over, preparations were on for the next phase starting 23 May, but an unfortunate incident put the further process under a cloud.

'WON'T DIE TWICE'

As the CEC, it did not matter to me whether Rajiv Gandhi won or lost. It was a matter of doing my duty without favouring anyone discriminately. I religiously maintained that nobody could touch the commission's work through personal influences. At the same time, as a friend and a well-wisher, I hoped for things to go well for Rajiv. Due to my interest in horoscopes, it was natural for me to see what the stars foretold about Rajiv. There were valid astrological reasons, apart from a host of other factors, to conclude well in advance that Rajiv's party was poised for victory. Ironically, that was what brought me intimations of fear.

On 10 May 1991, I called on Rajiv around daybreak. There was no agenda; it was a personal chat to convey my concern, to which Rajiv replied, laughing: 'I won't die twice'.

I cautioned him again, beseeching him to reconsider his decision to campaign so freely, but to no avail.

Four days later, on 14 May, there was a message for me from Kanchipuram Shankara Mutt, asking Rajiv to be careful. I told the Kanchi seer that Rajiv was taking the risk lightly in spite of being cautioned by me. A fax to this effect was again sent directly to him and that reached his table on 17 May. However, before he could read it, he was killed in the bomb blast in Sriperumbudur late in the evening on 21 May. I was grief-stricken again. I did not attend the cremation and spent the entire day at home.

THE AFTERMATH OF RAJIV'S ASSASSINATION

Once the president notifies that Parliament is dissolved, the CEC and the ECI come into the picture. It is the job of the CEC to notify the dates of a national election, keeping in view the question of law and order, deployment of adequate forces in sensitive and trouble-prone areas, the weather, harvesting seasons and religious festivals. So, there are three touchstones on which the decision is taken: the facts on the ground, the views of all concerned, and the responsibility to conduct free and fair polls. Having considered all these issues, the commission has to decide the dates. It is like feeding a lot of information—solid chunks as well as bits and pieces—into a large computer and waiting for it to respond.

The tragedy of Rajiv's death was a personal loss. On the professional side, we were right in the middle of an election for the conduct of which I was chiefly responsible. In 30-odd hours from then, the next round of polling was to commence. A decision regarding the conduct of the poll had to be taken quickly, so that the entire state machinery involved in the election could be spared wasteful effort. However, there was more to it than just making needless efforts. The aftermath of the 1984 assassination of Indira Gandhi was still fresh in everyone's mind. It is prudent at such times to not leave anything as ambiguous, so that the people in an organization clearly know what is to be done.

While I made my way to the President's house that night, much had already happened at Delhi. According to press reports, that I read only later, at around 11.20 p.m., the President was informed of the assassination. At that time, PM Chandra Shekhar was campaigning at Bhubaneshwar. On being informed, he left for Delhi immediately. He was to arrive at Delhi only after 2.30 in the morning. Some of his cabinet colleagues were also informed and called to the Rashtrapati Bhavan.

Meanwhile, the President tried to go to 10 Janpath to personally convey his condolences to the Gandhi family. But his car was mobbed by mourners who forced him to return without meeting the bereaved family. Clearly fearful of a repeat of the events of November 1984, the President summoned the three service chiefs and the cabinet secretary and directed them to take immediate steps to prevent any outbreak of violence. Flag marches were planned and the paramilitary forces were asked to be on full alert.

With the arrival of the PM in Delhi, a meeting was held to consider the law and order situation, the security arrangements and the future course of the Lok Sabha elections. Law minister Swamy and cabinet secretary Naresh Chandra were present at the meeting.

Rajiv had been the leader of the leading national party. With the environment being charged up with the murder of a person of the stature of Rajiv Gandhi, I considered that it would not be appropriate to rush things. On 6 and 8 June, Assam was originally scheduled to go to polls. And on 22 June, it was to be Punjab's turn. These dates were best left unchanged. Monsoon loomed on the horizon, and elections could not be delayed for long. Therefore, we arrived at two possible slots for the elections: one in the beginning of June and the other in mid-June. Given the fluidity of the situation, the mourning period and the required preparation time, I felt that the first two to three days of June would be too close and preferred the second option.

The cabinet secretary and senior bureaucrats related to law and order felt that the government would be able to bring the situation under control in about three days and therefore polling could be put off by about a week. They said that they were better placed to judge the law and order situation than me and suggested 31 May and 2 June as the revised dates. As the CEC, I was of the view that the situation was not conducive for holding free and fair elections.

The President and the political leadership seemed to be more inclined to the latter set of dates. The PM thought that since I now had everyone's point of view, the decision should be left to me. More or less, agreeing to mid-June, he suggested that it would be good if I asked the opinion of other political parties before announcing the decision.

I made phone calls between 3.00 a.m. and 5.00 a.m. to the leaders of important parties and could get only Pranab Mukherjee on the line. When I suggested that elections should be held in mid-June, he was non-committal. Looking at the situation, I thought that it would be futile to waste any more time. Moreover, based on how the situation evolved in the following two or three days, there would be an opportunity to review the decision and advance the date if necessary. Even the parties could be consulted on this. So, early in the morning of 22 May, I announced over the television that the second and third segments of the general election would be postponed to 12 and 15 June, respectively.

Reactions came in thick and fast. Sunderlal Patwa, the CM of Madhya Pradesh, and Biju Patnaik of Orissa reportedly told the press that keeping in view the duration of national mourning, there was no need to postpone elections for such a long time. On the other hand, Chimanbhai Patel, Sharad Pawar and P. Chidambaram either wrote to me, called me on the phone or met me personally to communicate that they would like the dates to be advanced.

The PM was sure that the dates should not be advanced. Advani spoke to me over the telephone and opposed against advancing the poll dates. On the other hand, the general secretary of the Congress (I), Ghulam Nabi Azad, pleaded for the advancement of the polls, pointing out that the situation in the country after the assassination of Rajiv was under control and that the candidates were anxious for the election process to be completed at the earliest. Taking everything into consideration, I finally decided that the poll dates were not to be advanced.

At the end of May, I received memoranda from the CMs of Andhra Pradesh, Goa, Karnataka and Maharashtra, as also from several leaders from Nagaland, Mizoram, Meghalaya, Arunachal Pradesh and Tripura, urging the commission to advance the poll dates in their respective states to the first week of June in view of the difficulty that the monsoon would create if the polls were to be held in mid-June. But I declined their request.

THE LOOMING THREAT OF A BANANA REPUBLIC

The first phase of elections that had already happened on 20 May was a mixed bag. In all, 204 parliamentary constituencies went to the polls on that day. While polling went off peacefully in most places, the situation was not good in particular states. From Kerala, Madhya Pradesh and Rajasthan, only one adverse incident each were reported. However, they were 28 incidents reported from Andhra Pradesh, 58 from Bihar, 26 from Haryana, 48 from Uttar Pradesh and nine from Bengal. These were a cause for concern since these incidents were more systematic than sporadic. There was an organized effort to defeat the free will of the people. Clearly, the rights of the voters were not being taken seriously in such constituencies.

The reports from Purnea in Bihar were a case in point. The henchman of a contestant resorted to terrorizing the people. In Rupauli sector in Haryana, about 200 men on horseback were reported to have gone on a spree of capturing booths, intimidating the supporters of rival parties and even officials of the police and the administration. Bombs were exploded at places to scare off genuine voters. At one place, the CRPF used lathis to disperse a group of militant youth supporters. But the youth were determined to capture the booths. We could not proactively stop the malpractice, but no one was going to benefit from it either.

No minister or his partymen can enter a polling booth when polling is going on. So, on 20 May, I passed an order that 'in the exercise of its power under Article 324 of the Constitution of India and Sections 58, 50A, 135A and 153 of the Representation of the People Act, 1951, and all other powers enabling it in this, the commission countermands elections for the parliamentary constituencies of Purnea, Patna, Etawah, Bulandshahar and Meerut'. Similar orders were passed for 15 other assembly constituencies.

The action kicked up a storm and I was accused of a lot of things. At a press conference, Bihar CM Lalu Prasad Yadav said that I was 'flouting' rules of constitutional propriety as a part of a Congress–BJP–SJP conspiracy to prevent the Janata Dal from gaining a 'majority' in the Lok Sabha.[17] He said that he would seek the 'personal intervention of the president to curb the anti-democratic functioning of Mr Seshan'.

Among other things, I was accused of targeting I.K. Gujral, the former minister of external affairs in the V.P. Singh government, in order to settle personal scores. One spokesperson accused me of committing crimes against the Constitution. One leader wanted that there should be independent observers and not the ones the CEC had appointed.

Besides press reports, a lot of communication also directly reached the ECI. There were requests to review the decision I had made. There were requests not to review the decisions, arguing that I had taken sufficient time to arrive at a stand on these primary issues. And on such matters too, I heard the views of the contestants. Let me take the example of two constituencies to explain how I addressed these issues.

[17]'Laloo Breathes Fire against Seshan', *The Indian Express*, 22 May 1991, p. 9, https://bit.ly/3mnfW3n. Accessed on 3 March 2023.

TEST EACH CHALLENGE ON THE TOUCHSTONE OF LAW

As regards Patna, the ECI received a very large number of complaints and reports orally—on the telephone, through telex or fax, in writing and through other means. The reports spoke of all kinds of electoral malpractices. I listed the 25 most important ones in the final countermanding order. In fact, the countermanding of Patna elections was ordered on 21 May 1991. It was challenged by I.K. Gujaral, raising points about the CEC's authority on the matter. And I gave the final countermanding order on 12 June 1991 after hearing the objections raised by Gujaral in person. In fact, one message of these 25 even indicated that I.K. Gujral himself was rather 'active' on polling day. The message received from C.P. Thakur, who later went on to become a cabinet minister in the Vajpayee government, and his lawyer Gopal Singh was a complaint which read: 'I.K. Gujral, JD candidate, along with the chief minister, Laloo Prasad Yadav and Ramanand Yadav, MLA Patna West, are capturing booth of Patna West.'

Subsequently, the returning officer, who had earlier admitted only minor incidents, informed us that there were some repoll cases as a result of booth capturing and violence. These changing statements of the returning officer on the day of the poll lent credence to the complaints.

That I had a right to countermand elections if I found that the situation was not conducive to free and fair polling was never in doubt. But as I considered the case, I found that I had to first address three preliminary questions that arose in the course of the hearings:

- Whether in countermanding elections, the commission can proceed ex parte under Section 58A (b) [Of Representation of the People Act 1951], without giving any pre-decisional hearing.
- Whether the commission, after having once passed the countermanding order under that section, can review, rescind or modify its own order.
- Whether a candidate could be allowed to appear through an advocate for a nominee.

On the first point, I said that the scheme under Section 58A 'as is apparent from the express provision thereof, is that the commission may pass the orders thereunder ex parte, i.e., without hearing the candidates'. The reason is that the relevant sub-section clearly puts the onus on the ECI to decide (on the first point) based on whether or not repolling should take place in several booths or whether or not elections need to be countermanded. Further, it would be well 'nigh impossible to conduct the election on any schedule' if the commission has to give a hearing to candidates from every nook and corner of the country before taking a decision whether the poll should be declared void at particular polling stations. Therefore, there was no need to first hear the candidates before taking a decision on countermanding.

As for the second point, I said that an administrative decision could be relocated, rescinded or modified. As countermanding was an administrative decision, under Section 58A, the commission also enjoyed this power available to every administrative authority.

As for the third point, only facts are to be placed before the commission and complex points of law are not involved. Therefore, the presence of the candidates is enough, and it is not necessary to permit them to present the factual position through their advocates or nominees. Therefore, I ruled that my ruling out of advocates to represent the contestants was correct.

Further considering the facts of the case, I said:

> ...What is causing serious concern for the commission is that the district authorities failed to bring the true situation as was obtaining in the constituency to the notice of the Commission. On the contrary, the Commission was being misled to believe that the poll passed off peacefully and that there were only a few minor incidents. Even when the Commission got disturbing reports and wanted the verification of these reports, there was a deliberate attempt to keep the Commission in the dark and the full facts were not forthcoming... the assessment of the Election Commission that the polls held on 20th May 1991 in Patna parliamentary constituency was not free and fair and did not reflect the true

wishes of the electorate, stands further reinforced. The evidence and materials which have now come into the possession of the Commission have further substantiated the evidence that was available to the Commission at the time of the passing of the order on 21 May 1991 and the Commission does not find even semblance of a cause to go back on the order.

Accordingly, I rejected Gujral's plea in which he had maintained that the polling in Patna was peaceful.

A similar case came up in respect of Etawah parliamentary constituency. Dr Subramanian Swamy, as the president of his party, brought up the matter before the commission on behalf of his party candidates, one of whom was Mulayam Singh Yadav, the CM of Uttar Pradesh. He, too, pleaded that that my countermanding of elections be reviewed for that particular constituency.

The information and complaints cell of the ECI also received a large number of complaints and reports in respect of the Etawah constituency. According to the returning officer, polling at as many as 10 per cent polling stations had been vitiated.

Vitiation of the poll in about 10 per cent of the polling booths across the length and breadth of the constituency left no doubt that the process had been irregular and could not reflect the views of the voters.

Overall, there was no consistency in the views of the parties and the candidates on this point of countermanding, and they expressed their views depending on the electoral fortunes in different constituencies. For example, Dr Subramanian Swamy, president, Janata Party, and Mulayam Singh Yadav, the party's candidate for Jaswant Nagar assembly constituency contended that the commission has the power and jurisdiction to review its order. But Yashwant Sinha, the party's candidate for Patna parliamentary constituency contended before the commission, saying the contrary. Similar examples could be given from other parties as well.

As I proceeded to review the Etawah case, I found that the irregularities were more extensive than were indicated in the information available to the commission when the countermanding was ordered. Therefore, finding no case made out for revoking the countermanding decisions, the supplication of Dr Swamy for seeking review of the order was rejected.

An interesting case in this process was that of a district magistrate against whom I had to take action. This incident happened in the parliamentary constituency of Chapra. After polling took place on 20 May, repolling was ordered in 22 polling booths. There were several conflicting reports from the district magistrate of Chapra and the chief election officer of Bihar. Initially, the returning officer (the DM) had stated that the presiding officers had not sealed the ballot boxes properly. Subsequently, he changed his story and said that the ballot boxes were lost. Owing to it, repoll was ordered in 26 more booths. After looking into the case, I said that the DM would be transferred and replaced by a suitable officer. He was removed the very next day, and I had a new officer. The subsequent round of election on 12 and 15 June were relatively more peaceful.

Repolls were also ordered in eight booths in Balia, the PM's constituency. There was not much delay, and it was taken care of in a matter of a few days.

Another interesting case was Davanagere constituency of Karnataka. In the parliamentary constituency, the final result showed that the difference between the winner and the runner-up was less than 20 votes. Twenty is a small figure when the total count in a constituency is close to a million votes.

After the declaration of election results, the Congress formed the government under Narasimha Rao with support of other parties.

HOLDING ELECTIONS IN TERRORISM-INFESTED STATES

Punjab missed the general elections of 1991; to understand why, let us retrace a little. This was one of the biggest stories of the 1991 general elections. And it was one of the most traumatic experiences of my years in the ECI.

In March 1991, when the President directed that a new House of the People should be constituted on or before 5 June 1991, elections became due in the state of Punjab. I said in a press conference that I was ready to hold elections everywhere in the country, including J&K, provided I felt assured that the polls would be free and fair.

So how bad was the situation in Punjab?

On 25 March, the home ministry was reported to be of the view, on the basis of intelligence reports, that the elections could not be conducted in a free and fair manner. But it became apparent very soon that the PM was keen on the elections taking place.

On 1 April, Atal Bihari Vajpayee of the BJP said it was not conducive to hold elections in Punjab and Assam.

A report appeared in *The Indian Express* on 3 April 1991.[18] According to it, the Punjab governor, Gen. (Retd) O.P. Malhotra, was probably planning to ask for 400 additional companies of paramilitary forces for election duty in the state, at a time when there were already 350 companies there. This amounted to almost 35 per cent of the total strength of the paramilitary forces in the entire country! And the report was not far off the mark. The governor eventually did ask for 300 more companies. If someone is asking for that much force, one can imagine what the assessment of the situation on the ground must have been.

A day later, Communist Party of India (Marxist) or the CPI (M) politburo member Harkishan Singh Surjeet said that the PM's stance was totally misplaced and did not reflect the truth. Shiromani Akali Dal (P)'s Mahant Sewa Das Singh in a letter to me, and senior Congress leaders of Punjab in a representation to the president, indicated that they were not up for elections, as there were looming secessionist fears.

On 7 April, the PM was reported to have said that the government would announce its decision for holding elections in Punjab shortly and that the decision would depend on the assessment of the law and order situation by the ECI on the basis of the reports that were to come to the ECI from the state government.

It was reported on 11 April that the PM had held discussions with the governors of Punjab, Assam and J&K. Apparently, after hectic

---

[18]'Punjab to Seek More Para-Military Forces', *The Indian Express*, 3 April 1991.

talks, the PM finally succeeded in persuading his cabinet colleagues to hold elections in Punjab.

Owing to that, on 11 April, I received a letter from the home secretary saying that the elections to the state legislative assembly (of Punjab) may be held along with the elections of the Lok Sabha.

As it turned out, the Janata Dal and the PM were isolated in this.

Considering all this, on 12 April, when the recommendations for notification were sent to the President by the commission, the details of elections in Punjab, Assam and J&K were deliberately excluded after consultation with all concerned, and a later date was recommended for elections in these states.

The exclusion of any state from the notification regarding the general elections required an amendment to Section 73 of the Representation of the People Act, 1951. Such an amendment could be made by the President by invoking his ordinance-making powers. The council of ministers advised the President that only the state of J&K should be brought within the purview of the ordinance. The President sent it back to the council for reconsideration, but the ministers returned it as it was. Thus, on 18 April, I had no option but to send revised proceedings to the President that Punjab and Assam should also be notified. Therefore, by a notification dated 19 April, with the exclusion of J&K, all other states were to go to polls on 20, 23 and 26 May. And some of the states, including Punjab, were also to elect their state assemblies.

USING THE ECI'S RIGHT TO RESCHEDULE

Just after this notification was issued, on that very day, I received a note from the governor of Punjab, forwarded by the home ministry, requesting that the dates for the Punjab polls be postponed until 20 June. The reason he gave was that there would be a large number of candidates and that more force would be needed to provide security for them. This additional force would not be available, since they would be required elsewhere in the country until 28 May. To protect the contestants during the period of canvassing, it would be desirable if the dates were postponed by three or four weeks to around 15 or 20 of June, he said.

This request amazed me for the reason that, until then, nobody in the government at the state or the Centre had considered this requirement of the protection of candidates at all. It reflected poorly on their assessment of the security situation. Another point of concern was that a postponement would stretch the process of electioneering, given that the poll process had already started. This meant that the candidates would be exposed to personal risk for a much longer duration.

In any case, after considering all the factors, the elections were rescheduled to 6 and 8 June for Assam and 22 June for Punjab. That would make it almost one month after the original schedule.

THE DOUBLE WARNING OF INSUFFICIENT SECURITY AND ENHANCED TERROR ACTIVITY

A complication arose when the second and third segments of elections were postponed after Rajiv's assassination. The home ministry could assure the Punjab government of enough forces for holding elections only after 19 June, since the election process in other parts of the country would be completed only on 18 June. The governor wrote to me again on 24 April saying that he wanted the elections to be further postponed from 22 June to 30 June.

I wondered what would be achieved by postponing the elections by a week. The forces protecting the candidates were already in place, and additional forces were to be positioned for the elections. These would be deployed in time for the 22 June elections in any case. No decision on this request was immediately taken, but we continued to closely monitor the situation in Punjab.

When I wrote to the home minister on 6 June, many candidates had already been killed and there were, on an average, anywhere between 10 to 20 other election-related killings a day. I asked the central and the Punjab governments for their assessment of the law and order situation in Punjab, specifically from the point of view of holding free and fair elections. In my letter dated 6 June, I first relayed the state of law and order in Punjab, specifically with the killing and attempts to kill the candidates as it had come to our notice. I then relayed the requests I had received for postponing the elections. In the reply sent, probably the next day, the home secretary wrote: '...as no decisions were forthcoming from your side despite the letter of Governor of Punjab dated 25 May 1991, the matter was examined by the MHA and action had been taken to provide as much force as possible to Punjab to enable the elections to take place on 22 June as scheduled.'[19]

The home secretary wrote again on 10 June. He referred back to his earlier letter in which he said he had: '...indicated the steps taken by the government to increase the strength of paramilitary forces in Punjab for internal security duties and also for providing protection to the candidates in the context of the elections scheduled to be held on 22 June as decided by the Election Commission.'[20]

Clearly, the home secretary again deliberately avoided replying to my primary question. On that day, the governor of Punjab came to meet me and pleaded with me that the elections be postponed, to which I replied that I will consider the request. After he met me, he went straight to the PM. When he came back, he said that he did not want a postponement; he wanted the original dates. And in a letter dated 10 June 1991, he said that he believed that a free and fair election can be conducted on 22 June 1991. I, however, was duty-bound to have a clear picture of what was happening on the ground before taking a call, even if the governor assured me that all was fine for free and fair polls.

As elsewhere, observers were sent to Punjab, and they had the specific mandate to find out whether the situation was conducive to a fair and free poll. The best of these reports was discouraging to the prospect of elections and the worst of them described sinister possibilities and the existence of fear psychosis. The reports indicated that to protect the candidates, they were kept behind bars in police stations. The candidates complained that they were being unfairly detained and not being allowed to campaign.

---

[19]The author has a copy of the letter in his private collections.
[20]The author has a copy of the letter in his private collections.

On 14 June, Punjab chief secretary, Tejinder Khanna said that the government would not allow the elections process in the state to be subverted and that it would not hesitate to take the assistance of the army as a last resort to ensure free and fair polls. He pointed out that army units had already staged a flag march in a few towns to instil confidence in the people. He went on to dispel rumours that candidates were being held by the police against their will. He said that the reports of 14 candidates being kidnapped were false and only three were missing, of which two were proclaimed offenders. The very next day, at the Ludhiana railway station, 110 passengers, of one particular community, travelling in a train were shot dead by militants.[21] The press reports indicated that it was a mindless act that was intended to polarize and spread fear.

When I was asked about the killings the next day, I refused to comment. On his part, Khanna again assured me that adequate security arrangements were made for the staff deployed for poll duty. He said that the staff would be taken from the point of distribution of election material to the polling booth under armed escort consisting of police and paramilitary forces.

Militants continued to issue threats, some of them printed and pasted as bills on walls, which read that they would chop off any finger seen carrying the election ink. Threats were issued to village headmen that their villages would undergo severe consequences if they participated in voting. The militants had also called a general strike on 21 and 22 June. On 18 June, the Shiromani Akali Dal (B) candidate for Faridkot was killed in a bomb blast.

In all, my assessment of the ground situation, based heavily on the opinions of the observers, could be summarized in the following points:

- The majority of the contesting candidates were not in a position to campaign at all or meet their voters without threat to their lives.

---

[21]'110 in Two Trains Gunned Down by Punjab Militants', *The Indian Express*, 16 June 1991.

- The administration was not in a position to ensure the security of the candidates except by keeping them behind bars or deporting them out of the constituencies, which was a situation totally inconsistent with the demands of any democratic elections.
- The electorate was gripped with fear created by the threats of militants, and the poll would not reflect the true will of the voters.
- Polling personnel were afraid of conducting polls.
- Even candidates of those political parties that, at the national level, opposed the postponement of poll in Punjab were unsure of the possibilities of conducting a free and fair poll.
- The call for bandh on the day of polls had brought into question the possibilities of movement of polling parties, transport of poll material, safety of poll personnel and the peaceful conduct of polls.
- The deployment of forces for the peaceful conduct of polls on 22 June was totally unsatisfactory.

One would have realized by now that the opinion of the government of the day was also an important consideration among the many I had to take into account before making an informed decision. During the course of the elections, PM Chandra Shekhar was incharge of government, but after the conclusion of elections, the Congress, under P.V. Narasimha Rao, was to take over and the swearing in ceremony was to be held on 21 June 1991.

I called up Narasimha Rao, over the phone, and in the short conversation, discussed several issues, including Punjab.

Giving due regard to the views of all the leaders of political parties and public servants, and also representations made by various persons to the ECI, and taking into account all relevant factors and the totality of the situation, I was satisfied that it may not be possible to hold free, fair and peaceful polls in the state of Punjab. I pulled out Section 30 and Section 153 in the Representation of the People Act, 1951, which nobody but me—none of my predecessors—had really thought of and postponed the elections by about three months, to 25 September. This

Section says that the ECI may, for reasons that it considers sufficient, postpone an election.

The decision was finally issued late on the night of 20 June, or rather early on the morning of 21 June. Once having decided, there was no point waiting. This was especially true because the task of moving of the entire machinery would begin early next morning, and that too on a day when the militants had called for a strike. So, early that morning, at 1.15 a.m., I announced the decision.

The decision to postpone the Punjab poll dates was taken entirely by me, independent of any extraneous influence, only on the basis of hard and undebatable information available to and in the possession of the ECI.

FACING THE MUSIC POST POSTPONEMENT

This decision went on to be the main plank on which I would be impeached later that year. Many people made a big song and dance about it and said that I deliberately postponed the Punjab elections, favouring the Congress.

One thing to note is that, after the postponement of the Punjab elections, when I called Narasimha Rao to congratulate him on his taking office as the PM, he stood up, walked around the table, came up to me and thanked me for having saved Punjab from going the secessionist way.

An immediate aftermath of this episode was that Gen. Malhotra resigned as the governor of Punjab. In his opinion, the CEC's decision to postpone the elections on the eve of the polling day would have a demoralizing effect on the people of Punjab. It would also give a boost to the terrorists who had opposed the holding of elections in the state. He complained that he was not informed about the decision before its announcement.

It was at this time that the calls for my impeachment suddenly grew louder, and there were many attempts to take the matter to court. Three candidates questioned my authority in putting off the elections by three months, terming it 'a constitutional fraud' at the behest of a minority government, which was yet to assume office.

Shortly after the postponement, in an interview, one reporter criticized me saying that I was biased against holding polls in the troubled border state. In reply, I said, 'Commission's advice to the government was for not holding the polls.' It was my duty to give advice, and I had to be objective and truthful about it.

On my part, I had no doubts about the righteousness of what I had done. To summarize, there was nothing illegal in the decision itself. It was surely in keeping with the provisions of the Constitution and the Representation of the People Act. As if to confirm it, the decision was challenged in the Supreme Court and adjudged correct.

NEED FOR ANOTHER POSTPONEMENT

Now that the elections were postponed, the next question was whether the elections had to be held in September after all or whether there was a possibility of cancelling the elections. And if elections could not be held in September, when would they be held?

Having studied the law carefully, I was sure that the elections in Punjab could not be cancelled even by the government. There was a requirement to amend the laws and even this amendment would not be simple. I said so in an interview on 25 June. In fact, this issue had come up for discussion in the beginning of the month when Pranab Mukherjee, who was then the chairman of the campaign committee of the All India Congress Committee, claimed that when the new government was formed, it would have the right to review elections in Punjab. At that time, I had expressed my view that it would not be easy to do so and laws would have to be changed for the purpose. The Opposition had criticized me for this, saying that I should not comment on political views. I said the same thing again when I was asked after the elections.

As the revised date for elections in Punjab neared, on 21 August, the new governor Surendra Nath called for the postponement of polls. In early September, the PM hinted that the poll would be postponed. On 18 September, Parliament approved the six-month extension of

President's Rule in the state. Only in January 1992, the PMO finally said that elections could be held in the state. Accordingly, it was decreed that Punjab elections would be held in February, and under exceptionally tight security, elections were eventually conducted in Punjab in February 1992.

Initial post-poll press reports projected a dismal picture of the elections, saying that there was general apathy in the rural areas and there were instances of villages where not a single vote was polled. In some cases, the locals even refused to give water to the polling agents. There was an environment of suspicion, along with sporadic instances of bomb explosions all over the state, with the intention to scare away voters. There were a few deaths and injuries.

Despite the negative reports, 30–35 per cent of the voters had cast their votes, which was quite good, given the situation. Reports eventually complimented the people of Punjab, with subsequent reports reflecting a positive picture.

The outcome was that the Congress sailed through the assembly elections with a thumping majority. It was able to strengthen its position in the Lok Sabha, as it won 12 out of the 13 seats and needed only eight more to reach simple majority in Parliament. Naturally, there was heartburn in the Opposition parties. S.R. Bommai of the Janata Dal said that the poll was rigged. Many from the Opposition said the same, but the charges did not stick. The BJP eventually expressed satisfaction over its poll performance. The Communist Part of India (CPI) said that it was a good beginning, while the CPI (M) thought that the outcome was bad.

However, when one examines the more subtle clues, it is clear that there was nothing euphoric about the picture in sight—even the celebrations in the Congress camp was subdued.

NINE

IMPEACHMENT BLUES OF 1991

Punjab remained in focus for a little over half a year after the general elections of 1991. While this was happening, I had been studying the reforms required in the electoral system and had written to the government about it. There was only so much a CEC could do within his powers. Beyond that, there was a need for Parliament to change the laws and I had called for many changes.

There were some useful outcomes of the Punjab polls in terms of poll reforms. In the interest of conducting such difficult elections better, certain ordinances were passed. One such ordinance was about reducing the period of canvassing, and another was to prevent the countermanding of elections on the death of independent candidates. And while the second ordinance seemed skewed against the Independents, it, in fact, protected them. People who wanted to stop elections would no longer target independent candidates to achieve their aim. The ordinances were taken up in Parliament in the second and third week of March 1992, and the relevant bill was passed.

In the debate preceding the passing of this Bill, law minister K. Vijaya Bhaskara Reddy said that the government was contemplating bringing a comprehensive electoral reforms bill by the next session of Parliament. Of the three bills that were already pending in Parliament, he said that this 'very important' legislation would be brought forth only after evolving a consensus with all political parties. He said that consultations would begin in April that year. It is another matter that nothing substantial came out of the promise. Even when the matter of reform was taken up in Parliament, there were motives other than bettering elections that seemed to be driving it.

As for the Bill that was passed to regularize the ordinance, it was challenged in the Supreme Court. But the next year, on 28 February 1993, the judiciary upheld the amendment. There was an important observation made by the court on that occasion.

The petitioner's contention was that, by the amendment, the government had made a distinction between a candidate set up by a recognized political party and any other (Independent) candidate. He said that the distinction was artificial, inconsistent with the spirit of the laws governing elections and was discriminatory. He said that the Constitution did not give special rights to party candidates, treated all candidates similarly and did not recognize any categorization.

In his judgement, justice L.M. Sharma of the three-judge bench of the Supreme Court said that, for a strong and vibrant democratic government, it was necessary to have a parliamentary majority as well as a parliamentary minority, so that different viewpoints on controversial issues were brought forth and debated on the floor of Parliament.

The petitioner had also challenged the reduction of the campaign period from 20 to 14 days by the amendment of the Representation of the People Act, 1951, as unconstitutional. The court rejected it by saying that the argument against the reduction was equally without any merit.

WHY I GOT SECURITY COVER

3 April 1991 was a dark day for me as the CEC. It is so vividly etched in my mind as if it was a recent event. On that fateful day, someone took potshots at my office with a gun from somewhere outside the building. I really don't know the reason behind the attack. This had occurred even before I had taken any major decisions in respect to postponing elections in Punjab or changing the election schedule in the general elections. On examination, it was found that two bullets had struck the building, one just above my office floor and one just

below. The result was that the security threat to me was reviewed and my security upgraded. I was given protection by the National Security Guard (NSG). A bulletproof car was also included in the arrangement. Questions were raised about this unprecedented measure for me. I had no answer expect that it was not I who should assess the threat. In fact, Deputy Election Commissioner, D.S Bagga, was also given special security cover.

Another security threat was reported on 18 July 1991. When the storm kicked up with the Punjab postponement issue at its peak, it was claimed that a certain terrorist group from Punjab had included me in their list of potential targets. As a result, my security cover was extended for the rest of my tenure. One must be thankful for the safety provided, but it was not without irritants. Sometimes, it felt as if my baiters were getting at me through the security personnel; several incidents that took place early in 1994 made one suspect so.

THE UNFOLDING DRAMA OF IMPEACHMENT

Soon after I had first postponed the elections in Punjab, PM Narasimha Rao had walked over to me to say that I had saved Punjab. However, the political reactions to my decision were largely negative. From what I have told you so far, you would have realized that everybody across the political spectrum had some grouse against me. I did not behave 'normally' by the then established CEC standards, and it was easy to single me out as some kind of maverick—just because I was going by the book in pursuit of my mandate. Even Dr Subramanian Swamy, a personal friend and law minister at that time, who many a time went out of his way to defend the CEC, had his reservations in one or two instances.

Circumstances leading to possible impeachment

Regardless of the results of my decisions and actions in all the issues that I mentioned before, did they lead to confrontation? Yes, they did—particularly so in the National Front (which consisted of parties associated with the Janata Dal) and the Left Front. They made it look like they were at the receiving end of a whimsical person's work.

An issue that raised the hackles of the Janata Dal was a matter relating to the then Lok Sabha Speaker who was from Orissa. On 12 May 1991, somebody had made an anonymous telephone call to the ECI, making some allegations about the Speaker related to the grants from the Speaker's fund and about some unspecified 'out of turn promotions in the Lok Sabha secretariat'. The commission forwarded the message to the Lok Sabha secretariat, requesting them to look into the matter and made a mention of it in a press conference that day, clearly stating that it was an anonymous call.

The next day, the Lok Sabha secretariat expressed shock. The Janata Dal described it as 'an indiscretion', and in their estimation, we were supposed to have verified the facts before going to the press. They were of the opinion that Dr R.P. Bhalla, the deputy election commissioner who addressed the press briefing on that day, had abetted in the designs of 'certain unscrupulous elements and vested interests including possibly counter political interests', who successfully secured 'through the good offices of the Election Commission, and through utterly condemnable means', adverse publicity against the Speaker. The Speaker was a candidate in the general elections of 1991. They wanted the ECI to 'announce, unequivocally, that the contents of the allegations are blatantly false and mala fide'.

On 13 June, the day after I gave my decision on the countermanding of polls in Patna, Jaipal Reddy, spokesman for the Janata Dal, was reported to have said, 'We need not come to power to impeach him. Nobody is happy with the functioning of the Chief Election Commissioner except the Congress and, of course, the law minister Subramanian Swamy.'[22]

On 15 June, a delegation of members of the Janata Dal met the President and reportedly brought to his notice the 'strange practice' and 'bad precedents' set by the ECI in recent weeks. In their opinion, I was supposed to go by the 'letter' in so far as the reports of the returning officers and observers were concerned. Among those who

---

[22]'Janata Dal to "Impeach" Seshan', *Political Observer*, 14 June 1991.

met the President were V.P. Singh, Ajit Singh and Surendra Mohan.

There was another incident that added fuel to the fire. One member of the Bihar legislative assembly spoke with me on the telephone. Unfortunately, there were only two words—his and mine—and no others were privy to this conversation. It is true that he called. I did not speak a single word which was derisive either of the member himself or of the dignity of the Bihar legislative assembly. But the member said that I had spoken ill of the Bihar legislative assembly. He raised a motion of privilege against me. Among many other things, he said that I had 'committed contempt of the House and its members by uttering derogatory, unprintable and unparliamentarily abuse against both'.

A notice was issued to me by Speaker Ghulam Sarwar, to which I duly replied and the reply reached him in the first two days of July. On 3 July 1991, there was another issue that came up in the Bihar Assembly: the Congress, which was in opposition, wanted to raise a privilege motion over the torture of a member during the recently concluded elections. The members of the ruling party countered it by voicing the privilege motion that was already raised against me (to which I had already replied). So, there was a ruckus in the House.

At this, the CM is said to have intervened: 'We all are people's representatives. Members have been hurt by the comment of Mr Seshan. But the Chair should go through all the aspects of the constitutional provisions before delivering the ruling.' It was decided that I had to be heard for my point of view. The issue just fizzled out.

By far, the most important reason for an impeachment attempt lay in the decision I took to postpone elections in Punjab. Apart from the CPI (M), the Congress was the only party that stood to benefit from the postponement. The decision triggered a chorus for my impeachment.

Incidentally, the national executive of the BJP had begun its two-day session to take stock of the party's performance in the elections. On the first day, 20 June, it passed a resolution, which read: 'We are extremely sorry to say that by his arbitrary behaviour, the CEC has lowered the dignity of his office and call upon the government to establish the convention of appointing the CEC in consultation with the leaders of the opposition.' It went on to say, 'We hope that Mr Seshan will realize the gravity of the situation and resign his office.'[23]

The next day, after the postponement decision was announced, the BJP said, 'This volte face by the Election Commission has proved beyond a doubt that instead of discharging its duties independently and impartially, it is functioning as an instrument of a political party.' The Punjab unit of the BJP described the postponement as the 'murder of democracy'.

On 27 June, BJP leader L.K. Advani called on the President to dismiss me for my 'illegal act' of postponing the Punjab poll. Since the National Front leaders had already spoken about initiating impeachment proceedings against me, this BJP statement was seen as added momentum for the move to impact me. On 2 July, the BJP said that it was ready for coordination in respect of my impeachment.

There were rumours that I would resign. On my part, I had no doubt. Of the rumours, I said, 'It was all balderdash.' I said, 'The thought of relinquishing my post has not crossed my mind. There is no question of my resigning.'

On 29 June, the Janata Dal asked me, through a notice, to either quit office on my own or face 'the ignominy of being impeached'. That was supposed to be an ultimatum. The same came in the form of a resolution by the national executive of the Janata Dal on 30 June. But then, it said that my 'earlier grave lapses pale into insignificance before my decision to postpone the Punjab elections barely 30 hours before the scheduled poll, a decision that has held the Indian state up to ridicule in the eyes of Punjab and the international committee.'[24]

The impeachment procedure

The CEC can be 'removed' from office after due procedure as is applicable to a judge of the Supreme Court. To put it briefly, either 100 members of the Lok Sabha or 50 members of the Rajya Sabha need to sign a notice for the CEC's removal and submit it to the Speaker

---

[23]'BJP Wants Seshan To Go', *The Hindu*, 21 June 1991.
[24]'Seshan Must Go, Asserts JD', *The Patriot*, 1 July 1991.

or chairman, respectively, whose personal discretion it is to decide whether or not to accept the notice. If he accepts, then a judicial panel of three members would have to be constituted, and which would have to be satisfied, following all procedures, that there was either 'misbehaviour' or 'incapacity' on the officer's part. If either of this is proven, the matter would then go to Parliament, where it has to be passed by a special majority. It meant that, in the Lower House, out 543 members at that time, at least 362 had to be present, of which at least 272 should support the motion of removal.

Given the composition of the House at that time, the combination of Opposition parties interested in my removal came to around 180 members. On including the Left Front, which was also showing inclinations at that time, the figure would reach around 250 members. In any case, the Congress and its supporters would need to support the motion. Or rather, it appeared as if those who wanted impeachment were only gunning for, as Janardhan Reddy put it, a tactical victory.

Once the monsoon session of Parliament began, the battlefront shifted into Parliament and moves were made, both inside and outside it, to force my ouster. On 19 July 1991, there was a discussion on the issue in the Rajya Sabha. A resolution had been moved by Satya Prakash, a formal parliamentary affairs minister, asking the government to urgently introduce legislation to amend the existing election laws. While participating in a discussion in relation to this motion, the members heavily criticized me for my decision to countermand elections in some constituencies and for ordering repoll in others.

The Minister of State for Law and Justice, and Parliamentary Affairs, Rangarajan Kumaramangalam, took strong objection to the members making allegations against me and said that they could do so only if they moved substantive motion for my impeachment. Failing this, it was not proper to make charges against me as I would not be able to defend myself.

Dr Subramanian Swamy supported the minister and objected to allegations made against me. Vice chairman Bhaskar Annaji Masodkar asked the members to desist from making allegations against an individual and restrict their speeches to the text of the resolution.

Satya Prakash Malaviya from the Samajwadi Janata Party (SJP) said that the House should recommend to the government to urgently amend existing election laws to prevent a repetition of such happenings, like the sudden postponement of general elections after Rajiv Gandhi's assassination or the sudden deferment of the Punjab elections.

On 2 August in the Rajya Sabha, Malaviya brought a private resolution that raised three points: the long postponement of polls following the assassination of Rajiv, the deferment of polls in Punjab and the countermanding of polls in several constituencies. He urged the government to introduce legislation to amend the existing electoral laws in the context of these events. There were also demands by others that polls should not be countermanded because of the death of an independent candidate. In the discussion that ensued, members were said to have raised the issue of the 'arbitrary and dictatorial' manner in which the polls of 1991 were conducted. Several members also demanded that the commission be made 'accountable'. The same issues again came up—it was 'shameful' on my part to have countermanded polls in several constituencies, and that I had lowered the dignity of the ECI by the partisan manner in which I had conducted the polls.

Law minister Vijaya Bhaskar Reddy intervened to say that the government was committed to bring a comprehensive legislation, incorporating major electoral reforms in the light of the experience of the last two elections. In his opinion, the Congress, too, was unhappy over the ECI's decision to defer the second and third rounds of polls and that the government would consult political parties before arriving at decisions on electoral reforms, including the decision to have a multi-member ECI in place of the one-man commission.

In the beginning of the second week of August, M. Padmanabhan of Telugu Desam Party demanded an inquiry into the installation of a dish antenna at my residence and at the residence of certain secretaries to the government and even ministers, all of which were permitted by the previous governments. Making a special mention, he said that I had a telephone in my car and wondered whether I needed hi-tech gadgets in the discharge of my official duties. He wanted to know how much money had been spent on providing these gadgets to me.

Jayanthi Natarajan of the Congress (I) objected to the discussion about the CEC in the House. However, deputy chairman Najma Heptullah ruled that the member was only referring to wasteful expenditures.

Even as all this was going on, a major incident in August and September added considerable fuel to the fire.

WAS HEGDE HOLDING AN OFFICE OF PROFIT OR NOT?

Let me take you back to the time when V.P. Singh assumed office as PM. I was still the cabinet secretary. An officer in the Planning Commission told me that the government proposed to appoint Ramakrishna Hegde, who was as recently as November elected as Member of the Karnataka Legislature, as the deputy chairman of the Planning Commission. The officer wished to know whether Hegde would undergo disqualification under the condition that the chairmanship of the Planning Commission was an 'office of profit'. I looked up the law and told him that, in my view, he would undergo disqualification. The officer said that it was their intention that Hegde would not draw any salary. I said the non-drawing of the salary prescribed for a post does not take away the mischief of the office of profit, and that he would still be subject to disqualification. This was in December 1989, long before I reached the ECI. They went ahead and appointed Hegde as the deputy chairman. It was ironical that a few days later, I found myself in the Planning Commission as a member.

Someone raised the issue of the 'office of profit' in Hegde's case with the ECI. The ECI asked Hegde to state his case, and there were a series of filing of replies, counter replies, rejoinders and more rejoinders, and the matter could be heard only seven months later on 10 July 1990. That hearing was inconclusive. At the date of the next hearing, the then CEC, my late predecessor, was indisposed. Thus, no hearing could be held. In the meantime, Hegde resigned from the post of deputy chairman of the Planning Commission.

The petitioner also approached the High Court of Karnataka with a petition to direct the ECI to hold an early hearing on this matter. By the time the petition came up for hearing, Hegde had already resigned and therefore, the court dismissed the petition saying that, as he was no longer the deputy chairman, he could not be disqualified in this case.

This was immediately challenged in the High Court, saying that this decision interfered within the jurisdiction of the governor and the ECI to adjudicate upon the matter. The contention was that it was related to a decision to be taken about Hegde being disqualified when he had joined as deputy chairman of the Planning Commission; what happened subsequently did not matter. Therefore, according to the law, this matter had to be decided upon by the governor on the advice of the ECI.

All of this had happened even before I had joined the commission. It was only on 13 March 1991 that the High Court, by its order, upheld the commission's contentions. So, the matter came up for hearing before me and, owing to everyone being busy otherwise, it could be heard only on 10 July 1991.

Roxna Swamy was the counsel for the petitioner while K.N. Bhat was the advocate on behalf of Hegde. I had to decide whether Hegde incurred a disqualification or not. The case hinged on two issues:

- Whether the office of deputy chairman of the Planning Commission is an 'office of profit' under the Government of India.
- If so, whether the said office is exempted under the provisions of the Karnataka Legislature (Prevention of Disqualification) Act, 1956.

As far as the first question was concerned, neither party contested the fact that it was an 'office' under the Government of India. The question was about it being one of 'profit'. It was Hegde's contention that, since he had declined to take any salary and had accepted only compensatory allowances, it was not an office of profit. The petitioner's claim, on the other hand, was that it was indeed an office of profit, as the office had a salary attached to it.

According to Hegde's appointment letter, it was agreed that he would draw no salary and would be entitled only to certain allowances that were listed. Citing this, in the order dated 24 July 1991, I said:

> The above-mentioned agreement, that the opposite party would draw no salary, obviously shows that the office of the deputy chairman of the Planning Commission was entitled to salary but that the opposite party would not draw such a salary. This amounts to a voluntarily giving up of salary by the opposite party. Had the opposite party demanded the salary, he would have drawn the same, as a definite salary is attached to that office and has been paid in the past.[25]

The next question was whether such an office of profit is declared by the Karnataka Legislative Assembly as one that does not attract disqualification. The law on the subject is the Karnataka Legislature (Prevention of Disqualification) Act, 1956, and the relevant provision is contained in Section 3(d) of that Act. Under this Section, the office of the chairman or member of a committee, which would include the Planning Commission by virtue of the definition in Section 2(a) of that Act, shall not be an office of profit if the holder is not in receipt of or entitled to any remuneration other than compensatory allowances.

So the matter was clear: He was not in receipt of a salary alright, but he was 'entitled' to such remuneration and that disqualified him. Thus, the fact that he did not take the salary did not absolve him of the qualification of receiving salary. So, you see, the conclusion was simple, you can read the law. Several posts had been added to the list of exemptions, but the deputy chairman of the Planning Commission was not one of them. Thus, for those reasons, I declared Hegde as disqualified.

This recommendation was signed on 24 July 1991, just the day before I left for my leave. The order was duly sent to the governor of Karnataka. On 6 August, Khurshed Alam Khan, the then governor of Karnataka, disqualified Hegde from the Karnataka Legislative Assembly. The reaction was immediate. The very next day, there was a great hue and cry about it. All those associated with Hegde and his

---

[25]The author has a copy of the order in his private collections.

party spoke against the verdict and decided to challenge it in court.

On 10 August, Hegde opined that his disqualification was legally absurd, constitutionally perverse and politically vindictive. He felt that even an institution like the ECI is being used as an institution for political vendetta.

On 15 August, Hegde's supporters in Bangalore burnt what was supposed to be my effigy. The next day, around 500 members of the Janata Dal staged a protest by marching from Jantar Mantar to Patel Chowk where the ECI's office is situated. They were led by the leader of the Opposition in the Rajya Sabha, Jaipal Reddy. Again in Bangalore on 19 August, about 3,000 people participated in a rally organized by the Janata Dal in a protest against the disqualification.

While the case of Hegde's disqualification was still pending in court, another issue related to it came up during the presidential elections in June and July the following year in 1992. I sent the list of eligible voters comprising MPs and MLAs from the state of Karnataka, in accordance with the records I had at that particular time. Hegde's name did not appear in the list. It again stirred up some protest. However, eventually on 17 September 1992, the court gave a ruling—it did not uphold my decision.

Much water has flown under the bridge since then on the question of what are offices of profit and what are not offices of profit. Varied decisions were made. Today, you can write a whole lot about offices of profit and disqualifications. In my view, at that time, the legislator had undergone a disqualification. I lost the judgement; the High Court of Karnataka rejected my decision. Anyway, I decided not to waste any more of either the ECI's or the courts' time on it.

IMPEACHMENT EFFORTS WITH RENEWED VIGOUR

With the Hegde issue, the impeachment calls took a shriller tone. Concrete steps were being taken to develop a consensus to impeach me. Between 20 and 26 August 1991, the Janata Dal began seriously working to prepare an impeachment motion. Meanwhile, the BJP said that it was against the idea of impeachment and that it was keeping the matter alive in discussions in party forums. On 24 August, the SJP decided not to back the move to impeach me. Two days later, it was reported that the Left parties were ready with a move. And reports on 28 August said that both the National Front and the Left Front had together finalized a motion.

The National Front and the Left Front were putting pressure on the PM to make me quit. Around this time, I was back in Delhi from a trip abroad. There was speculation in the press that I would quit soon. Among other things, they suggested that I would leave if I were made ambassador either to the Soviet Union or to USA. Simultaneously, the newspaper began to talk about my successor. Rama Devi was brought back as one of the contenders. On 20 September, they bought in competition for Rama Devi. M.M. Rajendran, the union sports secretary, found his name floated as a possible contender for the post.

In this intervening period, calls for my impeachment decreased in intensity. On 4 September, the National Front and the Left Front together in Parliament reportedly agreed to go slow on its move for my impeachment on assurances from the government that a way would be found soon, so that I would leave my office as the CEC. Again, on 13 September, another report said that the two party combined may drop its move on my impeachment. These were based on the assurances from the PM that the government was looking into the possibility of giving me some other assignment. The net effect was that there was a lull in hostilities between the politicians and myself regarding the impeachment.

I AM NOT A CO-OPERATIVE SOCIETY

The bad blood between PM Narasimha Rao and me probably started with an incident in October 1991. The office of the then law minister, Vijaya Bhaskara Reddy, would routinely ask the ECI to prepare replies to parliamentary questions to which I would object. I made it clear to them that the poll panel was no appendage of the ministry. Reddy was angered by my instructions to my office not to prepare any replies, and that it should only provide the relevant details which the ministry needed for its reply in Parliament. He took up the matter with the PM who summoned me to his office. In the presence of the PM, Reddy told me, 'You are not co-operative.'

I replied, 'I am not a co-operative society. I represent the Election Commission.' Apparently, the PM was stunned. Then, turning to him, I said: 'Mr Prime Minister, I cannot do business with your minister if this is his attitude.'

More trouble followed. Narasimha Rao had become the PM in June 1991, and he had to be elected to Parliament before December. The law was that if he did not have a seat in Parliament in six months, he stood to lose the appointment. Having been appointed PM in the third week of June, he had to get elected by the third week of December.

The entire process of electioneering takes about 45–50 days, and we had to finish this by the middle of December. Early in October, I mentioned to the PM that he had to stand for election from wherever he wanted and the dates were under discussion.

Completely unrelated to me, there was a dispute going on in the High Court of Delhi about the disqualification of some members of the Nagaland Legislative Assembly. It had happened much earlier, much before I become the CEC. On 8 October 1991, the attorney general of India, G. Ramaswamy, who was the EC counsel in that case, rang me up in the evening to inform me something the judge had mentioned in court that day.

There is a common misconception that the attorney general of India is ipso facto ex-officio lawyer of the ECI. He is not; he is appointed by the ECI. I found it beneficial to seek Ramaswamy's help as my lawyer since he was willing to do so. The benefit was that you did not have to haggle about the fees and, for a case of the ECI, I could pay him whatever the government would pay him for a similar case. He took a very active interest in the whole business. So, there he was, in connection with the Nagaland members' case.

On that day, while I was at home, between 6.30 p.m. and 7.00 p.m., Ramaswamy rang me up and said that when he was in the High Court of Delhi that day, the judge sent for him and asked whether he would give them an assurance that a certain constituency—Etawah—which was coming up for by-elections would not be notified. Ramaswamy told the court that he was not the standing counsel of the ECI and that he would refer it to me. So, he wrote me a letter, which reached my house late in the evening at seven or eight.

What happened was that someone had moved the High Court of Delhi that day to stop the by-election being notified in Etawah, where there was a vacancy. The lawyers moving it had asked for assurance of some kind that the elections would not be notified. So, the court had asked G. Ramaswamy to do so, and he, in turn, passed it on to me.

The next morning, I was getting ready to go to the office when one of my secretaries at the ECI—there are half a dozen of them of the rank of deputy secretary to the Government of India—rang me up and reported a call from Rama Devi, saying that the government wanted Etawah to not be notified.

I have explained earlier that the procedure for the issue of a notification starts at the ECI. A draft notification is sent by the ECI to the law ministry. The law ministry sends it for approval to the President. The President approves it, and then it is issued as a notification. That notification issued by the President is a signal for the ECI to start the work.

Rama Devi was the officer who processed all the notifications in the law ministry. I had sent a whole bunch of notifications to be approved by the President. When my deputy asked me for a response to Rama Devi's message about the government wanting a constituency to be excluded, I said, 'Tell her that this is not a matter to be decided at her level. She should talk to me if she wants to.'

Rama Devi then talked to Bagga, the deputy election commissioner, and repeated the same request, mentioning that the minister of state for law, Rangarajan Kumaramangalam, desired it. What had happened was that Ramaswamy had written a letter to me and had marked a copy of it to the law minister. In the law minister's copy, the minister had said that a certain constituency should be excluded. It is not within the power of anybody in government to exclude a constituency. Not even the President can order such a thing unless there is something legally wrong. Nobody has the authority to decide when the notification for a particular constituency is to be issued except the ECI.

This was my first real test of autonomy.

I rang up Rama Devi and informed her that this was unacceptable to me as a CEC and that it is the ECI that decides when a particular constituency is to be notified or not. The government has no role in it.

The courts had given a stay order for elections in the case of Patna, Purnea and Meerut constituencies, but there was no stay on polls in Etawah. Therefore, there was no reason why polls for Etawah should not be notified. That a reply had to be given to the High Court judge was another matter, but as far as the decision of notifying Etawah was concerned, the law had put the ball in the ECI's court.

It is not open to elected representatives either to delete a constituency from the list or to demand that the ECI delete it, unless it senses a legal foul play. If they had given reasons explaining why it would be legally wrong to notify polls in the constituency, I could understand. But in this case, no clear reasons were mentioned. The only reason mentioned was that the Congress would not win the election. That is no reason for the ECI to accept the non-inclusion of the constituency.

However, Rama Devi hummed and hawed, and said that it was the minister's decision and that she could not do anything about it. Understandably, she couldn't oppose the minister. I rang up the PM, and to make a very difficult conversation short, I said, 'In the government, there seems to be a misconception that I am the horse and the government is a rider.' These were my exact words, 'I won't accept this. Nobody in the government has the right to dictate what I should do. If you have a good reason, please tell me. I'll listen to the reason. I'll not listen to dictates.'

The PM, after carefully listening to my words, said, 'Yes, yes, you settle it with Rangarajan.'

I said, 'No, I am not going to settle it with him. I am going to settle it with you. I need an apology from Mr Rangarajan for having tried to overrule the ECI, which he does not have the power to do. With great respect, even the President does not have the power to overrule the ECI. That is a critical issue; the critical issue is the authority of the ECI. If we do something wrong, you can come back and say we need to change it. If there is something we are not aware of—a famine, a flood, a plague, cholera—you can say we cannot hold the election because there are a lot of administrative problems. But you can't direct me to delete or include anything.'

Rangarajan telephoned me and, breaking into Tamil, he asked, 'What is the problem?'

I said, 'I have no problem. I want an apology. I want an apology from the government for trying to overrule me.'

He said, 'Shall I send it?'

I said, 'I don't mind it if you send it. But as a person who has worked in the government for 30–40 years, I know that normally the communications are sent by the civil services and not by the minister. I have no objections to either one of them. But I want it by one o'clock.'

I further said, 'If I don't get the letter by one o'clock, I am going to scrap the entire lot of elections and one of the persons to be affected would be the PM, because his elections have to be completed by December, and I won't do it. I'll say until the issue is resolved, I won't hold the election. There is nothing the PM or anybody can do about it.'[26]

To make a long story short, by 12 or 12.30 p.m. that day, there was a joint secretary coming up the stairs to my office with the letter from Rama Devi. In the letter, she had written, 'If you think that there was anything improper in whatever I did or said or if anything has been informed to you in this regard that you think is improper, I wholly apologize.' It further read, 'If anything I've said or done has caused any offence, I am sorry.'

Having obtained this apology, I appended it to a letter to the minister of law and justice, recounting the incidents of the day as well as the previous day. In it, I also informed that the commission had not received any kind of notice or order from the High Court about petitions pertaining to the Etawah elections. I was standing by

---

[26]The author has a copy of the letter in his private collections.

my earlier advice to the president of issuing a notification of fresh election in Etawah too.

As I said, one of the constituencies notified in the by-elections was of PM Narasimha Rao. He decided to contest the election from the Nandyal Lok Sabha seat in Andhra Pradesh. To enable him to contest the seat, the sitting member resigned.

Narasimha Rao was in an extraordinarily comfortable position. He was a Congress candidate, but he was being openly supported by N.T. Rama Rao, who was the CM, and belonged to the other powerful party in the state. Since he was supported by the Congress and the Telugu Desam Party, it was a foregone conclusion that Narasimha Rao would win the election hands down.

Even so, some Congressmen in Andhra Pradesh went overboard and engaged in all kinds of irregularities in the Nandyal elections. One candidate was captured, taken 482 km from Nandyal, left in the forest and asked to walk back. Another candidate was kept confined in a room in the collector's office until 3.00 p.m., which was the last hour for filing nominations.

It was but natural for members of the Opposition parties to complain of large irregularities, but there was no evidence. There were no major irregularities, in my opinion, which would have justified the cancellation of the elections. Narasimha Rao won by a huge margin.

In Bihar, the by-polls did not go smoothly. This time, repoll was ordered in 331 booths. On 18 November, immediately after the by-polls, V.P. Singh was again reported to have threatened to impeach me. He was reported to have threatened to revive proceedings of the impeachment in Parliament if I delayed announcing the date for repoll and recounting of votes in the by-elections in Bihar. He is reported to have said that the requisite number of signatures of MPs were already with him to move the motion of impeachment against me.

From press reports of 20 November 1991, it was evident that the Janata Dal MPs had disrupted proceedings in the Lok Sabha. These members are said to have defiantly shouted '*T.N. Seshan ko barkhast karo* (Remove T.N. Seshan).'

In the midst of the sloganeering, the leader of the Opposition,

L.K. Advani, was reported to have risen to demand a full discussion on the 'serious malpractices' in Andhra Pradesh and Bihar during the recent by-elections.

On 26 November, there were reports in the press that the National Front–Left Front combine had arrived at the decision to go ahead with the impeachment when the matter was discussed in its coordination committee. While addressing reporters, the concerned leaders were reported to have said that, on the PM's assurance, they had withdrawn the impeachment move before the by-elections. He had assured them not once, but thrice. But this time, around 120 members of the Lower House had already signed the motion.

The next day, when reporters asked me about it, I said, 'Fear is not a word in my dictionary.' I was certainly not afraid of impeachment. On the contrary, to a suggestion by the Gujarat CM that there should be reforms in the electoral process, I informed him that work on electoral reforms was underway and that I would submit a report to the Centre very soon. In other words, I was looking forward to my task, unmindful of the chorus of impeachment.

Finally, nothing came of it in that particular session of Parliament. On 11 December, the Opposition combine again said that it was all for impeachment, but it also stressed its 'unhappiness' over the PM's 'non-responsive' attitude towards their request.

On 13 December, when members of the press asked about it, I said that 'impeachment does not worry me'. By that time, the impeachment chorus had hit a temporary lull.

CUSHY UN JOB OR TURBULENT CEC JOB?

At no time did I intend to do a less-than-good job at the ECI. But the truth remained that I had taken up the post of CEC with no great love for it. Within weeks of of my being appointed, I had met Chandra Shekar, Rajiv Gandhi and President R. Venkataraman and requested them to 'relieve me'.

In a similar manner, I had asked to be a relieved of that office of responsibility several times throughout the year 1991. So, when an offer came from the United Nations (UN), it got me thinking.

An official high-up in the UN hierarchy called me up one day to make an attractive offer. The proposal was that I could become the deputy secretary general with all the departments of development administration under me. I would receive two lakh dollars as an annual salary, an executive aircraft for personal use and so on. I was impressed, and my wife even started thinking of packing.

The Kanchi Math had always been important to our family and if you remember, I had taken up even this post on the advice of the Kanchi Seer. So, I had a permission to seek. I went to Kanchi and sat at the feet of Paramacharya. After some minutes of silence, during which the Paramacharya seemed to be in a state of incomprehension, he said, 'No'. He said it with utter finality. No questions asked, no clarifications given. That spelt the end of the would-be assignment.

My friends and I decided to find out why the Paramacharya took that position. The only way to know his mind was to consult Namboodiri of Guruvayur in whose astrological skills and clairvoyance everyone, including myself, had trust. I and some friends made plans to go there, but the plan was dropped again and again for some reason. When we thought we were really going to make it at last, my friend in Chennai was suddenly summoned to Kanchi.

The Paramacharya jolted him with a question. Was he going to Guruvayur to find out why Paramacharya had said what he said? 'No, give up the plan. Ask Seshan to come down to Kanchi', he said. When I went, I sat with the saint for five long hours without a single word shared between us. I did not dare ask any questions. As the time crawled on beyond five hours, the Paramacharya dismissed me with a silent gesture full of affection. It was then that I knew it was pointless pursuing the UN offer.

TEN

THE SECOND YEAR AT THE COMMISSION

I f a party violates the constitutional code, does the ECI have the authority to deregister the party after verifying the facts about the violations? This was a question that was on my mind, especially when the symbol related issue came up again in 1992.

Prior to the general elections, in connection with the case that Arjun Singh had brought up, I had found that a third party could intervene and bring a symbol-related matter before the commission. But the main question about whether the commission could deregister a party could not be settled before the elections. This was the reason behind why the matter of the BJP lotus symbol was taken up again in the beginning of 1992.

CAN THE EC DEREGISTER A POLITICAL PARTY?

Counsel for Arjun Singh argued that the power to deregister a party, though not explicitly stated in the laws, actually flowed, by implication, from the Constitution and the available laws. All parties, by their actions and deeds, bear true faith and allegiance to the Constitution of India and to the principles of socialism, secularism and democracy, and uphold the sovereignty, unity and integrity of India. Therefore, the power to deregister a party if it, by its action, policies and programmes, violates the provisions of the relevant Section 29A (5) of the Representation of the People Act, 1951, has to be read as having been conferred on the commission by necessary implication, even if not expressly stated. Article 324 of the Constitution provided a reservoir of powers for the commission to deal with such surprise situations, and this has been upheld by the Supreme Court in several cases. Arjun Singh's counsel added that if an individual or a candidate makes any appeal on the grounds of religion or using religious symbols, he or she may become liable for action under the provisions relating to corrupt practices and electoral offences. But if a political party indulges in such practices, the complaint against such a party will lie with the commission that has registered and granted the symbol on its recognition.

On his part, BJP leader Arun Jaitley first took an extreme stand that once a party is registered, the ECI has no right whatsoever to deregister it but finally conceded that the ECI could definitely directly deregister a party under two conditions: first, if the information supplied by the party during the registration was proven to be false; and second, if the political party itself wrote to the ECI saying that they would not abide by Section 29A of the Representation of the People Act, 1951.

The Unlawful Activities (Prevention) Act of 1967 provides for regular machinery for keeping watch over the activities of all the associations including political parties. If it indulges in any unlawful activity, an association can be declared unlawful by the central government. Once declared as indulging in unlawful activities, the association or party ceases to exist as a registered party under Section 29A of the 1951 Act because the party then ceases to exist in the eyes of the law.

So, I found that, when arrangements are already in place to monitor the activities of the political parties, it would be superfluous for another organization, such as the ECI, to monitor the same thing. Therefore, I determined that the ECI has not been empowered in this respect by Parliament. Besides, if such monitoring were done by the ECI, it would have to adjudicate upon ideologies, policies and programmes of political parties.

Two further issues remained: one of the registration of a party and the other of recognizing it as a national party. The allotment of a symbol to a political party also acknowledges its recognition as either a state party or a national party. The rules for such recognition are laid down in terms of percentage of vote shares that a party gains in a general election. There are no other criteria. Arjun Singh himself admitted that the BJP has used its symbol to improve its electoral prospects by appealing to a certain section of society. The symbol, however, could be taken away only if the relevant percentages are not achieved by the political parties.

I concluded that if anyone feels that the political party has indulged in certain acts that are not in keeping with the law of the land, there are remedies elsewhere but not with the commission. So saying, I dismissed the petitions.

In this case, 'the duty' and 'the power' of the commission were interpreted—interpreted to mean that there was no power to take away the symbol.

AT THE RECEIVING END OF INACCURATE REPORTING

In the heat of the 1991 general elections, I became a victim of improper reporting by the press. In a TV interview, I communicated the dates for the elections. I had clearly said that there were a set of factors that together dictated the decision that I took. The subject of the word 'dictated' that I had used was 'set of factors'. True that the PM's opinion also constituted one of the various factors. But the press went to town saying that I had said that the 'Prime Minister' dictated it. It creates a world of difference; in fact, it negated the very first principle of autonomy that I fought for. And when the press reported it, whether the distortion was inadvertent or deliberate, it reflected lack of excellence on the media's part. In like manner, there were other notable instances in 1992 that reflected this.

One such instance was based on an incident that occurred on 28 February 1992. I was under NSG protection at that time.

As we were driving home that day, I was in a bulletproof car, the pilot car preceded mine and an escort car carrying more guards brought up the rear. There was a white Maruti in front of our little convoy, and it was not letting our cars pass. The whole row of cars had slowed down; every time the pilot car switched on its siren, the Maruti would deliberately not let it go by.

Having worked as the officer incharge of the PM's security, I was well versed with security drills, security threat perception and such matters. I understood the dilemma the driver of the pilot car faced, thwarted as he was in his attempts to overtake the white Maruti. I told my driver to overtake the pilot car because it was having problems. At this point, the commando in the front seat placed his gun on my driver's neck and said, 'Overtake karega to goli mar doonga (I'll shoot you if you overtake).' This was the commando's response to an order from me to my driver in my own car.

I turned to the personal security officer (PSO) sitting beside me and asked what was going on. True. I had not asked the security personnel for permission to overtake the pilot car. The PSO explained that overtaking the pilot car was not allowed. I accepted; but I said that threatening to shoot my driver was not right.

We were close to India Gate at that time. I told the driver to stop, and the car came to a slow halt near Andhra Pradesh Bhavan. The pilot car had also stopped and suddenly reversed and banged into my vehicle. The ranking officer rushed out and asked what the problem was. On being apprised of the situation, he apologized on behalf of the offending guard. But I stood my ground saying that a man who threatened my driver had no place in my car. I got the security guard to leave my vehicle, and my driver drove me to the house.

After I reached home, the officer said he would have to submit a report of the incident to his superiors. I said that he could do whatever he wanted. In the meantime, I spoke to Dr Subramanian, the head of the NSG. He apologized and sent his deputy along. I told him that anyone who threatened my driver was not acceptable to me as part of my security detail. Soon afterwards, I forgot about the incident as the guards were changed.

About three weeks later, on 17 March, a completely distorted version appeared in the press.

Apparently, there was a report by the United News of India that was picked up and published by many papers. It was interesting to see how various newspapers went about the story with relish. Among the interesting things they said about the incident were the following:

'Mr Seshan's car finally managed to overtake the car and screeched to a halt in front of it.'
　　'Mr Seshan ordered his guards "to fire" on the occupants for their insolence.'

The report did matter to me because it described and published a version of me that was designed by someone who was out to harm my reputation. But it is more telling about the credibility of the press in performing what it calls its 'dharma'.

THE ELECTIONS OF 1992

In addition to Punjab Legislative Assembly Elections of 1992, there were other by-polls in some Lok Sabha and Vidhan Sabha seats, elections to the Upper House and the election of the President and Vice President.

Of the two Lok Sabha seats going to by-polls in 1992, one was in Bihar and the other was in Delhi. There were 125 candidates in the fray in Delhi. The pick of the lot included actors Rajesh Khanna and Shatrughan Sinha, on the Congress and BJP tickets, respectively. People who wanted to vote for them had to search for their names and symbols on a sheet that was 86 cm by 69 cm in size, almost as big as a broadsheet newspaper. In all, there were three national parties, 16 registered parties and 106 Independents in the fray.

The constituency of Vaishali in Bihar was particularly sensitive because a candidate and his supporters had been killed and another candidate had been attacked allegedly by some miscreants favouring the ruling party in Bihar. So, in Vaishali, there were calls for countermanding elections.

Elections were conducted, and counting took place immediately in most constituencies. In Delhi, Rajesh Khanna won the Lok Sabha seat comfortably, but the result was interesting for other reasons. Out of the independent candidates in the fray, more than 100 did not reach the three-digit mark. And a surprise was Phoolan Devi, an ex-dacoit, who had filed her papers from jail as an independent candidate. She polled 753 votes in all, and these votes came from all over the constituency. Interestingly, the Lajpat Nagar segment, considered to be the elitist segment of all, gave her a maximum of 173 votes. It is another matter that 753 was a small figure in comparison to Rajesh Khanna's a little over one lakh votes out of the nearly two lakh votes cast. But it was a significant result, considering the fact that she got it all on her own strength.

There was election-related trouble in many places. Counting was put off in Vaishali and Danapur in Bihar, Ballygunj in West Bengal, and Allagada and Himayatnagar in Andhra Pradesh. The one constituency of Malkangiri in Orissa was Naxalite-violence prone, and the Naxals had called for a boycott. Repolling was ordered in 15 booths spread out over various constituencies in other states. Finally, only in Ballygunj, Danapur (Bihar) and Himayatnagar (now in Telangana), the counting remained suspended beyond 10 June. Shortly, repoll was ordered in 40 booths of Danapur, elections were held on 14 June, and the Janata Dal candidate was eventually elected.

The case in Himayatnagar was peculiar. Himayatnagar was important because the Congress candidate contesting from there was supposedly handpicked by the PM and was known to nurture chief ministerial ambitions. Janardhan Reddy, who was the Congress CM at that time, was reported to be a worried man. The BJP demanded a repoll in 52 booths and the Telugu Desam Party in 46 booths. The Congress (I) candidate asked for a repoll in the entire constituency claiming that the administration (headed by his own party) had conspired to help the BJP win. The returning officer recommended repoll in 10 booths on 10 June, which was accepted by the commission. After the counting, the BJP candidate was declared victorious.

Ballygunj in Kolkata, West Bengal, was a unique case. The political situation was complex. It was a seat that the CPI (M) had won just a year earlier and the winning candidate had passed away. The party had put in a new man, but another member of that party who had recently been expelled was contesting as an Independent. The Congress, under Mamata Banerjee, was in the fray, too, but press reports suggested that it was a divided house and there was scheming within the party against Banerjee's candidate. Finally, the BJP had put up its state secretary as a candidate there. It was a four-cornered contest that had become a prestige issue, and the parties were sure to fire on all cylinders.

Midway through polling on 8 June, the Congress candidate declared that he had withdrawn from the contest. He attributed his withdrawal to the large-scale rigging by the CPI (M) cadres. Three other Independents, including the rebel CPI (M) candidate also withdrew.

The CM, on his part, addressed reporters and said that the polling was generally peaceful except for some stray incident in Ballygunj. It was officially stated that three rounds had been fired by policemen attached to a radio (wireless) telephone when it came under attack from Congress supporters.

Counting of votes was postponed. And subsequently, the commission was accused by the CM of doing so 'on the basis of baseless allegations of the Congress'. A 24-hour bandh was called for the next day by the Left Front in protest 'against Delhi's sinister design to dictate'. The claim was that 'absolutely peaceful polling was held yesterday, despite the Congress efforts to disturb it...'[27]

The situation in Ballygunj was to get further complicated. A four-member team led by S.D. Prasad of the ECI was dispatched on 9 June, but it was prevented from conducting a full inquiry. The next day, 10 June, was declared a bandh, and nothing could be done on that day. The team of officers were constantly followed by party workers and newsmen, and there was no possibility of recording oral evidence of complaints.

The CM denied the charges of creating hindrances and the chief electoral officer feigned ignorance on the matter. A notification was issued, extending the end date of the election process to 18 June. It was stated that the inquiry should continue in order to arrive at proper facts. But this could be done only if the government of West Bengal gave an assurance on providing essential facilities to the commission's team to conduct the inquiry in a free and fair manner. Only after

---

[27]'Basu Decries EC Decision', *The Patriot*, 10 June 1992.

the complete report of the inquiry team was submitted would the commission decide on the future course of action.

According to the report that was finally submitted by the team, an enraged elderly gentleman and his neighbour had said: 'Imbecile policemen stood as mute witness while armed CPI (M) cadres resorted to false voting and other irregularities in my area.' They went on to give a no holds barred account of how the cadres unleashed a reign of terror that day. One of them said: 'Take my advice. If you wish to conduct an independent inquiry, do not come to us escorted by policemen. Avoid traveling in the state government's car; instead, use a hired car wherever you go.'

The CPI (M) eventually won the election with a margin of around 30,000 votes, the Congress candidate who had withdrawn came second with around 31,000 votes. In the previous elections, the margin was as small as 4,300 votes.

THE OBLIGATION TO STOP A COMPROMISED VOTING PROCESS

By the time the by-elections came to a close, the election of the President had already taken centre stage as also had polls for filling vacancies in the Rajya Sabha. This time, it was Bihar that drew the limelight. On 25 June 1992, commencing from 1.30 p.m., several complaints from Bihar reached the ECI. The chief electoral officer of Bihar, who was the observer for the poll there, had received a complaint from an independent candidate alleging the snatching of votes. The officer also reported that there was shouting and counter-shouting and that he was not present at the polling station between 12.15 p.m. and 1.30 p.m., as he was away on another duty.

In view of the complaints and allegations, the commission directed the returning officer not to start the counting of votes and wait for direction from the commission. Two senior officers—Deputy Election Commissioner D.S. Bagga, and Secretary S.K. Mendiratta—reached Patna the next day, on 26 June, to inquire into the allegations. They submitted their report on 30 June 1992.

The report indicated utter chaos when elections were held. The arrangements did not ensure an orderly flow of voters. There was crowding and, as a result, the secrecy of the ballot was compromised. Unauthorized persons were present when voting was going on. In at least two instances, and possibly more, voting ballets were snatched from voters, marked and put in the box. The CM and the leader of the Opposition, along with many others, were among the unauthorized individuals who frequented the polling station.

On 1 July, I passed an order: 'In exercise of the powers under Article 324 of the constitution and Section 58(2)(a) of the Representation of the People Act, 1951, the poll taken at Patna on 25.6.1992 for the Biennial elections to the Council of States and the Bihar Legislative Council by the members of the Bihar Legislative Assembly is declared void.'[28]

I added that, subject to the ECI being enabled by Bihar government to appoint a new returning officer by 3 July, the poll could be held for the Rajya Sabha on 7 July and for the legislative council on 21 July.

As requested, the Bihar government provided the ECI with a list of names of IAS officers. On 3 July, the secretary of the Bihar legislative council was appointed as the returning officer.

In the meantime, the Rajya Sabha elections took place on 7 July 1992, on schedule, and went off without a hitch. The results were duly declared. The results went mostly in favour of the Janata Dal, which was in majority in the House. But a notice was issued against me for having undermined the dignity of the House.

The demand for the notice triggered noisy scenes and 10 ruling party members were said to have trooped into the well of the House shouting slogans against me. The Speaker is said to have admonished the ruling party members for creating a disturbance. He informed them that a letter had already been sent summoning me to the House. Unruly scenes continued and culminated in a noisy walkout by the Congress.

The Bihar election matter was also taken in Parliament, accusing me of having done something 'undemocratic'. The minister of state for law and justice, H.R. Bharadwaj, in defence of my stand in the matter, gave a written reply to the Rajya Sabha. It was a mostly accurate

---

[28]The author has a copy of the order in his private collections.

reflection of what I had ruled. As for me, I never had any doubts about the correctness of my action.

The election of 11 seats of the legislative council of Bihar scheduled for 21 July went off smoothly.

AN EVENTFUL ELECTION OF THE INDIAN PRESIDENT

President R. Venkataraman was to be at his post until 24 July, and Vice President Dr Shankar Dayal Sharma's term was ending on 2 September. Therefore, elections for these posts were required to take place between June and September 1992. These elections became interesting for some odd reasons.

Elections for the president's post were notified on 10 June, and polling was to be held on 13 July. A total of six people filed nominations, of which two were initially rejected because their papers were found faulty. Mr Shankar Dayal Sharma was put up as a presidential candidate by the Congress. Apparently, he also had the support of the CPI (M). The National Front tried its best to wean away the Left from supporting Mr Sharma, but it did not succeed. Finally, Prof. George Gilbert Swell joined the contest as an Independent and was supported by both the BJP and the National Front. Advocate Ram Jethmalani, who also joined the contest, tried to raise the issue of 'conscience vote'. He wrote to me asking me to clarify whether seeking votes in the name of caste for the highest office would be a corrupt practice under the ordinary election law. Though his approach did generate some reflections in the media, he did not have the requisite support. A day before the elections, he withdrew in favour of Prof. Swell because the BJP and Janata Dal told him that Prof. Swell had a fair chance of winning. In fact, on tallying the total number of value votes before elections, it was found that the combined Opposition had a slight edge over the Congress. The Congress was looking for a consensus.

The other person who remained in the fray was Kaka Joginder Singh, otherwise known as 'Dharti Pakad'.

Both the presidential and vice presidential elections saw a string of cases being taken to the courts. Early on, there was a petition seeking the election of a woman as vice president. The division bench of the court turned down the petition since the petitioner had failed to make out a prima facie case to substantiate his claim that fielding female candidates to the exclusion of males had constitutional sanction.

Shortly after the elections, on 20 July, Dharti Pakad petitioned in the Supreme Court challenging the election of Dr Shankar Dayal Sharma. He asked the Chief Justice to not administer the oath of office to Dr Sharma on 25 July. In his petition, he raised objections on several grounds including the fact that Dr Sharma was holding an office of profit at the time of contesting elections. Another ground for objection was that the returning officer had 'illegally and unconstitutionally' accepted the nominations of Dr Sharma and the Opposition- sponsored candidate Dr G.G. Swell. He said that both were above 65 years old and therefore were ineligible. Yet another objection was that there was only one proposer in the case of Sharma and Swell, while 10 proposers were required.

Though the Supreme Court accepted their claims for hearing, it did not stop Dr Sharma from taking the oath of office, and he became the president.

The election of the vice president is not as elaborate a process as that of the president. Only the MPs, including the nominated members, elect the vice president. The counting for the presidential poll was scheduled on 16 July. A day before that, I notified that the vice president's elections were to take a month later on 19 August.

Dr S.D. Sharma, the then incumbent in the vice president's chair, was to relinquish office only on 2 September. But he was a frontrunner in the presidential race and would have to resign on 24 July if he were elected as the president. Some people tried to create a controversy saying that I had jumped the gun and the new vice president would be elected 14 days before the due date. I had nothing to say to them except that the notification was done following the normal course.

Many persons filed their papers but most were rejected because they did not have the five proposers and five seconders required. Finally, it turned out to be a contest between K.R. Narayanan and Dharti Pakad, with the result that Narayanan was elected as the ninth vice president of India.

THE 1992 ROUND OF IMPEACHMENT EFFORTS

The year 1992 also saw a whole lot of impeachment moves against me. In this, the presidential elections featured in a small way. On its sidelines, seeds were sown for the second big fight between the commission and the government.

The two major events between December 1991 and February 1992 relating to the derecognition of political parties and elections in Punjab added to the political drama. Many parties had lost their symbols after the 1991 general elections. In Punjab, the Congress had made a clean sweep, getting a landslide majority in the state assembly and almost all the parliamentary seats. This was the same party that had boycotted the elections in May–June 1991. I assume this added salt to other parties' wounds.

On 4 March 1992, the National Front and the Left Front parties finally initiated formal moves to seek my impeachment and submitted a notice signed by 122 Lok Sabha members to the Speaker Shivraj Patil. An article that appeared the next day in the *Hindustan Times*, 5 March 1992, Delhi, elaborated: 'The notice has charged Mr Seshan with acting in an arbitrary, partisan and authoritarian manner and says acts of misbehaviour made him totally unfit for the high office... The signatories wanted to urge the president to remove Mr Seshan for his various acts of misbehaviour, particularly in dealing with elections in Punjab, Bihar, Uttar Pradesh and Tripura.'[29]

Besides, it said that the notice accused me of having a desire to create difficulties for non-Congress governments. The notice is supposed to have charged me with arbitrariness and illegally holding repoll or withholding results in various constituencies. Seemingly, the notice also charged me with overlooking the 'reign of terror in Tripura'.

On 5 March, the Janata Party stated that it did not support the impeachment motion. Instead, it asked the Speaker to suo moto reject the notice of impeachment.[30]

---

[29]'NF, Left Submit Notice to Speaker', *Hindustan Times*, 5 March 1992.
[30]'Reject NF, LF Move on Seshan, Says JP', *National Herald*, 6 March 1992.

The notice to the Speaker remained under his consideration for more than a month. The budget session was almost coming to an end. Around 24 April, the leaders of the Janata Dal took up the matter with the Speaker again. Two of the leaders had personally met the Speaker, and a question in this regard was also raised by Ram Vilas Paswan, MP from Rosera in Bihar, at zero hour.

Around this time, there was speculation that the Speaker was yet to make up his mind on the basis on which the matter could be taken before a judicial team for ascertaining whether I had violated the Constitution.

The budget session came to an end without any further movement on the notice. If at all the matter was to be taken up, as the law stood, the process had to be started all over again in the next session.

The Left Front was displeased with the development in Ballygunj. Their grouse was that the ECI was not going entirely by the words of the returning officers and the chief electoral officer of West Bengal. They intensified their campaign against me. But all of a sudden, the intensity dropped a couple of days before the repoll in Ballygunj.

Even as all this was going on, the snatching of votes in Bihar happened. I stopped the counting on the evening of 25 June. The knee-jerk reaction was that the next day, there were statements in the press that I should be impeached. On 27 June, there was a protest outside the ECI office in New Delhi by about 2,000 members of the Janata Dal who courted arrest. Among the protesters were V.P. Singh (former PM) and Mr Sharad Joshi who also addressed the protesting workers.[31]

On 1 July, there was a disturbance over the issue in the Bihar assembly, and my reported telephonic conversation with a member for which a privilege notice had been issued to me was also dragged into the debate. On this occasion, the CM and the leader of the Opposition were supposed to have been involved in a heated exchange when the BJP staged a walkout saying that the debate was not being conducted in a democratic manner.

---

[31]'Staying of Counting Undemocratic: VP', *The Indian Express*, 28 June 1993.

Interestingly, two days later, even the Left parties denounced my decision to declare the election null and void. The CPI (M) politburo member, Prakash Karat, said that my decision was tantamount to the murder of democracy and added that there was no other way to safeguard Parliament institutions but to remove me from my constitutional position.

On 3 July, it was again reported that the Janata Dal and the CPI (M) would be pursuing an impeachment motion against me. They were reported to have said that the PM was 'honour bound' to support the Seshan impeachment motion. Shivraj Patil called the National Front and Left Front leaders to hear their case on the pending impeachment notice against me.

What may have sealed that fate of the impeachment issue is probably a statement made by the PM at a press conference in Delhi. The remark did not get much press coverage, but it was significant. An article in the *Patriot*, dated 4 July 1992, reported that the PM in a press conference said, 'I have not come across any constitutional provisions where the Prime Minister can remove the Chief Election Commissioner. Unless one quotes chapter and verse to me, I cannot respond to that.'[32]

This was seen by the sponsors of the motion as a breach of promise by the PM. But it also acted as a dampener of sorts. Nothing finally came of the impeachment move that year but the friction continued.

The end of 1992 and probably the whole of 1993 also saw another important issue hitting the limelight: electoral rolls and their purity. And the ECI had a fight with various state governments over it.

INDIAN DEMOCRACY AND THE QUALITY OF ELECTORAL ROLLS

Making electoral rolls is an important part of elections in any democracy. In India, it is the responsibility of the ECI, and for that purpose, it needs to use the state's machinery. Needless to say, the electoral rolls can be only as accurate as a process of enumeration. It

---

[32]'NF, Left to Insist on Seshan Impeachment', *The Patriot*, 4 July 1992.

is sad that there are many loopholes that need plugging in this regard.

While I was in office, there was a relentless struggle against these loopholes, and within the power available to me, I did everything I could to set things right. It should also be clear why it is important for the ECI to have disciplinary power over the staff deputed for such election work. The power, in any case, was there, but the government wanted to deny it to me.

A typical example would be of West Bengal. I found many inconsistencies in the lists prepared and ordered that the lists be remade. Naturally, the government of West Bengal was appalled. So, there was a lot of back and forth and the attempt to improve the purity of the electoral roles had to be taken on with a lot of focussed effort. I would recommend that the reader should look into an article written by Poonam Kaushik for the Indian News and Feature Alliance, titled 'Megalomaniac CEC or CM?', dated 21 November 1992. It is a representation of the ground realities of that time and it gives a fair idea of what I was up against.

In December 1992, there was one instance that came to light in Andhra Pradesh where the number of voters in a constituency was more than the population of that constituency. It even got coverage in the press. The issue of the revision of rolls is a regular feature, and the rolls need to be updated from time to time. Beginning from August 1992, specific steps were taken, particularly in the identification of foreign nationals in the electoral rolls in West Bengal, Delhi, Bihar and several northeastern states. It is because of obtaining these adverse inputs about the rolls in West Bengal, that a complete revision was ordered there.

In the case of Assam, the ECI had to wage a perpetual struggle. A string of orders had to be passed to attempt to purify both the process of enumeration and the electoral rolls produced. In Assam, there was the issue of foreign nationals who had come from Bangladesh. Complexities in the case arose in fixing the acceptable immigration year, in fixing the enumeration and census that was to form the base, in determining whether people illegally living on government land were to be included in the rolls, and many more such questions. The All-Assam Students' Union did not want the foreigners in Assam. The

BJP, for obvious reasons, was against the poll lists that were being generated. The Saikia government of the Congress party was finding great difficulty in selectively excluding a certain community from the rolls. The Muslim associations of Assam were up in arms against the injustice being meted out to 'genuine' citizens and the harassment of Muslims in the name of preparing electoral rolls. In short, it was a mess. With the courts coming in and decisions going this way and that, the struggle persisted and the problems continue to this day.

The problem in Nagaland and Tripura were the same. In Tripura, it was again a case of bloated electoral rolls and other law and order problems. There was a problem of infiltration in Bihar, too.

Let alone the border states, there was a problem in the capital itself. Many complaints were received after the draft rolls were published on 25 January 1993 in Delhi. The complaints said that the names of foreign nationals were included and genuine Indian citizens were excluded. It was decided by the commission that action would be taken against the Delhi administration for 'lapses' in its procedures for including the names of foreign nationals, particularly Bangladeshis, in the revised electoral rolls. The final lists were to be out by 25 March in 13 sectors where a large population of illegal immigrants was supposed to be living. The result was that in the final roll, only 17,000 could be declared as voters from one area where there were 128,000 in the draft rolls. These figures were alarming. The publication of final rolls was held up for some time. In fact, according to police sources, there were possibly around 400,000 illegal immigrants in Delhi at that time. There were speculations in the press suggesting that this was just the tip of the iceberg. It took up to November for elections to be held.

It cannot be said that the ECI did not do its best nor can it be said that the problem was solved. I only say that, like many others, this problem probably was not something that could be handled with the limited mandate the ECI had. Solutions for such problems lie elsewhere. Eventually, many of the firm steps taken up by the ECI in this regard went to the courts and the ECI hit a roadblock two years down the line where many of these decisions were reversed by the Supreme Court for various reasons. But that is another story...

ELEVEN

FIGHT FOR EFFECTIVE
AUTONOMY OF THE ECI

By mid-1992, the Opposition was gunning for me at full throttle. I had already had one major fight with the government, which ended in the apology penned by Rama Devi. Cleaning up of the electoral rolls rubbed all kinds of people the wrong way. But that was only the start. The fight was about to climb up to a completely different level.

The word 'fight' might give an impression of 'squabbling'. That was not the case. While the opponents were standing up for tradition and practice on my part, I was standing up for the law, which, in turn, was integral to the way the Constitution had envisaged the Indian democracy. Effectively, I was prosecuting my prime responsibility as the CEC. The practices and traditions were going down the wrong way; it had to stop somewhere, the Republic had to fight back.

THE TURNING POINT

Up to mid-July 1992, there had been several cases of breach of discipline by government staff deputed for election-related work, which the ECI had taken up with the government. These did not become big issues, though they left something wanting. A particular case precipitated an unprecedented sequence of events.

It started when observers were being appointed for the president's elections in July 1992. As is customary, the government gives a list of officers who could be appointed for election duties and the ECI appoints from amongst these. One such officer was X, joint secretary in the ministry of urban development. In a letter signed by K.P.G. Kutty, the secretary to the commission, X was informed about his appointment and about his further action. The letter, amongst other things, read: 'You are statutorily obliged to perform the duties as observer and any refusal to perform these duties will be viewed seriously by the Commission.' After being given further details about the concerned duty, he was instructed: 'You are requested to attend the briefing by the Commission at 12:00 hrs on 6th July, 1992. Kindly note that the attendance in the briefing is compulsory and not optional.'[33]

A set of guidelines was also attached with the letter. The letter was delivered to the officer on Friday evening, 3 July. It was followed by holidays on Saturday and Sunday, and thus, the meeting was scheduled for 6 July, Monday, at noon. This officer, along with one or two others, did not turn up for the meeting on that day.

Immediately, articles of charges and a statement of imputations were framed in respect of all defaulting officers and were dispatched on that very day. The charges in respect of the joint secretary read:

Shri X [name kept anonymous] did not comply with the summons and failed to be present during the briefing by the Chief Election Commissioner on the date and time mentioned above. He did not even intimate a reason for his absence in the meeting.

...While duly appointed as an observer... [he] wilfully abstained from the briefing and showed complete lack of devotion to duty, which is unbecoming of a member of the All India Services.[34]

After the decisions were made and dispatched, it came to light that the ministry of urban development had written a letter that was received at the commission just 15 minutes prior to the commencement of the

---

[33]The author has a copy of the letter in his private collections.
[34]The author has a copy of the letter in his private collections.

meeting. The letter said that the officer was engaged in some workshop in Thailand from 6 to 11 July and that the intimation regarding his deputation by the commission as observer was received very late and that it was imperative for a representative of the ministry to attend the workshop.

Post receiving this letter from the ministry, seeking to excuse X, the commission wrote back stating emphatically that it found the explanation given by the ministry of urban development as unacceptable. As a result, the request made by the ministry, seeking to excuse X from the meeting and duties, was rejected. That left them with the necessity to respond to the articles of charges and statement of imputations against X.

On 9 July, the additional secretary from the ministry of urban development again wrote trying to clarify that according to his records, the letter of X's unavailability was delivered at 11.45 a.m., while the meeting was at noon. He also attached a photocopy of the relevant page of the peon book that recorded receipt of the letter by the commission.

The additional secretary's point was that when the commission passed the order, it was not aware that the said letter was sent well before the briefing meeting itself and not after the issue of the charge sheet. Therefore, the matter may be looked into and the charges be dropped.

X was given time until 8 July to reply, but no reply came. On 17 July, the commission received a reply that was apparently written on 14 July, the day after the presidential elections were held. He began by saying that he was on an official tour and returned to office only on 14 July and therefore could not make a representation before the deadline. In the letter, he wrote that the intimation from the ECI was received very late and after office hours, and thus there was no time to make any alternative arrangement.

Then he said that his ministry wrote to the commission and that the letter reached before the noon briefing. And so he pleaded that the charges against him be dropped.

The explanation given by him was found unacceptable by the commission and accordingly, the commission decided to proceed against him. The statement of imputation of charges was framed, in which it was stated:

> ...according to his own admission, Mr X got the appointment letter on the 3rd July, 1992 and he was to leave for Thailand on the night of 5th July, 1992. Full two days were available for him to communicate with the Election Commission.... He has not adopted either of the above two courses of action. He is thus guilty of gross dereliction of duty and breach of Commission's orders.[35]

It was proposed that the commission proceed against X under Article 324 of the Constitution of India, Section 13CC of the Representation of the People Act, 1950, and the All India Services (Conduct) Rules, 1968. He was given time until 2 August 1992 to make a representation failing which the commission would proceed to pass and order ex parte.

X did not reply directly to the commission this time. Instead, he forwarded his reply through his ministry. The reply reached the commission on 6 August, four days after the deadline had elapsed. In any case, he had nothing new to say.

Meanwhile, another issue was unfolding. I had to send a memorandum to the joint secretary in the ministry of welfare regarding his interference in the functioning of the commission. The matter reached the cabinet secretary and the two of us communicated over the phone. Following that, the cabinet secretary wrote a letter to me on 25 September:

Dear Shri Seshan,

i. Kindly recall our telephonic conversation regarding the performance of duties by officers of Government of India in connection with elections conducted by the Election Commission.

ii. I learn that the Election Commission has issued communications to certain joint secretaries in the ministries of welfare and urban development in respect of alleged

---

[35]The author has a copy of the letter in his private collections.

dereliction of duties in connection with appointments as observers for elections. It is also learnt that a memorandum has been sent to a joint secretary in the ministry of welfare for alleged interference in the functioning of the Commission.

iii. As you are aware, Government of India has issued detailed instructions regarding performance by government servants of the duties they may be called upon to discharge in connection with elections. These instructions are now being reiterated. Position with regard to 'observers' will also be covered in these instructions.

Please be assured that due priority will always be given sparing officers for election work. However, circumstances may arise occasionally when government is unable to spare particular officers. The departments of government are being informed that whenever such eventualities arise, the Election Commission should be informed and alternative arrangements suggested in advance.

In view of the above, I am sure you will agree that we will treat the above cases as closed...[36]

Three days later, I wrote back to him. Calling his attention to what had happened and saying that these were not the first instances of their kind, I stated in a clear manner that 'the President, or governor of the state, shall, when so requested by the Election Commission, make available to the Election Commission or to a regional commissioner such staff as may be necessary for the discharge of the functions, conferred on the Election Commission by Clause (1).' I further stated in response:

You have mentioned kindly that these instructions are being reiterated. I would urge that it should be made clear that when a person is appointed as an officer for election duties, the discharge of such duties is not on a voluntary basis. I say this because if at the highest levels of the government, an impression gets around

---

[36]The author has a copy of the letter in his private collections.

that the election duties can be performed at will, the implications for the conduct of elections can be enormous. I refrain from expatiating on this because it is not my intention to unnecessarily exacerbate the position.

If you kindly confirm that these positions are clearly accepted, the two or three cases mentioned by you can be treated as closed. There are other pending cases and unless a specific reference is made, these will continue to be proceeded with.[37]

The difference of opinion, as brought out by these two letters exchanged, represents the crux of the disagreement with the government. While I was certain that the Constitution vests in the ECI the relevant powers, the government was not willing to concede it. There was no reply to my letter.

So, the ECI decided to go ahead with taking action on erring officers. On 2 December that year, a letter was dispatched to the secretary of the ministry of urban development according X an opportunity to make his case to the commission in person and hence directing him to appear before the commission on 8 December 1992. He did not appear and also failed to send any communication, seeking an alternative date or making any other request. Therefore, the commission proceeded with the available papers.

In the order, I highlighted that the commission had to give important instructions to the observers in the matter of the performance of their duties as observer in the election to the highest elective office, namely, that of the president of the country. But X did not attach importance to his duties as observer for such an important election in the country and instead preferred to attend the workshop in a foreign country. It is true that the country's international commitments have to be honoured, but the country's internal commitments can also not be overlooked and the matters cannot be left to be decided by the officers according to their own will and choice. But this is precisely what X did:

---

[37]The author has a copy of the letter in his private collections.

[...] Mr X obviously deliberately did not utilise the above facilities provided to him at the government expense as I did not contact any of the offices of the Commission before proceeding to Thailand. The explanation furnished by him also does not show that he obtained any direction of the additional secretary of his ministry...

[...] Nor does that explanation show that he was directed by the additional secretary to attend the said workshop and not to perform the duties as observer of the Commission...

[...] Mr X asked his ministry to take up the matter with the Commission for making an alternative arrangement in his place as observer, taking for granted that the Commission must make alternative arrangements. This shows utter disregard and disrespect on his part towards the Commission, a high authority created by the Constitution and vested with the sacred functions of superintendence, direction and control, inter alia, of elections to the highest elective office of the land, that is, the president of India.[38]

Shifting focus to the debate over the powers enjoyed by the commission in this regard, I referred to Article 324 in the Constitution, which I had mentioned earlier and to the concerned Section 13CC of the Representation of the People Act, 1950, which clinches the issue:

The officers referred to in his part and any other officer or staff employed in connection with the preparations, revision and correction of the electoral rolls for and the conduct of all elections shall be deemed to be on deputation to the Election Commission for that period during which they are so employed and such officers and staff shall, during that period, be subjected to the control, superintendence and discipline of the Election Commission.[39]

Therefore, I added: '...If any occasion arises in which an officer is unable to perform his duties, such officers must seek exemption from the Commission.'

---

[38]The author has a copy of the order in his private collections.
[39]The author has a copy of the order in his private collections.

Referring to the letters exchanged with the cabinet secretary and their contents, I said that since I received no response for over three months from the secretary, I could presume that the position of the commission is correct and accepted by the government. Therefore, it was my duty to discipline said officer for his non-performance of duties.

If senior IAS officers are unwilling to do election duties, others too can refuse. In that case, how could one conduct an election in a country where there are six lakh polling booths, and each booth needs six officials besides policemen? The ECI needed 35 lakh officials for an election.

All this had happened in the latter half of 1992.

In the beginning of 1993, there were other matters that put a question mark on the authority of the ECI. These were not matters related to the control over election staff. Rather, these two matters had to do with the status of the ECI in relation to the status of the courts in the country. You will see that my taking a firm stand on these issues could easily be perceived as an ego-instigated/childish tantrum. And that is how the detractors presented it. But the truth was that it had to do with the violation of systemic order in which the authority of the ECI was being adversely affected. Check out for yourselves.

REJECTING THE THOUGHTLESS ORDER ON DELIMITATIONS OF J&K

Delimitation of electoral constituencies is an exercise that takes place once in a while to respond to factors such as demographic changes or formation of a new state. Two delimitation cases that came up early in my tenure as CEC were those of the delimitation of the constituencies of Delhi and J&K. While the delimitation exercise in Delhi was eventless, the delimitation process in J&K ended in controversy just because people could not follow simple rules and procedures.

The problem had originated even before I took office as the CEC. In January 1991, the J&K government had reconstituted the state delimitation commission compromising two judges of the state High Court and the CEC. One of the judges was made the chairman, and I was to be an ex-officio member. I forwarded to the J&K government a copy of the salary and conditions of service of the CEC, which stated that they were the same as those of a Supreme Court judge. I pointed out that the anomalous position of the CEC being a member of a committee in which a High Court judge was the chairman had to be rectified. The state government did not act on it. The delimitation commission asked me, instead, to nominate a junior person, namely the deputy election commissioner for the limited purpose of having the ECI represented in the body. I decided that I would not nominate an officer.

I said that the ECI has to superintend, direct and control the preparation of electoral rolls for, and conduct of, elections of the legislative assembly of J&K on the basis of the assembly constituencies validly and legally determined by the delimitation commission and not on the basis of a fraudulent and deceitful document that is a nullity and non est. I was referring to the document that reconstituted the state delimitation commission. I said:

> Therefore, the Election Commission, in exercise of the powers conferred by Section 138 of the Constitution of Jammu and Kashmir, the Jammu and Kashmir Representation of the People Act, 1957, and all other powers enabling it in the behalf, hereby totally rejects the purported order of the Jammu and Kashmir Delimitation Commission as being without jurisdiction, without authority, a nullity, and non-est for any purpose whatsoever.[40]

ASSERTING THE EC'S CONSTITUTIONAL AUTHORITY VIS-À-VIS THE MODEL CODE

I postponed the April–May 1993 Kalka (Haryana) election as the CM had violated the model code of conduct by announcing several development schemes after the election process was set in motion. It was for the first time that the ECI was invoking powers conferred

---

[40]The author has a copy of the letter in his private collections.

on it under Article 324 and 329(b) of the Constitution and the Representation of the People Act, 1951, to rescind an election on the grounds of violation of the model code of conduct. In that sense, we were breaking new ground. The Punjab and Haryana High Court stayed my order and ordered that the election be held as per the schedule decided by the ECI. However, I did not leave the matter at that. I immediately filed a special leave petition in the Supreme Court challenging the High Court order.

The matter was heard in the Supreme Court on 5 May by a two-judge bench comprising Chief Justice M.N. Venkatachaliah and Justice S. Mohan. I raised several questions of law in my petition. One of the points was whether, in view of the specific bar under Article 329 (b) of the Constitution, judicial interference in an election process was justified. Then, in such a case, only an election petition could be filed under Section 80 of the Representation of the People Act, 1951, after completion of the election process. I said that the High Court's order was ultra vires of the power and jurisdiction it had under Article 226 of the Constitution, in view of the Supreme Court's earlier decisions.

The Supreme Court set aside the order of the Punjab and Haryana High Court. It merely said that the High Court's order was 'inappropriate'. It was inappropriate in the sense that such an important order was passed ex parte. The matter was sent back to the High Court, and it was asked to hear the ECI as well. The High Court passed an order saying that the commission's position was wrong, and it ordered the continuation of the electoral process in Kalka. The commission took up the matter again in the Supreme Court. The Supreme Court, on 11 May, upheld the order of the ECI. With that, the elections to the Kalka assembly seat came to a decisive halt. This case is important because an important power of the commission, which was given to it in any case, was well established in the process. I had even challenged the extent of jurisdiction of the courts on election-related matters and the Supreme Court itself clarified in the ECI's favour. True that, in this case, the position of the ECI was established with respect to the courts but the issue was of the implementation of the code of conduct, and the ruling disposition had more to lose in the proper implementation of the model code. It added to their grouse against the ECI.

Around that time, I also had friction with the Tripura and the West Bengal governments over the appointmentof election officials. Parliament was in session at that time and there was an unstarred question in the Rajya Sabha to which the ministry of personnel, public grievances and pensions replied that 'the government did not ipso facto consider expression of inability to spare the services of a particular officer for election duty to be deliberate defiance of the Commission's order.'

On 26 March 1993, I wrote to the cabinet secretary on this account. Referring to the answer in Parliament, I said that the position was unacceptable to the commission. I added that legally, once a person is appointed as an officer of the ECI in accordance with the law, he comes under the disciplinary control of the commission. Such an officer appointed for election duties has to discharge his duties not on voluntary basis but is bound by law to do so. Therefore, it did not matter what the government decided to do. As for the officers who disobeyed the commission, they were to be punished and there was no going back on this. According to the mandatory provisions of Clause (6) of Article 324 of the Constitution, the law will be obeyed in toto by all concerned on whom the law makes it incumbent to do so. '...Such an unequivocal assurance of the government should be received by the Commission within fifteen days of the receipt of this letter or on the 15th of April, 1993 whichever is earlier...'

As you can see, I was threatening that I would stop 'all' work related even to the conduct of elections. But would it come to that?

This triggered a series of letters exchanged between the government and the ECI in which the government was not ready to concede.

Before we try to understand the issues, let us first review the four articles of law that matter in this debate.

1. **Article 324(1) of the Constitution:** The superintendence, direction and control of the preparation of electoral rolls for, and the conduct of, all elections to Parliament and to the legislature of every state and of elections to the offices of the President and Vice President held under this Constitution, shall

be vested in a Commission (referred to in this Constitution as the Election Commission).

2. **Article 324(b) of the Constitution:** The President or the governor of the state, shall, when so requested by the Election Commission, make available to the Election Commission or to a regional commissioner such staff as may be necessary for the discharge of the functions conferred on the Election Commission by Clause (1).

3. **Section 13CC in the Representation of the People Act, 1950:** Chief electoral officers, district election officer, etc., deemed to be on deputation to Election Commission: the officers referred to in this part and any other officer of staff employees in connection with the preparation, revision and correction of the electoral rolls for, and the conduct of, all elections shall be deemed to be on deputation to the Election Commission for the period during which they are so employed and such officers and staff shall, during that period, be subjected to the control, superintendence and discipline of the Election Commission.

4. **Section 28A of the Representation of the People Act, 1951:** Returning officer, presiding officer, etc., deemed to be on deputation to Election Commission: The returning officer, assistant returning officer, presiding office, polling officer and any other officer appointed under this part, and any police officer designated, for the time being, by the state government, for the conduct of any election, shall be deemed to be on deputation to the Election Commission for the period commencing on and from the date of the notification calling for such election and ending with the date of declaration of a result of such election and accordingly, such officers shall during that period, be subject to the control, superintendence and discipline of the Election Commission.

The two important things that the government was not willing to concede was: first, that the ECI had the right to appoint whom it wanted and second, that the ECI had the right to discipline officers who did not act in consonance with the ECI's orders. Let's take up these points one by one.

RIGHT TO APPOINT

The government's argument in relating to the ECI's right to appoint the officers it wanted arose from Article 324(b) of the Constitution quoted above. By selectively emphasizing the phrases 'when so requested by the Election Commission' and 'such staff as may be necessary', it was concluded that the ECI only had a right to 'request', while the government would determine whether the staff was necessary and then make that staff available. The ECI should take whatever it gets.

In simple words, the government said that when elections come, it would make an assessment of the requirement of officers for holding elections. Having received a 'request' from the ECI, the government could then make up its own mind on what the actual needs are and provide staff according to its own assessment. It is important to see that it is plain common sense that if holding elections was the ECI's job, then it would know better what was needed. Even if, for argument's sake, the ECI's assessment of necessity did not take priority—meaning that, even if the government was finally responsible for free and fair elections— the commission's perception of 'necessity' had to be accepted by the government. Whatever the ECI asked for, they had to give, subject only to conditions of availability.

I said that the government's position was unacceptable. My contention was that it was the prerogative of the commission to decide what 'staff maybe necessary'. Whatever my 'request' may be, the government 'shall' provide.

RIGHT TO DISCIPLINE

As for the exercise of disciplinary jurisdiction, the cabinet secretary latched onto the phrase 'shall be deemed to be on deputation to the Election Commission'. According to him, the officer was only 'deemed to be deputed' and therefore did not cease to be government officers to become officers of the ECI.

With reference to the two clauses of the Representation of the People Act excerpted above, he concluded that the mention in them that officers were 'subject to the superintendence, control and discipline of the Election Commission' did not mean that the commission had a right to undertake disciplinary proceedings on erring officers. All the commission could do was to give a 'preliminary inquiry' report.

In his opinion, service rules for these officers said that there was one particular predetermined disciplining authority for each officer of the government and therefore an officer could not be placed under the discipline of an authority other than that designated.

How can fairness of elections be assured if punishment powers over officers on election duty, instead of being with the ECI, were in the hands of government officials, which means in the hands of the executive, which means in the hands of the minister, which means in the hands of politicians who were going to be elected? By no logic can we accept the position that the ECI has no authority over the staff deputed to it.

If it is determined that the election staff cannot be disciplined by the ECI, it would necessarily imply that the government is responsible for elections. That is not the position of the Constitution.

When I wrote back to the cabinet secretary, I brought out these points clearly. To add emphasis, I directly quoted from the debates that took place in Parliament in 1988 prior to the passing of the amendment bill that inducted Clause 13CC and 29A into the relevant Representation of the People Act. Though reference to parliamentary debates is not considered in a court of law, as the courts have decreed that the statutes stand on their own weight, in a communication like this, the reference was appropriate in order to make myself as clear as possible.

Hans Raj Bhardwaj was the Union minister of law and justice who was piloting the Bill in the Rajya Sabha. He spoke on exactly this issue and the point was defended by B. Shankaranand, (then minister of health and family welfare) in the Lok Sabha. Bharadwaj said that he took the responsibility to put all the poll machinery incharge of the ECI, if the question arose as to whether it should be under the CM or under the ECI.

On 14 December 1988, Shankaranand said in the Lok Sabha that the ECI was 'dependent' on government staff: '...As the honourable members are aware, the Election Commission is dependent on the machinery of the state government concerned, both in respect of the work of preparation, revision and correction of the electoral rolls, and annual process, and the work in connection with the actual conduct of elections...'

These members were from the same party that was running the governments and this government was stating the opposite and was in conflict with the ECI on this very point. When letters excerpted above were being exchanged, the law minister in the central government was the very same Hans Raj Bhardwaj who had brought the amendments.

In my letters, I also quoted from an opinion officially tendered earlier by the attorney general on 8 August 1992, which was forwarded to us by the ministry of personnel and training. He had opined:

'...The words in this section are very clear that the disciplinary control is only during this period (election); and after this period is over the Election Commission becomes functus officio as far as government servants are concerned... He only can report to the government and government alone can take action.'

So, he had said in writing that he had no doubt that the commission alone could take disciplinary action against election officers during the period of his deemed deputation. He had expressed reservations about the exercise of disciplinary jurisdiction by the commission after the period of the deemed deputation. I had not even accepted this limitation and had written back citing the concerned Clause and Act, explaining why I did not agree, and I was still waiting for the reply. But now the government, quoting the advice of the same attorney general, was denying even what the attorney general had agreed to.

I ended by saying that the commission would like to give yet another opportunity to the government to provide an unequivocal assurance that my stand in respect of appointing and disciplining officers was accepted. Such assurance should be received by the commission by

5 May 1993, failing which the 'Commission would be constrained to take all steps available to it, including but not restricted to the total stoppage of all works relating to preparation of electoral rolls or conduct of elections with which it is concerned...' And I warned them that it was a serious matter, by not mincing my words in pointing out that the responsibility, of the creation of such major constitutional and statutory crisis, would be the government's alone; this would be owing to the failure of the government to work in accordance with the constitution and the laws.

The cabinet secretary rejected this contention.

ELECTORAL AHIMSA: ALL ELECTIONS POSTPONED!

The executive was trying to bully the ECI into a subservient position in relation to the elections. The constitutional scheme clearly laid out that it was a body called the Election Commission of India, with a high degree of autonomy, which would hold elections, and not the government.

I had been cautioning the government with two alternatives open to me: one, that I would stop all election processes; and two, that I would take the matter to court with suitable jurisdiction to obtain a decision on the matter.

While this was on, elections were due in Tamil Nadu, and again questions regarding the assessment of security appointment of electoral staff and superintendence and control came up. There was no way this could continue. Thus, I decided it was time for me to put my foot down. I chose to exercise total stoppage of all works in connection with the preparation of electoral rolls. Deep in thought and fully aware of the consequences of my action, I drafted the order on 2 August 1993.

It would lead to a constitutional crisis. But it was not I who would be responsible for it; the responsibility would squarely rest on the central government, which was taking an illegal view of the matter and was not accepting a position that was so obviously constitutional.

Then I quoted from the relevant Supreme Court orders and made it clear that the position of the government was unconstitutional:

55. In the above circumstances it is absolutely imperative that the constitutional position of the Commission, particularly in regard to its constitutional prerogative of securing the assistance of necessary staff, is unequivocally and clearly accepted by the government of India.

56. Accordingly, till such a time as the present deadlock, which is solely the making of the Government of India, is resolved, the Commission does not find itself in a position to carry out its constitutional obligations in the manner envisaged by the makers of the Constitution, and has accordingly decided that all and every election under its control, including biennial and by-elections to the council of states, by-elections to the state legislative council, by-elections to the house of the people and by-elections to the state legislative assemblies, as have been announced or notified or are in progress, shall remain postponed until further orders.[41]

AND ALL HELL BROKE LOOSE

Stopping all elections in a modern democracy, and that too by the person who was to conduct elections—this was unheard of! The politicians, of course, reacted in a knee-jerk fashion... and to put it mildly, 'negatively'. It kicked up a storm. Some newspapers prophesied that I was heading for impeachment again.

Petitions were filed against my orders in the Kolkata, Chennai and Mumbai high courts. They, in turn, issued interim orders against me. The ECI moved the Supreme Court to transfer to itself the cases that were in Kolkata, Mumbai, Chennai and Patna high courts since all of them involved the same question of law of general importance.

THE SUPREME COURT TOOK ITS STAND

After initially turning down this request, Chief Justice M.N. Venkatachaliah and Justice S. Mohan heard the petition on

---

[41]The author has a copy of the letter in his private collections.

A friend and I (on the right) in front of Ghoom Monastery, Darjeeling, on 29 June 1955 during our IAS training

My wife Jayalakshmi before our wedding. She played the veena quite well.

Jayalakshmi and I, in our post-wedding shoot. We were married on 9 February 1959.

My brother (standing) and I with our respective wives and our father in 1959

On stage with Chief Minister (CM) of Tamil Nadu M. Bhakthavatsalam (first from left) in the early 1960s. The loss of his party is usually attributed to the anti-Hindi sentiment, but the main cause was mishandling of fair price shops and dry weather conditions leading to rice shortage.

K. Kamaraj, Indira Gandhi and I (first from left, behind Kamaraj) during our visit to the Meenakshi Temple in 1967. Kamaraj was the CM of Madras when I joined, and Indira Gandhi was the Prime Minister (PM) when I served in atomic and space departments.

As the collector of Madurai in 1967

(Clockwise from left) Subramanian Swamy, myself, a mutual acquaintance and Roxna Swamy, in Harvard in 1968. We enjoyed good mutual camaraderie. The Swamis loved the dosas my wife made.

At the convocation ceremony at Harvard in 1968 where I earned a master's degree in public administration

Meeting with the Pontiff of Sarada Math Sri Abhinava Vidyatirtha Mahaswami (third from left) in Madurai in 1965. His successor Sri Bharathi Teertha Mahaswami's advice in 1995 helped me reconcile myself to the two election commissioners' verdict.

Rajiv Gandhi and I at the Red Fort on 15 August 1988. We enjoyed great mutual camaraderie and respect.

Prime Minister P.V. Narasimha Rao and I shortly after he became the PM in June 1991. There was no discord with the government at that time.

R. Venkataraman, former president of India, and his wife, Janaki Venkataraman (seated second and third from left) interacting with me and my wife (standing) at the sashtiapthapoorthi function (Hindu ceremony celebrating my sixtieth birthday) in June 1993. We enjoyed a good personal rapport even beyond his presidential years.

Watching my voter ID card being made in 1994, as Jaya (first from left) looks on

(From left to right) The three election commissioners: K.P.S. Gill, I and G.V.G. Krishnamurty back in 1996

With my grandniece, Aditi, in my arms and surrounded by other relatives in 1997. Keeping with what the stars foretold, my wife (second from left) and I did not have any children of our own, but children were a joy to both of us.

Receiving the Ramon Magsasay Award (fifth from left) for government service in August 1996 in Manila, Philippines. Fidel V. Ramos, president of the Philippines, (fourth from left) presented the award to me.

6 August. The Chief Justice observed that, undoubtedly, the ECI alone could decide what constituted damage to a free and fair poll: 'The High Court cannot decide it.'

It was the Chief Justice's view that 'Mr Seshan has got a good point which involves interpretation of the Constitution. He may be right and the Union government may be wrong. But can he say that he will stop all elections?' He went on to tell my counsel that I should adopt all means that are constitutional and asked me to find some solution to the constitutional crisis.

Finally, the Chief Justice said that the Supreme Court was ready to transfer to itself all cases pending before the state high courts challenging my 2 August order, '...but this depends upon the response from the election commission.' He mentioned that, 'The whole purpose is to maintain and preserve the sanctity of the Election Commission which has been, under the Constitution, assigned the task of conducting free and fair elections.'[42]

The Supreme Court gave me time until 13 August to reconsider my decision of postponing all elections and by-elections across the country. Matters took a turn on 10 August, and it was dramatic.

That morning, I went to the Supreme Court. All kinds of mediators came to me saying that the PM wanted me to find a solution. I said I had the following answers: I was willing to quit, elegantly, with no noise and no controversies. Otherwise, the government should yield to my point that the ECI was entitled to staff and entitled to disciplining them.

Nothing came of this. At 2.30 p.m, the Chief Justice started the hearing. At 4.45 p.m, I got the decision saying that my position was correct, at least in the interim order. The court said:

> [...] Whether the blanket suspension of the electoral process purported in the order dated 2 August 1993 is justifiable on that principle of judicial review is eminently arguable. But one thing seems clear: the jurisdiction of the court would not extend to issuing directions to the Election Commission for the conduct of particular elections on particular dates independently of the perception of the

---

[42]"SC Asks CEC to Reconsider Poll Decision', *Hindustan Times*, 7 August 1993.

Commission as to their feasibility and practicability consistent with what may be needed to ensure the purity of the electoral process. On this aspect we have reservations about the permissibility of the various interlocutory orders of the High Court which may have the effect and implications of compelling the Election Commission to conduct polls on particular dates and also to follow those events up to their sequential and logical ends. But in the light of the submissions made by Shri G Ramaswamy, it becomes unnecessary to consider these aspects any further at this stage.

Shri G. Ramaswamy, learned senior counsel for the ECI, submitted that the commission will reconsider the question of continuance of the embargo imposed by its order dated 2 August 1993, and, in all likelihood, might withdraw that notification. The effect of this restriction is, it is submitted, that all other notifications issued pursuant to the order of 2 August 1993 postponing the polls in individual elections would also come to an end. However, the Election Commission, it was submitted, would reserve to itself its constitutional function to notify such suitable dates for the polling as the circumstances and exigencies obtaining in the respective constituencies may permit. The stand of the Election Commission is proper and reassuring. The fixing of the days of polling is a matter for the informed judgement of the Election Commission consistent with its perception of the law-and-order situation and of the ensurement of the requisite precautionary and remedial measures.[43]

Effectively:

1. The Supreme Court stayed all proceedings in the Mumbai, Kolkata and Chennai High Court challenging the 2 August order.
2. The Supreme Court admitted a writ petition of the ECI seeking an authoritative decision of the ECI in conducting elections and ordering deployment of forces to maintain law and order.

---

[43]The author has a copy of the letter in his private collections.

3. The commission filed for the transfer of petitions, seeking the transfer of all the petitions pending before the high courts of Mumbai, Kolkata, Ahmedabad, Chennai relating to the matters.

On 19 August, the Supreme Court ruled, in another case related to the state of J&K, that the 'superintendence, direction and control' of all elections were not 'unbridled'. It said: 'Power under Article 324 is not altogether unreviewable'. And it wanted to say that the actions of the commission should be in keeping with the law. By now, most write-ups in newspapers more or less reflected that I was right after all. Except a few who were critical of my ways, most agreed that I was striving to clean up the system.

When one looks at electoral reforms, 2–19 August 1993 should be considered red-letter days in the history of the commission. It was important because it clarified that the constitutional scheme gave control to the ECI. Otherwise, conducting free and fair elections would not have been possible.

There I was. I had this 'observation' that the Supreme Court made on 7 August 1993: 'There is no doubt that the Election Commission is the authority which will decide about the law and order situation and what forces are necessary for free and fair elections.'[44] In fact, the court went a step further and on 10 August 1993 and observed that 'the commission had exclusive jurisdiction to oversee free and fair elections [and] should not be lightly interfered with even by the courts.'[45] On the basis of these, I was exerting my authority over the polling staff. But the matter remained sub judice in the Supreme Court. It wasn't heard for a long time after August 1993, and I continued working on the basis of only the interim order. Even so, things were not offered to me on a platter, and I had to push time and again for the commission's rights. The matter resulted in a tussle with the central and state governments, which continued for a long time. It was not that I won every time. Efforts had to be made to wean the state machinery

[44]'Seshan Lauded for His Stand by CJ', *The Indian Express*, 8 August 1993.
[45]'Good Sense Has Prevailed: Seshan; Bypolls by September 10; Status Quo in TN', *The Indian Express*, 11 August 1993.

away from the executive in respect of all election-related duties. In this pursuit, many feathers were ruffled. One had the thankless, or rather the enemy-making job of taking on the established political leadership—and were they annoyed!

TWELVE

TWO MORE COMMISSIONERS TO SHARE 15 MINUTES OF WORK

O
n 1 October 1993, while I was in Pune on a private visit, there was a telephone call for me at my host's place: 'Sir, there is a new ordinance. Two gentlemen, G.V.G. Krishnamurty and Dr M.S. Gill, have come to join as election commissioners.'

It was sometime in late afternoon when Krishnamurty arrived, accompanied by someone from the law ministry. Someone ran up to Deputy Election Commissioner Bagga, the seniormost officer present, and told him that there was a gentleman sitting in his room saying that he was the new election commissioner.

'This is the ordinance,' Krishnamurty said, 'and here I am.'

Bagga said, 'Fine,' and got him to sign the necessary papers. Half an hour later or so, Dr Gill arrived and the process was repeated. Bagga spoke to me at 7.30 p.m., and I asked him to extend all courtesies to the new election commissioners and to take them around the building to select their rooms. While Dr Gill had left immediately after signing his papers, Krishnamurty had stayed. Bagga took him around the office. Krishnamurty selected his own room and was told that the room would be ready as quickly as possible. Meanwhile, Bagga gave him the anteroom to the main conference room that was fully equipped and could be used temporarily as an office.

When questioned on the decision later, Congress spokesperson

Vitthalrao Gadgil sarcastically said that the decision was taken to assist me in my work. Yes, indeed, assistants had been appointed because my shoulders were thin, my work was excessive, I was unable to deal with it, and the entire country was complaining that the ECI was sitting on hundreds of files, that it was not sending replies! My workload took about 10 minutes in the morning and three minutes in the afternoon. For the rest of the day, I used to spend my time solving *The Times of India* crossword. On one occasion, I dozed off, for the first time in my life, in my office chair and that was not because of my approaching age. I had no illness that would justify going to sleep in the office chair other than sheer boredom.

I used to reach home by 12.30 or one in the afternoon. Until very recently, when television became more varied in its programme content, I used to watch 'Rasoi', the cookery show. Unfortunately, it used to teach how to cook lobster and crab, but I was a vegetarian. So, that was the level of my 'excessive' work, and someone was being extremely kind to me and ensuring that my burden was shared.

THE RUN-UP TO THEIR ARRIVAL

It would be an understatement to say that I was disliked by the political class. After the many failed attempts to impeach me and my non-acceptance of alternate posts like governorship and ambassadorship, there was a campaign to think of other ways to get at me, and one of these was the possibility of creating a three-member ECI. On 11 June, the CPI (M) had decided that it would campaign for a three-member poll panel.

There were reports in the press one day, in the month of July, that the Congress was planning to 'tame' me. But the very next day, the spokesperson denied the move of a constitutional amendment to repeal my powers.

After the order of 2 August 1993, there was a great hue and cry about my being impeached. During a debate in Parliament on the very next day, members had asked for a multi-member ECI. On 4 August, even the BJP had called for more election commissioners.

One prominent person who had countered the suggestion of a three-member commission, however, was the former CEC R.K. Trivedi. He was very clear that appointing two more commissioners was not necessarily the best method. As for me, I made it clear that it was pointless and there was not enough work for even one officer.

From the end of July to the end of September 1993, the advocate general of various states took to conducting 'informal' meetings. This was unprecedented. Particularly in the last 10 days of September, they had met twice under the initiative of the advocate general of West Bengal. Among the many things they were reported to have discussed was how wrongly the word 'superintendent' was being interpreted by the ECI in the context of holding elections. They were also said to have considered the option of a multi-member commission and had recommended the same.

The decision was supposedly made on the morning of 1 October, and the government immediately had it approved by the President. It was reported that Dr Gill was in Gwalior and had gone there by train, but he was flown back that morning on a BSF plane and kept on standby while the Cabinet was deciding the issue. Everything was timed in such a way that I would not be in office when the officers arrived. Everything was kept hidden from me.

Interestingly, that very morning, when the Cabinet was supposedly going ahead with the decision, the Supreme Court was hearing arguments about the powers of the commission in regard to deployment of forces and discipline of poll staff. At that time, the attorney general, Milon K. Banerjee, was telling the Supreme Court that the government would work out a way to establish 'harmonious relations' with the ECI.

This was, shall we say, 'breaking news', except, of course, for the devastating earthquake in Latur, Maharashtra. The very next day, the press was questioning me about the appointment of the commissioners. I said that it would really make no difference if 101 election commissioners were appointed. Even then, we will fail to reform the entire election process, which stood corrupted with the erosion of values, unless we introduce better laws and give the ECI more powers for conducting free and fair elections.

Anyway, the fact that two commissioners had been appointed and were installed in Nirvachan Sadan had taken me completely by surprise in Pune that evening. I had to look for everything for them, a place to sit, facilities, a car and, most importantly, work.

The ordinance that enabled the appointment of the two election commissioners was called the Chief Election Commissioner and Other Election Commissioners (Condition of Service) Ordinance, amending the 1991 Act. The earlier Act was silent on how decisions were to be taken, but the amendment inserted two clauses that sought to lay down how business was to be transacted among the three members 'unanimously' and in the case of difference of opinion, the majority would hold sway.

Effectively, the ordinance sought to redefine the conditions of service of the election commissioners, placing them on a par with the CEC and Supreme Court judges and the status of cabinet ministers. It fixed the terms of the election commissioners as six years and stipulated the age of superannuation at 65. It also fixed the pay of the other officers as equal to mine.

The question arose as to what was the actual position of the CEC vis-à-vis the other commissioners? The position, as the Act of 1991 revealed, on 30 September and the position after 1 October were different. Prior to the ordinance, the position was not subject to any interpretation except the order of the Supreme Court in the Dhanoa case[46]. The court said that, even though Article 324 says that the ECI shall consist of the CEC and other election commissioners, the CEC was not *primus inter pares*, or first among equals. He was to be on a pedestal.

The question now was to what extent the ordinance had altered this situation. The two most important questions relating to the 1 October ordinance were: What was its impact? Was it legally valid?

I was in no hurry to arrive at any conclusion on this. I took measured steps. I had decided that if the situation affected the election

---

[46]'S.S. Dhanoa vs Union Of India and Ors', *India Kanoon*, 24 July 1991, https://bit.ly/42AOTlM. Accessed on 20 March 2023.

process, I would surely ask the courts for directions.

The Janata Dal reacted through one of its leaders, Mufti Mohammad Sayeed, saying that the party had always strongly pleaded for making the ECI a multi-member body. This would ensure free and fair elections and not leave the election process to the whims of a single individual.

The BJP came out with the statement opposing the appointment the next day. They cited two reasons why they felt that the way it was carried out was wrong. The first was that since elections were already on, it was improper. The second was that such appointment should have been made in consultation with the leader of the Opposition, the Chief Justice of the Supreme Court and other such functionaries. So, they had no problem with a three-member commission except that many others should have had a say in choosing the other two persons.

Constitutional experts mostly disagreed. Only two constitutional experts who were in favour of the change, P.P. Rao and D.D. Thakur, said that the power to issue ordinances was enshrined in the Constitution. According to them, it could not be constructed that the ordinance was infringing upon the powers of the CEC. Rao was of the view that it was no attack on the office of the CEC; the powers were given to the ECI and not to the CEC.

The rest of the constitutional experts were reported to have said that it was a backward step. Former Supreme Court judge, H.R. Khanna, felt that the ordinance was avoidable and should have been discussed by Parliament before such a major change was introduced.

Ram Jethmalani, MP and senior advocate, felt that it was a fraud that had been perpetrated and that the whole system of introducing ordinances had been abused.

Fali Sam Nariman, noted Indian jurist, is reported to have said: 'The ordinance dilutes the power of the Chief Election Commissioner. It would definitely hamper the independence of the EC. If they had three commissioners instead of one, it is tantamount to diluting authority.'[47]

---

[47]'Ordinance a Mockery of Statute: Experts', *The Indian Express*, 20 April 1993.

CAN THE CEC ARBITRARILY MISUSE POWER?

The CEC has a span of control that is far lesser than that is enjoyed by many executives in the government. And that power is wielded for the limited period and scope of elections only. Then again, is it possible to do anything unlawful and get away with it even within the limited scope of elections? Could a CEC arbitrarily breach the limits of 'rule of law'? And if the law is not broken, how can a charge of arbitrariness be levied?

When a CEC is powerful, the persons who would be directly affected would be the politician. And if a CEC acts within the law, then only those politicians would face a hard time who were using unfair means to win elections. In truth, what this vocal group of people saw as arbitrary was actually my departure from tradition. And I am sure that the departure was 'towards' the firm implementation of law as revealed by the framers of the Constitution and 'not away' from it. I was determined not to allow any wrongdoing. I put my foot down when I could and where it was right.

Then again, if a politician could not create an impression, by playing to the gallery, that I was being 'arbitrary', he would not have been a politician in the first place. So, though I got excellent support from critics, many members of the press and the public in general, there was a constant barrage of abuse and misinformation targeting me and decrying my 'whimsical' ways. And my penchant for being curt and intolerant of sloppiness did not help either.

How can one who swears by the law be arbitrary? It is no rocket science to understand the game behind the move. When reporters asked them about the purpose of appointing two more election commissioners, I said: 'They have sent two colleagues to assist me. No, no, not to assist me since they have the same powers, but to assist themselves.'

I returned to Delhi on the night of 4 October. That very night, the secretary to the commission, K.P.G. Kutty, came and told me that they had been asked to change the lawyer for a case relating to the Delhi elections. Krishnamurty had directed the officer incharge of legal work to put K. Parasaran incharge. The officer went to Parasaran, who, I believe, told him they had picked the wrong lawyer and suggested that he go to some other advocate named Gopalaswami. But he was unreachable. When I came in, at about nine that night, I was told that the case had been adjourned solely because the ECI had no lawyer.

'What do we do tomorrow?' they asked me, and I told them to go back to Ramaswamy.

How can one member of the ECI change an existing decision completely bypassing the CEC, without as much as a word, a whisper, or a piece of paper to the CEC?

TRYING TO MAKE THE THREE-MEMBER COMMISSION WORK

On 5 October, I was feeling a little out of sorts because of the unaccustomed physical activity in Pune, so I didn't go to office at all. Gill rang me up at eight in the morning. He said he didn't want to join until he had talked to me and asked if he could come to my house. I said I was feeling unwell and asked to meet the following day. But Gill wanted to meet on that day and came over and spent three and a half hours with me. My wife gave him three cups of good South Indian coffee. At the end of it all, he said, 'I think, we can make this work.'

Running the commission was my responsibility one way or the other. With the new ordinance in place, there was bound to be confusion ahead. Reading the ordinance together with the Constitution did not produce a harmonious or clear outcome. There was the need to resolve a contentious issue. In fact, as *The Indian Express* article dated 4 October 1993 puts it, 'Ordinance a Mockery of Statue: Experts', knowing that the matter could only be resolved by the courts, I wanted to make sure that the normal functioning of the commission would not be derailed. I gave directions to my staff in writing. I quoted the provisions 10(1), (2), (3) of the amended Act and said that according to it, the 'Commission, should, by unanimous decision, regulate the procedure for transaction of business as also its allocation of business' amongst the three commissioners. Until that was done, things would carry on as before. My staff was to follow the normal channel of communication until the allocation of business was done.

Section 19A of the Representation of the People Act, 1951, says that all the functions of the ECI may be discharged by a deputy election commissioner or a secretary. I quoted this section in the directions and told the staff to follow the law and carry on the designated tasks.

The next day, on 6 October, I went to the office and even drafted the notice for the first meeting. I had told Gill that I would meet him in the office that day to show the world that I had no animus. When I arrived, he came and sat with me, and we had another long chat. 'We have to make this work,' he said, to which I replied, 'I have no problem.' We shared a warm and cordial relationship. We even discussed astrology. He told me about his family and later got a chart prepared for himself and for his eldest daughter. I didn't pay for it, he did. That was the kind of warm, friendly relation we had.

After he left, I had a BJP delegation waiting for me. Sushma Swaraj, Pramod Mahajan and a few others were there. They were rather detailed in the exposition of all the ills they were facing. But my normal method is to not make people feel I'm throwing them out. So, I listened patiently. While this was going on, my deputy walked into my room and said that Gill and Krishnamurty wanted to meet me. Since I was already in a meeting, I told him that I'll call him as soon as I am free. The moment I was free, half an hour later, I rang up Bagga. 'They've both left,' he said. Gill had gone to select his room, and Krishnamurty had gone to his temporary office. Five minutes later, Bagga rang up to say all hell had broke loose.

Krishnamurty had gone to his temporary room, found it locked and assumed that I had got it done deliberately. Then he found that his telephone wire had been disconnected and made the same assumption. He returned to Bagga's room and spoke, shall we say, less than amiably. Word spread, God knows how, that all kinds of disastrous things had happened in the ECI that day.

On 7 October, I issued a one-sentence note to the two commissioners: 'Shall we meet at 11.00 a.m. on Monday, 11 October, in my room, please?' There was no reply even up till the morning of the intended meeting.

My room is normally kept closed, but on the morning of 11 October, I kept the door open from 10.45 in the morning, so that nobody would feel that the door was closed against them. I was sitting there when, at five minutes to eleven, Krishnamurty walked in. 'Ha! What now?' he said. I didn't say anything.

There were two chairs in front of my desk, which were certainly not inferior to mine in weight or size or height or upholstery or colour. He sat down on the sofa in the corner and said, in exactly these words: 'Come here!'

I folded my hands in a namaste and said, 'I prefer to sit where I am.'

'I'm not going to come and sit there,' he said, adding, 'those chairs are intended for your *chaprasis* (peon).'

That meant that whoever visited me and sat in those chairs became my chaprasi. Anyway, I put both hands on my mouth, so I wouldn't say anything even by accident. Gill hadn't come, so I sent a word through his PA. He arrived and stood in the middle of the room.

'Gill,' Krishnamurty said, 'you don't sit there; that is meant for his chaprasis. Ask him to come and sit here.'

Gill asked me if I would have any objections to sit on the sofa. 'On any other day,' I replied, 'I would have come and sat not only on the sofa but also on the carpet. But today, I will not.'

Then started a torrent of abuse from Krishnamurty: 'stupid', 'asinine', all spelt out for my benefit.

Gill was left standing, unable to sit on the sofa or on the visitor's chair. The poor man was caught between the devil and the deep sea. After several minutes of this, Krishnamurty was in a somewhat agitated state. Gill reminded him that he had a heart surgery only the previous year and that the excitement was not good for him. 'Yes,' he said, 'excitement is not good for me.'

Then, Krishnamurty pulled up his left leg and put his booted foot on top of an office table. He lifted his trousers and said, 'This is where my vein was cut in order to do bypass surgery.' He then walked up to my table: 'Are you willing to shake hands?' Then he came around the table and said, 'Are you willing to embrace me?'

I keep my mouth shut. He went back and sat down on the sofa.

'What is the agenda?' he said suddenly. I had not thought of a formal agenda, since this was not a formal meeting, so I kept quiet.

The meeting ended on a cordial note. Gill told me that he did not want to give rise to the feeling that he had walked out. It was true; Gill had not walked out at all; he had got into his car and gone home. However, it was announced in the newspapers that both Krishnamurty and he had staged a walkout.

On 12 October, I got a letter from Gill. 'You know,' it read, 'yesterday's meeting was a disaster.' He didn't say why it was a disaster—very nice of him—so any reader may think that I was the great contributor to the disaster.

On 14 October, the matter related to the powers of ECI vis-à-vis the government came up in court. The Supreme Court ordered that a joint consultative committee meet should take place with the government to coordinate about the forces and observers required. It also said that all three commissioners were to attend it. The meet was to be organized on 16 October, just two days later. It was conducted in a cordial atmosphere. The other members had complained about them being informed at the last minute. This was one of the matters Krishnamurty had written about in a letter to me. But even my attending was decided at short notice. I was initially not to attend; on that day, I was supposed to be in Chennai in relation to a court case. I had to cancel that visit.

I asked for 400 observers, the government was willing to offer 165 and Krishnamurty suggested 300 as a compromise, which was accepted. Several other decisions related to the posting of security staff were taken. Accordingly, a compliance report was sent to the Supreme Court.

On 18 October, I sent out another, more official looking, notice to the new commissioners, which reproduced what Section 9 and Section 10 of the ordinance said. I said I had hoped to discuss this on 11 October, but the meeting had not transacted any business. I wanted them to let me know their views on the relevant sections and make suggestions as regards to what could be done.

As for their comments, they suggested things like meeting every day or periodically. Both of them had marked copies to each other, as they had marked copies to me, and I honestly didn't know what to say.

THIS IS NOT WHAT THE CONSTITUTION SAYS: AN APPEAL TO THE SUPREME COURT

That the two commissioners were Gill and Krishnamurty was only incidental. I had nothing personal against them. When I had almost no work and when two other persons were sent to share the load, what motive do I read behind such an appointment? If, as most papers agreed, the intention was to 'clip my wings', would I get cooperation from the other officers or would they be prejudiced about my being a nuisance and serve the purpose for which they had been appointed by the government?

I filed a writ petition in the Supreme Court on 27 October. The petition was filed in the public interest and in the interest of free, fair and independent functioning of the ECI. The Union of India, through its cabinet secretary, as well as Gill and Krishnamurty, were made respondents.

In the petition, I contended that presidential powers had been misused by issuing the ordinance and the notification for collateral purpose, vitally affecting the scheme of the Constitution, thereby infringing on independence of the ECI and fair electoral process. I said that the attempt to equate the three commissioners was totally contrary to the letter and spirit of Article 324 and therefore unconstitutional. I said that there had been a constant tussle between the executive and I and that the ordinance seemed to have been brought out on that account. The purpose of the entire effort was to create a stalemate within the ECI.

I also said that there was no question of the election commissioners functioning or taking decisions in any manner without involving or going against the views of the CEC and, in view of Article 324(3), the question of allocation of work amongst the CEC and other election commissioners can never arise.

I drew attention to the fact that Krishnamurty had directed the commission staff to withdraw a brief regarding the Delhi High Court case on the postponement of Delhi elections from the senior counsel G. Ramaswamy at the last moment. This had led the courts to adjourn the matters for want of counsel.

I was not the only one who petitioned. There were others, and one of them was Cho Ramaswami (Srinivasa Iyer Ramaswamy) who had filed a public interest litigation on the same matter even before I did.

The two-judge bench comprising justices P.B. Sawat and Yogeshwar Dayal granted a stay on that ordinance on 15 November 1993, though the appointments continued. In their order, the judge said:

> Until further orders, to ensure smooth and effective working of the commission and also to avoid confusion both in administration as well as the electoral process, we direct that the Chief Election Commissioner shall remain in complete overall control of the commission's work. He may ascertain the views of other commissioners or such of them as he chooses, on the issues that may come up before the commission from time to time. However, he will not be bound by their views. It is also made clear that the Chief Election Commissioner alone will be entitled to issue instructions to the commission's stuff as well as to the outside agencies and that no other commissioner will issues such instructions.[48]

As it turned out, the interim order was in effect for close to two years till the Supreme Court passed an order on it in mid-1995. Until then, I continued to extend authority and was able to pursue my work at the commission as earlier. Gill was mostly on leave in this period and used this opportunity to pursue his interests. Both commissioners did express their views from time to time, but I faced no interference from them.

---

[48]'Seshan to Have Final Say: SC', *National Herald*, 16 November 1993.

THIRTEEN

THE MINI GENERAL ELECTIONS: TANGIBLE IMPROVEMENT

The responsibility of a CEC is not only to run the electoral process efficiently but also to identify and implement ways and means by which the electoral process would improve. In fact, one aspect of the responsibility cannot be separated from the other and therefore in everything I did as the CEC, there was always a lookout for opportunities to reform. And, of course, I believed in doing my work efficiently and with favour to none.

As I have indicated earlier, it started with setting the environment within the commission in proper order while improving on the efficiency and discipline. And then came the symbols cases and the related processes. Though these were handled according to law, the situation did improvize as we went along, be it through case laws or through managing the symbols better. The election process itself provided many opportunities, and much of the early improvements were focussed on better implementation of the laws.

I also took special steps, exclusively focussed at reforming the process. The first year, 1991, gave me ample opportunities to study the loopholes in the system in detail. It was not that this insight was not already available with the commission, but a comprehensive view was taken now. We listed different ways in which the integrity of election was being compromised. This ranged from impersonation while voting, collusion of polling staff with contestants, the use of muscle power, to illegal use of government machinery, and so on. The list had 150 items. Even after conducting many elections, I still had a list of 150 possible defects in Indian elections.

Some of the defects were repairable by what the ECI could do. Others were curable only if Parliament would change the laws. There were some that were treatable only if the political parties and individuals would change their character.

In respect to one set of defects, I needed to go to the government. A booklet had been printed and forwarded to the government in February 1992. This 34-page document contained a set of ECI proposals for electoral reforms. In nine chapters, it dealt with various aspects of elections, ranging from the delimitation of constituencies, of preparing electoral rolls, to the actual process of election and declaration of results. Each chapter discussed various issues pertaining to organizational structure, disciplinary powers, code of conduct, security, and so on. The document even detailed who should do what to affect the proposed reforms and what laws or rules should be changed by Parliament in each case.

The government did precious little about it. Let alone make a reply, the government did not even send an acknowledgement. Even two years later, when I spoke about the suggested reforms and the inaction of the government at countless public gatherings, the government did not take up the matter.

This did not mean that the entire exercise of documenting the suggested reforms had no benefits. It did make a difference in the ECI's approach to the challenges obstructing free and fair elections. It helped the commission define and visualize its goal, and sharpened its focus. Beginning in late 1992, I had used every legitimate means at my disposal to fine-tune the processes involved in elections in the country, so that loopholes could be plugged, and free and fair polls could be conducted.

It took a good team, a great deal of ingenuity and consistent work. In the latter half of 1993, a total of nine states, including a large part of the Hindi belt, went for elections, so it was generally termed as mini general elections. At the end of these mini general elections, the general report was that it was one of the most peaceful elections, despite the fact that one of the states that went to polls was the 'difficult' Uttar Pradesh. The commission received a great deal of praise for the handling of this election.

The actual election work is done by millions of ordinary Indians who diligently work, whether as security personnel, as poll booth staff, counting staff, enumerators, etc. Then there was the good work of my staff in the commission itself. All in all, the team worked well, and finally the newspapers agreed too without any reservations.

The Pioneer on 23 November 1993 had an editorial titled 'Thank You, Mr Seshan'. An article in *The Statesman*, dated 17 December 1993, read:

> [...] Though the ruling party is recalling the Frankenstein parallel [for appointing Seshan], what is frustrating most political parties is perhaps the fact that the CEC is yet to provide the parliament with a cause justified enough to constitutionally move an impeachment motion against him.
>
> Here is an extraordinary man who, for a change, is exercising the authority that a CEC, though empowered to, has perhaps seldom exercised before [...][49]

India Today, in its article dated 15 December 1993, reflected violence-related statistics in its article, showing a near 80 per cent fall in booth capturing and 90 per cent fall in deaths in comparison to the data for the 1991 elections. It went on to read:

> [...] Seshan's big stick clearly motivated the police forces in all the states going to the polls to wield their own sticks with more than the usual zeal and uncharacteristic good judgement. In Uttar Pradesh alone, some 50,000 history-sheeters were given the choice of filing for anticipatory bail or facing preventive detention. More spectacularly, in Himachal Pradesh, at least

---

[49]Panda, Koustubh, 'Two Cheers for Mr. Seshan', *The Statesman*, 17 December 1993.

eighteen gunmen of errant Punjab ministers were stopped and disarmed while crossing the state border on polling day.[50]

In these elections of 1993, even MLA Pappu Yadav was reported to have been stopped from entering Uttar Pradesh by Nagaland policemen posted there; they were enforcing the rule that was in place at that time.

The report is consistent with what I personally found on ground. My wife was on a visit to Mathura with a group of women when a police hawaldar there gifted her an image of Lord Krishna, which I have with myself even today. He said that he was grateful for what I had done because now, they could do what was right and what was their duty, without any fear as they had the commission backing them.

On my part, I had the powers that I had been asking for, and which the courts gave to me at that time. There was no doubt that there was enough character and substance in the polling officials and the police to run an excellent show. I could, therefore, focus on other matters related to reforming the polling process.

THE POLISHED CALL GIRL CONTROVERSY

As the time in the commission went by, I got many opportunities to address various groups, forums and the like on issues mostly connected with elections and but not restricted to elections alone. The instances increased with my months in the commission and could have easily been in the hundreds in the final years. I also gave numerous interviews.

One interview with *The Pioneer* on 26 November 1993 kicked up a big row. It was a three-hour interview, and the discussion strayed into the functioning of the bureaucracy. In the course of the interview, I said that if we took into account officers, of the level of secretary to the Government of India, one could find only one or two who were not willing to be collusive with their political masters. I said that, though I knew of secretary-level officers who were monetarily corrupt, the

---

[50]Ghimire, Yubaraj, 'T.N. Seshan Passes Most Crucial Test of His Term as Chief Election Commissioner', *India Today*, 15 December 1993, https://bit.ly/3Qnu73o. Accessed on 15 December 2023.

percentage of officers falling in this category might be just about 10 or 20 per cent. But I also pointed out that all corruption is not linked to taking bribes. I said that most bureaucrats are also morally corrupt since they do not stand up to politicians and ministers. I put the figure of this form of corruption at around 98 per cent of all bureaucrats. In the process, I ended up describing the IAS officers as 'no better than polished call girls because they continuously prostitute their position.'[51] I said that there was a basic lack of character and it was evident during the time of elections or at a time when big financial decisions were being taken by a government.

'The perks could be in the form of a bureaucrat settling his children in foreign companies here or getting them admitted to universities abroad. From this, it goes on to his receiving carpets, electronic goods and, on Diwali and Dussehra, gifts that are not normal dry fruits but solid fruits. The lowest form is getting hard liquor of every sort of label,' I said.[52]

I later clarified in a subsequent meeting with the press that all this was said in a fit of anger, but it is difficult to deny something that has so much truth in it. Referring to the bureaucracy, I said in my clarification: '...but the bureaucracy has realised the nadir of its existence. The spines have been broken because of multiple fractures...'

I also added that 'Civil servants have decided not to protest. There are members who do stand up, but *afsos hai* (regret to say) that a large number of them do not.'[53]

As one would expect, there was great indignation and a storm kicked up, but it turned into a debate with people expressing opposing views and doing some introspection.

---

[51]Dahlburg, John-Thor, 'Election Umpire Calls Them as He Sees Them: Shyness Isn't a Problem for India's T. N. Seshan, Who is Proud of Driving "the Fear of God" into Law-Breakers', *Los Angeles Times*, 25 January 1994, https://lat.ms/3vJ0zDI. Accessed on 6 January 2023.

[52]Ritu Sarin, 'Bureaucrats Polished Call-Girls: Seshan', *The Pioneer*, 27 November 1993.

[53]Srinivasan, K., 'TN Seshan, Bureaucrats and Call Girls', *Onlooker*, 31 December 1993.

The matter was first informally discussed by senior IAS officers, and they had reportedly expressed concern and a wish to retaliate. They wanted to take up the matter jointly against me for utterances 'without any basis'. Some officers wrote to the Cabinet Secretary Zafar Saifullah to take action. S.P. Bagla, who was the secretary at the ministry of surface transport, took the initiative of writing a letter to the cabinet secretary and to other secretaries in the government. He wrote that he considered my opinion not only irresponsible but highly reprehensible: 'The obsession of Shri Seshan with the "call girls" deserves to be publicly condemned, as, in my view, ignoring it as an opinion of an unpolished megalomaniac will neither be morally justified nor tactically correct.'[54] He wanted Saifullah to call for an urgent meeting.

Most officers saw many of my actions as that of a bully to juniors and a flatterer to seniors. Some others thought that having a public fight with me would give ammunition to the media and result in greater damage. But in the second half of the article, there were other views suggesting that I was not totally off the mark. Retired IAS officer J.C. Jetli was reported to have said: 'There is no denying that the bureaucracy has also deteriorated over the years, as most institutions have in the country to some extent. But with all its faults, the administrative structure is still very sound and can rise to the occasion provided it is given proper direction and support.'[55]

Former foreign secretary, S.K. Singh, on the other hand, was peeved at me for having violated his copyright on the epithet of 'call girls' in relation to diplomats.

K. Natwar Singh, who had served in the external affairs ministry for over 30 years, added, 'Seshan is absolutely right and, mind you, there's a lot of public support. There has been a general deterioration in the service over the last 15 to 20 years.'[56]

Bagla, however, did not relent. As late as 28 December, when he

---

[54]Srinivasan, K., and T.N. Seshan, 'Bureaucrats and Call Girls', *Onlooker*, 31 December 1993.
[55]Ibid.
[56]Ibid.

was retiring, he defended his point and dared me to tell who the incorruptible 2 per cent were. The media did not bother much though; the comment was reflected in one newspaper somewhere.

In the beginning of the second week of December, one P.R. Chari wrote a letter to the editor of *The Pioneer*, trying to quote the instances of me becoming the cabinet secretary after superseding other officers and me becoming the CEC as proofs of my 'collision' with the powers-that-be (sic). In that letter, aspersions were also cast in respect of the use of official vehicles and improving the furnishings at my office and in respect of some furniture that was supposedly issued to me from the environment ministry. In 1991, there was another attempt to dig up the things from the past; as always, nothing substantial came of it.

So, the matter simmered for some time and eventually died.

All in all, despite all the controversies, by the end of 1993, I received a lot of appreciation from the press. The *Eastern Clarion* of Assam adjudged me 'Man of the Year'. Another magazine, *Rashtriyadharma*, also selected me as 'Man of the Year'. In January of the next year, Rotary International gave their Man of Destiny Award to K.P.S. Gill and me.

FOURTEEN

A CONTINUUM OF REFORMS:
PRESSING HARD FOR THE ADVANTAGE

As the CEC, I had an upper hand by the end of 1993. Though the two orders from the Supreme Court—one concerning the powers to conduct elections vis-à-vis the government and the other concerning the powers of the CEC with respect to the election commissioners—were only interim orders, they provided the requisite leverage to continue the process of reform. One could say it was like a gift from the Supreme Court for my pursuit. Many members of the press, public figures (including some politicians), common citizens, various civic society organizations and government officials also responded positively and encouraged the ECI's attempts at change. Eventually, many changes did get formalized.

BETTER CONFIDENTIALITY THROUGH MIXING OF BALLOTS

Election watchers in India know that in certain pockets across the country, there is incredible pressure put on the voter to vote for certain groups, and the pressure could include threats to their life. Using muscle and crime, whole communities (settlements or villages) would be threatened with dire consequences if they voted in an undesired manner.

The whole idea of a secret ballot is that no one should be singled out for punishment because he or she has exercised the franchise in a manner that the local goon does not approve of. Extending that concept, nobody, goon or otherwise, should know how a certain person or community votes. But what was happening was exactly the opposite, owing to the fact that counting was done booth-wise. It became clear which way a community voted, and that made them susceptible to attacks of all kinds. This did not augur well for free elections, and it had to be stopped.

In April 1993, Tripura went to polls. There were areas in the state where polling materials and personnel could be sent only using horses, elephants and boats. The area was militancy-prone, and communities could be singled out for attack. In fact, out of the 1,953 polling stations, more than 208 were identified as sensitive and 542 as vulnerable. Traditionally, too, Tripura was excessively violence-prone.

It was decided that the ballot papers of all the booths of the constituency would be first mixed and then counted. The plan was successfully executed.

Later, in September, Ranipet in Tamil Nadu went to polls. The system of mixing of ballots was applied there, too. The voters welcomed the new method of counting, but the political parties were not quite happy.

Later in the same year, for the first phase of elections, the ECI issued the same kind of orders regarding the mixing of ballots before counting.

Several political parties criticized the decision. The reasons they gave were: first, it would be impossible to identify bogus voting at a particular polling station. This reason was indeed valid, but bogus voting could be tackled through other available means. The second was that the parties would not be able to know what the latest trends in different parts of the constituencies were. In this case, of course, my interest was exactly opposite to theirs—I did not want them to know their relative strength in different parts of the constituency. The need of the political parties to know this was of little significance in comparison to assuring voters of elections that were free of intimidation.

STEPS TO IMPROVE SECURITY DURING ELECTIONS

An important aspect—a vital aspect—of elections is the maintenance of law and order. Elections are not genuine if there is no maintenance of law and order—not when parties have no scruples about using money and muscle and everything illegal to win in the polls, and innovatively each time, too. Therefore, in every election, a set of orders dealing with the maintenance of law and order was more or less inevitable.

The elections of December 1993 were variously praised as the quietest elections until that day because of the minimal violence. The reason was the specific steps taken for improving security measures. One step that definitely helped was staggering the election over several days in order to facilitate adequate deployment of forces. The Tamil Nadu by-elections, which had precipitated the order of 2 August 1993 to stop all election work, had also just taken place. Following that, the ECI had full say in the deployment of forces. Apart from these, owing to the fact that, by then, I had reasonable control over the staff performing election duties, I could be firm in my orders and reasonably assured that they would be followed. The net result was that the probability of violent elections was drastically reduced. That was not all. It was important to tackle the menace of criminals being active on that day, and important steps had to be taken in this regard. Directions were given to the central and state governments on 20 October 1993 on the subject of maintenance of law and order during elections.

One specific area was targeted in the order—the unearthing and seizure of unlicensed arms and the selective surrendering of licensed arms. One should note that by this time, it was reasonably well established that we could firmly give 'directions' to the governments. This authority was put to good use to tackle the rampant use of firearms during elections. Specific instructions were issued, and the police and the district administration were mainly responsible for carrying out the required tasks. It became part of the standard procedure. One incidental exception was the Kodava community in Karnataka, who were exempted from surrendering their arms for reasons of established spiritual tradition.

STREAMLINING THE MEDIA–ECI INTERACTION AND COVERAGE OF ELECTIONS

The media has an active role to play in elections. There is always a keenness and enthusiasm in the general public for knowing who is going to take over the reins of office. That enthusiasm gets transferred to the press reporters as well.

The matter of media in elections first came up in a significant way during the elections of November and December 1993. It was related to the permission accorded to the press to cover elections.

Often, there were law and order problems in election areas in which the media people were the difficult component to handle in the crowds. Up to that time, there was an established procedure that press reporters would apply for passes, which would be issued by the commission, but not directly to the reporters. Blank signed passes would be given to state governments, according to their request. The state governments would then issue the passes to reporters and journalists. This procedure involved a breach of law. The procedure had to be rectified.

While examining this issue, it came to light that it was humanly impossible for a single reporter to cover more than five constituencies in one day. So, what was the point in handing out a use-it-everywhere pass? Besides, it directly affected security restrictions in polling and counting areas. So, a decision was taken to change the procedure of issuing press passes.

According to the new procedure, media personnel were asked to apply for passes specifying a maximum of five constituencies they would like to visit. These applications were to be addressed to the ECI through concerned government departments dealing with the press.

The commission quickly switched over to the new procedure, and passes were issued only to those who had followed the instructions for applications properly. Those who had applied for more than five constituencies were not issued passes. Certain publications had not applied in time and did not receive the passes. Switching over to the new system came with its share of minor teething problems too. I am sure it caused some discomfort and discontent.

In response, I was accused of behaving in an anti-media fashion and arbitrarily applying a gag order on the press. Even Gill used the opportunity to criticize my functioning. In fact, both commissioners came up with a joint statement. The tussle was still on in the commission at that time, and the Supreme Court had yet not passed the interim order putting the CEC in control.

Eventually, some press people affiliated with the Delhi Union of Journalists went to court over the new procedure and obtained interim relief on 26 November 1993. In accordance with the court orders, the passes were provided to those who had missed getting passes within the new system. The Supreme Court, however, did not change the restriction on the maximum number of constituencies being five.

Instructions were given with respect to the procedure to be followed to obtain the necessary passes from the ECI for covering the elections. Press persons were to forward their applications to the principal information officer in New Delhi or the chief electoral officers of the states. These officers were to recommend to the commission the names and addresses, along with the names of the organization for the issue of authority letters. No direct requests from any journalist would be entertained. No piecemeal recommendations would be accepted. No recommendation for preferential treatment for the government or foreign media would be accepted. The formal requests had to reach the commission on the fixed deadline. These authority letters would be issued to specific persons and would be non-transferable.

It was made clear again that there would be no restriction on covering elections in a constituency. However, in respect to polling stations and counting centres, only a maximum of five constituencies would be allowed for each journalist.

Orders were also issued prohibiting photographing of the interior of a polling booth from any position and audio or video interviews of electors standing in a queue in front of the polling booths, coming out of the polling station or within a radius of 100 m of a polling station.

These steps ensured that the confusion that occurred during counting and polling was taken care of. The media had their freedom and facility but were subject to the need for order and security. The commission had asserted its right to control the activities within the polling booths and counting centres. Not that there was no other issue relating to the press, but as far as media-related orders were concerned, they were consolidated and the discrepancies were removed.

INTRODUCTION OF VIDEOGRAPHY TO RECORD POTENTIAL VIOLATIONS

The commission broke new grounds in connection with the use of videography in the by-elections of early 1994. A directive was issued to district officials to videograph the proceedings at the polling booths.

The teething problems were aplenty. For example, in the sensitive Kurnool constituency in Andhra Pradesh, there were a total of 1,126 polling booths in 59 zones in 26 mandals, and there were so many questions: Whether to buy or rent the 26 cameras needed? If one were to buy, what would be the consequences if a camera was damaged? Would the commission hire private agencies for the security of the camerapersons?

All these difficulties had to be overcome. The belief was that the cameras recording the polling would act as a strong deterrent. People would refrain from illegal activities, as evidence would naturally be captured on video.

The process was evolving quickly even then. Anticipating the hurdles along the way, the commission adapted. On 20 May, just six days before the polling, I addressed a press conference in Kolkata, giving more information. I said: 'Hired video cameramen will try to cover as many booths as possible according to the instruction of the returning officer of the concerned seat. The ECI will use the videotape, along with other inputs, received from the central observers and security agencies besides political parties for the decision-making process.' I said that the video cameramen would tour the constituencies in a car and would be provided with adequate security.

The video films thus prepared would be viewed by the returning officer immediately after polling. If he were to find any violation that he was capable of attending to himself, he would take immediate corrective action against those found guilty and intimate the commission of the same. In cases wherein the violations were serious and he or she could not take corrective actions, the officer would send the video film to the commission through the quickest possible means, along with a note detailing the approximate content, the nature of the offence, the persons involved and the action recommended.

In the elections to four states that followed, the process was implemented smoothly. Using that experience, an order was issued on 26 December, in furtherance to the September order, with the expressed intention to 'fortify the existing order'. In this order, the returning officers were also asked to ensure that all kinds of public meetings addressed by the senior leaders of the various parties were also suitably videographed in due consultation with the observers and election expenditure observers. Once the video films were prepared, they would be viewed immediately by the returning officer to see if the speakers had committed any violation or infractions of statutory provisions and of the direction of the commission on the model code of conduct. If the returning officers were to find a violation of such kind, they were to bring it to the notice of the commission immediately.

Over the period of a year, the process of videography was effectively brought into the electoral process and hammered into a form that was suitable to the context. It is very difficult to assess its impact independently, but without a doubt, it made a big difference. It made an important contribution to ensuring free and fair elections. It acted as an excellent support structure and gave more teeth to help enforce other reform initiatives, like putting a ceiling on expenses and implementing the model code of conduct.

FURTHERING THE ELECTRONIC VOTING MACHINE AGENDA

An attempt was made to introduce the electronic voting machines (EVMs) into the electoral process. I had been familiar with EVMs even before I took charge in the ECI. The EVMs have an even longer history.

The decision to make and buy EVMs was taken long before I came anywhere near the job of holding elections. Bharat Electronic Limited and Electronic Corporation of India Limited (ECIL), both public sector undertakings, were asked to devise an EVM much earlier. Somewhere in the late 1980s, during Rajiv Gandhi's time, a few thousand voting machines were ordered to be made.

Much later, when I came to the ECI in 1991, there were not enough machines to be even put to trial. It is on record that I went to PM Narasimha Rao and explained that I wanted a specific number of machines and what would be the expenses.

When I wrote to the PM, the government's reply was that there was a financial constraint; the government did not have the kind of money to buy lakhs of machines. By then, the cost had also gone up. The rupee had devalued against the dollar, and the chip had to be imported.

Today, there are some people who still doubt the integrity of the EVM, thinking that it can be tampered with. I can certainly tell you that, in the last few general elections, they have been successfully used all over the country. After my tenure, the government was kind enough to listen to my successor Dr Gill and purchase lakhs of machines. Today, while they are used across the country, including the most backward areas, nobody has had difficulty identifying the button and pressing it. The whole thing is that easy. In addition, you get the result in no time at all. Today, if the counting starts at 7.00 a.m. or 8.00 a.m., by noon, all the Assembly results are out. The machine offers that kind of advantage.

My successors Gill and James Michael Lyngdoh used the machine exclusively in all parts of the country. The ECI had, for a long period of time, received no complaints from anybody stating that anything wrong happened because of the machine.

CHECKING THE ANTECEDENTS OF POLLING OFFICIALS

In August 1994, a large number of complaints against district magistrates, district election officers and returning officers were received by the commission. Therefore, it was decided that their antecedents would be checked. Over the following six months, 10 states were to go to the polls. The chief electoral officers of these states were asked to send reports about the election work within 15 days. The reports were to have a confidential note detailing whether any complaints were received from any political party reflecting on the official's impartiality during the previous elections. A report format was finalized for the purpose.

Part of the requirement was for the chief electoral officers concerned to issue certificates that they were sure that the officers would be 'totally impartial' and would conduct elections in a free and fair manner. A warning was also issued that serious action would be taken if it was found there had been a wilful misrepresentation of any information about the election officials.

As expected, the decision was met with resistance. On 16 September, West Bengal Advocate General Naranarayan Gooptu criticized the circular and said the chief electoral officers had no machinery to issue such confidential reports, which would be 'only subjective and nothing but witch-hunting'. They had decided to file a writ petition in the Calcutta High Court. I had no problem with it.

As a follow-up to this order of 31 August, another order on similar lines had been sent on 12 September in which it was elaborated that immediately after the announcement of the elections, the commission would scrutinize the antecedents of each and every 'statutory and election related officer' and seek a replacement for the officers who have suspected political leanings.

In another order, dated 20 September, further clarifications were given that officials against whom disciplinary action had been taken earlier should not be drafted for election work. It was also indicated that wide publicity should be given to the order and special efforts be made to inform the local units about the national political parties.

Communications were sent to the chief electoral officers of the 10 states that it had come to the ECI's notice that mala fide oral executive instructions were sometimes issued from certain quarters in some states that returning officers should not bring election-related developments to the ECI's notice in their reports. In this connection, a warning was issued that the commission would take a very serious view of the matter. Warnings were issued to the returning officers that any attempt at holding back any relevant information from the commission or failure to bring it immediately to its notice would be tantamount to a grave act of omission and would invite the severest penalty.

This new system of obtaining preliminary feedback had a good effect, and the commission was further able to gain control over the quality of the officers deputed for election duties.

EDUCATING THE VOTER

A suggestion had been set afloat that the commission should involve itself in educating voters about matters regarding elections. Needless to say, it was to be a new initiative. After giving it some thought, the commission decided to move ahead with it. Early in 1994, it was decided, and declared, that a poll awareness drive would be launched across the country from 15 August that year.

As I had mentioned earlier, there was a set of election-related problems that could be corrected only by changing the character of the voters and the contestants. The voter awareness drive was possibly the one modest attempt on the part of the commission to address this problem directly. We decided that we should aim to keep the ECI out of it and considered using non-governmental organizations and other apolitical organizations to make it a people's movement with the least possible official intervention.

In early June, a set of 22 guidelines were developed and the chief electoral officers of the states were informed of these guidelines. It was decided that the expenditure for the campaign would be met by the commission, but the real expenses would be met by NGOs, and no state was to exceed the limit allotted to them. While a state like Uttar Pradesh was to get a sum of ₹1.28 lakh, smaller states that had only one parliament constituency would get about ₹5,000 each for the campaign. The total expenditure was estimated at around ₹8–9 lakh.

The motive was to improve general awareness about the provisions of the Constitution of India, the Representation of the People Act, 1950 and 1951, and all related rules and orders, besides other laws related to the exercise of the franchise.

The aim was also to identify shortcomings in our election-related laws that render the result of the elections not truly reflective of the choice of the people and to improve awareness of the laws among the masses, particularly the deprived classes in remote areas.

Another aim was to familiarize the electorate with the factors that have a vitiating impact on the purity of the election process, including the 'buying' of votes, and to exchange views with the electorate on ways to remove or reduce the impact of all such factors.

The initiative also aimed at familiarizing the electorate with the election management practices of successful democracies of the world that were relevant to India. It would also make office bearers of registered unrecognized political parties and their agents aware of the legal and statutory requirements of election law and fundamentals of 'electorate attitude'.

In this awareness initiative, it was clearly stipulated that the chief electoral officer would not consult or take the approval or direction of the state government and the political executive of the state or a union territory, or make a reference to any political party, including the party in power at the state or central level.

The campaign was to begin in August 1994, and no targets were fixed for its completion.

The ECI also wanted to involve the universities of India in research related to elections. They were to be facilitated to take up projects devoted to the subject of election management and the right of franchise.

EXECUTING THE VOTERS AWARENESS PROGRAMME

The voter awareness programme was launched on 15 August 1994 as scheduled, and the function was organized by a voluntary organization. The general thrust of my address on that day was a call for people to 'wake up and fight.' I said that there was nothing right about our elections. All the efforts made at reforming the system had come to naught. It was time for people to act. I asked them to vote for this country to survive. I said that I had pinned hopes on them to help cleanse the system by getting young voters to register and to vote judiciously. I said: 'When good things are done, you do not stand up and applaud. And when bad things are done, you do not try to prevent it.' I added that I would continue my efforts to bring reform in the election system.

On 12 November, speaking of what was achievable while addressing a meeting of intellectuals organized under the campaign at the residence of Justice Gopinath, I pointed out: 'If only 15 per cent of the voters were awakened towards their rights, the country would be transformed by 100 per cent in 15 years.'

These programmes were held all over the country, but it was difficult to gauge their effect because of the intangible nature of the exercise. It definitely did not capture the imagination of the nation in a big way, but at the same time, one could not say that it had no effect at all. I personally addressed meetings across the country on this issue.

One directly tangible benefit of it was, of course, that it was a good learning experience for me and the commission. The programme could not be sustained for long, but we did try.

ENFORCING THE LAW ON RESIDENCY OF THE RAJYA SABHA MPs

As the years have gone by, some practices and traditions have slowly crept into the governance systems of the Indian states, which may be blatantly illegal and yet may not ruffle any feathers or hold the mighty who indulge in it, accountable.

A problem of this kind, with respect to the members elected to the Council of State (the Rajya Sabha), had come into focus somewhere at the end of 1993. There was a blatant violation of law and a dilution of a constitutional position. Once it came into the reckoning of the ECI that it was a defect in the electoral process that could possibly be addressed, steps were taken to rectify the malady.

First, let's take a look at the provisions of the Constitution and the law as it existed at that time.

Two significant articles in the Constitution related to this matter read as follows:

Article 80: Composition of the Council of States (The Rajya Sabha or the Upper House of Parliament) – (1) the Council of States shall consists of (B) Not more than two hundred and thirty-eight representatives of the states and of the union territories [...]

Article 84: Qualification for membership of Parliament—a person shall not be qualified to be chosen to fill a seat in Parliament unless he—

- (C) Possesses such other qualification as may be prescribed in that behalf by or under any law made by Parliament.

Section 3 of the Representation of the People Act, 1951, stated: 'Qualification for membership of the council of states—A person shall not be qualified to be chosen as a representative of any state...or union territory in the council of states unless he is an elector for a parliamentary constituency in that state or territory.'

Further, Section 19 of the Representation of the People Act, 1950, laid down the condition for registration as an elector as follows:

19. Conditions of registration—subject to the foregoing provisions of this part, every person who

(b) Is ordinarily resident in a constituency shall be entitled to be registered in the electoral roll for that constituency.

The difficulty here was that the law did not define the term 'ordinarily resident'. However, the law did lay down that the question had to be determined with reference to all facts of the case.

Section 20(7) of the Representation of the People Act, 1950, stated as follows: 20. (7) if in any case the question arises as to where a person is ordinarily resident at any relevant time, the question shall be determined with reference to all facts of the case and to such rules as may be made in this behalf by the central government in consultation with the Election Commission.

All the above clauses taken together yield the following conclusions.

First, that the general idea of the Council of State was that it should be a representative body of the various states that formed the union.

Second, qualifications were to be defined by law made by Parliament, and Parliament law clearly said that the person should be an elector for a parliamentary constituency in that state or territory in order to be able to contest.

Third, for being an elector, the necessary condition is that a person should be ordinarily resident in a constituency.

Finally, to determine whether a person is ordinarily resident, all the facts of the case needed to be examined.

The last point meant that a study was to be made as to whether the person was 'ordinarily' staying at that place. Letters, visits, telephone connection, ration card, bank passbook and other such things had to be reviewed to determine whether a person was indeed staying where he claimed to be.

A far less rigorous way of looking at it is to take note of how the Lok Sabha and the Rajya Sabha were treated differently under the Representation of the People Act, 1950. A candidate for the Rajya Sabha must belong to, and be registered as a voter in, the concerned state. This rule is not, however, applicable to candidates for the Lok Sabha. The implication that the domicile status is an additional constraint for the Rajya Sabha follows logically. Therefore, the members of the Rajya Sabha were expected to be from the respective states in both letter and spirit.

When the commission looked into the matter in mid-1993, a lot of discrepancies were uncovered. An internal enquiry into the election of 41 members, who had been elected since I took charge of the ECI, found that many had shown false residence.

On 21 December 1993, the commission sent out a directive banning false declaration. It was communicated that the ECI had decided to take the sternest action, including cancellation of the election of the winning candidate, in case of a false declaration of residence.

Anticipating that people would go to court over this issue, a caveat was filed by the commission in the Supreme Court requesting it to hear the commission before taking any action, in the event of anyone seeking a stay of the ECI order on the residential status of the members.

Welfare minister Sitaram Kesari, Minister of State in the PMO, Bhuvnesh Chaturvedi, Ministers of State, H.R. Bharadwaj and K.C. Lenka were due to retire in April and were hoping to get re-elected. The Lok Sabha member Gurudas Dasgupta pointed out that Finance Minister Manmohan Singh was not a resident of Assam, from where he was elected to the Rajya Sabha. My good friend Dr Subramanian Swamy, who was the law minister when I was appointed as the CEC, was also on the list.

I was quite certain that not much could be done in this respect. I did not intend to disqualify those MPs who had violated the rules laid down in this regard. I could not disqualify them because the commission did not have such powers. Effectively, I was merely exposing a blatant corrupt practice.

VIOLATORS TO BE BOOKED FOR FORGERY[57]

On 18 January 1994, I announced that cases of forgery would be filed against those who had given wrong information about their residential addresses to get elected to the Rajya Sabha.

On January 20, six persons were put under the scanner over this issue in addition to those who were already on the list. The returning officers had been instructed to ensure that no wrong information was given by any candidate for the Rajya Sabha. They would take necessary action against the person who was found to be erring.

As per the orders passed, the district magistrates responsible for the various constituencies got on the task of making inquiries regarding

---

[57]For a detailed understanding of the topic, please refer to the following citation: 'Chapter 21: "Strangers" in the Rajya Sabha', Noorani, A.G., *Constitutional Questions And Citizens' Rights: An Omnibus Comprising Constitutional Questions in India and Citizens' Rights, Judges and State Accountability*, Oxford University Press, 2006.

the bona fides of the MPs who were suspects. Show cause notices were issued to the concerned MPs. By the first week of February, the first of such show cause notices were issued.

The MPs from various parties ended up receiving these notices. Some examples were party vice president of BJP, O. Rajgopal, union law minister H.R. Bharadwaj, another BJP leader J.K. Jain, union minister Dinesh Singh, finance minister Manmohan Singh and union civil aviation minister Ghulam Nabi Azad.

The pattern was more or less the same. Some convenient address, from the constituency they were to represent, was declared by them as their place of ordinary residence. On inquiry, the place would turn out to be some shed in a village, or a room in a CM's home, or some temporary place, in respect of which some or the other documents would be created and presented as proof that they were 'ordinarily resident' there.

So, as per the commission's orders, the concerned district magistrates inquired into the matter and submitted their findings. Based on the findings, the commission issued the show cause notices.

There is no gainsaying that the district authorities, who were tasked to make inquires would be under various kinds of pressure. In the case of one district magistrate form Punjab, there were two contradictory reports that he sent to the commission. Eventually, while the concerned MP was taken to task, even the district magistrate was pulled up. Likewise, each case presented its own challenges and some of this was reflected in the show cause notices and orders passed by the commission in this regard. I am quoting here from one of these orders concerning an MP from Haryana. This example is a good indicator of what we were up against and how the entire issue was dealt with. This particular example relates to an MP who was shown to be on the electoral rolls of a particular constituency and the ground evidence gathered showed that the MP was not residing there actually.

21. The Commission intends to direct the electoral registration officer of XXXX assembly constituency of the state of Haryana to reconsider the entire episode in light of what had been stated above and, in case, in his judicial wisdom, the learned electoral

registration officer is prima facie satisfied that an error has been committed, he should proceed to take appropriate action under the provisions of Section 22 of the Representation of the People Act, 1950.

22. The Commission is painfully aware that under any provision of the Constitution, any law or rules in force as at present, the Commission cannot set aside the election of YYYY at this stage. Perhaps a case cannot be made out for his disqualification since lack of qualification is not a disqualification. The Commission is also aware that even if at this stage, after a further inquiry under Section 22 of the Representation of the People Act, 1950 (43 of 1950), the electoral registration officer amends, transposes or deletes the relevant entry...of the electoral rolls relating to village ZZZZ, the membership of the council of states in respect of YYYY cannot be terminated under the Constitution, the Representation of the People Act, 1950, the Representation of the People Act, 1951 or any other law in force for the time being or rules made thereunder.

23. Without prejudice or disrespect to the particular person or the high office held by him, the circumstances narrated above are being published for general information since they are of great national importance. The Commission hopes that the electorate, at an appropriate forum, and the parliament might like to look at the existing provisions of law and the extent to which they are being observed or flouted. It is up to the country at large to decide how far the said observance of the said law or its manipulative abuse in conducive to facilitating the exercise of their choice of representatives, and what changes in our fortification of the existing law are necessary to achieve the sacred intent behind them.[58]

As I said, these cases brought out many instances of open violations of electoral laws, committed with impunity. It presents the evidence of how there is a widespread cynical acceptance of falsehood as an inescapable aspect of political life in India.

---

[58]The author has a copy of the order in his private collections.

I have very often said in public that I am actually holding up a mirror to the nation. This instance showed how lawlessness was found even among the highest in the land. The markers of the law themselves were flouting it and dodging it.

Eventually, the law was 'successfully' amended, and the goal post was effectively shifted. Congress member V.N. Gadgil introduced a bill seeking to enable a person who sought election to the Rajya Sabha if he was a citizen of India, irrespective of whether he was an elector in the particular state or union territory from where he was contesting. It was introduced as part of the private members' business in Parliament.

Today, one can get elected to the Rajya Sabha from anywhere in the country, regardless of whether one is a voter in that state.

When the law is inconvenient, change the law. That is how the political class went about it. But I can take pride in the fact that I was able to push one open violation of the law into being seen as an illegal activity—until the law itself was changed to declare that it was fine.

But what should have been the motive, convenience or protection of the constitutional scheme? Was the new law really in synchrony with the spirit of the Constitution? I couldn't care less. I guess it is fine if Bihar legislators want a Malayali or a Kannadiga to protect the interest of the state. But at least now, in doing that, there is no violation of the law.

But this initiative must have added a great deal to the angst the political fraternity harboured against me. It is unfortunate that they were caught up in this. In fact, my good friend and vocal supporter Mr Subramanian Swamy himself was at the other end. But how could I help that? A practice or custom that was not consistent with the spirit or letter of the law was to be moved against, and it was done as it was the proper thing to do.

The response was along expected lines. While there were renewed efforts at getting me impeached later in the year, one other incident that happened early in 1994 showed the lengths to which the baiters would go to discredit me. And of all things, this happened in connection with attending a seer's funeral.

DIVERTING A PLANE TO PAY RESPECTS TO PARAMACHARYA

On 8 January 1994, I was in Trivandrum (now Thiruvananthapuram) on an invitation and to do some routine work of the ECI when I got intimation that the Paramacharya of Kanchi had passed away and that the other acharyas in Kanchi wanted my presence. And there was no way to reach there unless I could catch a flight.

To make a long story short, I looked for every way to reach Kanchi. There were no commercial flights available. I even checked up with the PM and he could not help me. Then I called up Subramanian Swamy who was in Madras and he suggested, 'Why don't you ask the Ambanis for a lift?'

I contacted Dhirubhai Ambani and he agreed to divert a plane, whose original route was from Bombay (now Mumbai) to Madras, to fly with a hop over to Kerala where I was 'stuck'.

So, I told Dhirubhai Ambani straight away that I would accept the offer only on the condition that he would accept payment of the cost involved in it. He tried to dissuade me saying that it would be a handsome amount. Some official found out and said 'it will cost you a lakh'.

I said, 'It is acceptable and within my ability to pay.'

So, I took the flight to Madras that morning and reached Kanchi in time for the ceremonies. That afternoon, when I was helping with the arrangements, the PM came around 3.00 p.m., and at the request of the Kanchi authorities, I showed him around.

The PM did not ask me how I reached but I anyway told him that I came by a Reliance plane, to which he replied with a 'fine'. That was the end of the story as far as I was concerned. On my way back, when I landed in Delhi, somebody on behalf of Dhirubhai Ambani came and told me that my said expenses for the trip had amounted to ₹95,500. I gave a cheque, and the next morning, I was given a proof of the realization of the cheque.

A few days later, this 'lift' matter became an 'issue' with the press going all out for me saying that I had taken favours from a private person, and that it was illegal to divert a flight of that kind. A study of the newspapers of those times would reveal how it was a concerted effort to show me in a bad light and possibly try to make a case for legal action against me. I eventually had to answer questions raised by the press. Slowly, the issue simmered out of focus when the answers I gave and the proofs that I presented brought closure to their write-ups. But the issue never died down; on and off, when the intention of a baiter was to show me in bad light, he would present half the truth. I would be left at the mercy of the reader.

Barely a few days after this incident happened, there was another that took place at my home in Delhi. I had two residential peons permanently authorized to the CEC. One of them went out into the pavement to pluck some flowers from our garden. He had to go out because some of the plants were leaning across the fence over to the pavement. The flowers were for a small pooja we usually do in the mornings.

I eventually found out that the peon was arrested, taken to a nearby park and interrogated as to why he was stealing flowers from my neighbour's house. My neighbour was an extremely good friend of mine—he would not have objected even if I had raided his house. But the security, my own security personnel, had the boy taken to the police station. He was tied up to a chair and beaten up. He was beaten up so badly that he had to be admitted to a hospital. Then rumours spread, specifically to the employees' union, that Mr Seshan had been misusing the services of the house peon and that the latter eventually got beaten up for that.

Not out of fear of the union or of anything else, I, of my own accord, said I would bear '100 per cent expenses of treating the boy and pay for his hospital stay'. The said employee's near and dear ones replied that it was a government hospital, and nothing was to be charged. Besides, the boy only had some bruises.

It did not end there. A story was made out that I was doing black magic, and the stolen flowers were required for the same.

Fortunately, I had proof that it could not be black magic because I was in Madras when the incident happened. Was it an attempt to terrorize my family? If so, who was behind it... No guesses... The issue, as any other, died its own death.

The point here is that if people resorted to such measures, one can only imagine what all they would have done—maybe even dig into my past to bring out some trace of misbehaviour or error to get at me.

All said and done, what did I do to deserve all the attention that I got from them, other than doing my duty and trying to excel at achieving my mandate? The reforms continued regardless...

FIFTEEN

HOW THE MODEL CODE OF CONDUCT CAME TO LIFE

So far, we have looked at various piecemeal reforms and observed how each aspect evolved as part of the process of change over the months. All these reforms were introduced to tackle various defects in the election process individually and to make elections better. But taken as a set, the entire package of reforms was affecting a tangible transformation in the process of elections.

In January–February 1994, there were a series of orders on various aspects of the elections, each of which was an improved version of an earlier order and/or dealing with a reform not addressed hitherto. When the combined impact of these reforms began to show, the reports indicated that the political parties were beginning to feel the heat.

By March, a stage had come when the total electoral reforms package was quite potent. In an interview with the *Sunday Observer*, this aspect was discussed. In the telephonic interview, the reporter asked me about the general progress of reforms. I said that the process had started a year back and I told him about the strict measures taken to ensure that poor voters were not intimidated and also to ensure that there were no cases of booth capturing. I also explained how we had postponed elections in a constituency of Madhya Pradesh since the governor of Himachal Pradesh had misused government facilities and governor privileges. I told him about the appointment of the inspector general, which we got cancelled in Rajasthan because it was too close to the impending elections.

The reporter chose to highlight the new aspect of videotaping. He had asked me if it was not an expensive proposition. I said it was not quite so and that it would be beneficial in cases of complaints of infringements of the model code of conduct.

The best way of looking at this entire package of reforms would be to consider the matter in light of the model code of conduct.

MODEL CODE OF CONDUCT: THE ORIGINAL THOUGHT AND THE OPPORTUNITIES

The model code of conduct had come into force in the fifth general elections held in 1971. It was a 12-point code then and was updated to include 23 more points in 1974. Later, in 1979, the ECI convened an all-party meeting to review the code. The then CEC is reported to have brought out how the party in power misused its position to an unfair advantage (monopolizing grounds, state guest houses, vehicles, etc.) and suggested more modifications in the code to tackle the problem. His suggestions found unanimous support from the political parties. So, changes were made in 1980, and more adjustments were made in November 1984.

Despite the existence of a model code of conduct, which was endorsed by the political parties, they still made a mockery of the ideal of free and fair elections. The commission, finding that no more points could be added to further expand the code, pressed for legal powers to enforce it.

With the aim of enforcing its observances, the commission had earlier (even before me) formulated a method of setting up district-level standing committees and constituency level committees. Any violation of the code was to be brought to the notice of these committees, and the committees were to take remedial action. These bodies were non-statutory in nature, comprising candidates of a particular constituency and certain government officials. With the statutes, there was no question of taking legal action against anyone violating the model code; in other words, there was no enforcement.

A LESSER ELECTIONEERING PROCESS

With the support of all political parties, I went ahead and enforced the model code of conduct. I issued orders to remove wall posters, check the use of loudspeakers, put restrictions on the use of government cars and vehicles, and enforced the limits on election expenses.

People talk about a 'carnival-like' atmosphere of elections as workers paint caricatures, write slogans, stick posters, etc., on every available wall, advertising the candidates in the area. Needless to say, it can be a source of great irritation for house owners. It gave an ugly look not only to the buildings but also to the whole town or city. The hapless owners of the building were compelled to tolerate this and to paint their walls or buildings at their own cost after the elections were over. In due course, the commission received numerous complaints from the public about it, along with the insistence that this was being done without the owners' permission.

This was an election-related matter and for obvious reasons, the person responsible for taking the initiative on this matter had to be me. I was in no mood for passing the buck to local governments.

Early in 1993, I wrote to the state governments to take legal action against parties indulging in such undesirable activities. The commission went to the extent of suggesting the enactment of special legislation to check this menace. The governments were not forthcoming, and thus the commission had to act. According to the model code of conduct, the parties did not have any right to deface or spoil any building, whether private or public. All parties were directed to immediately clean the walls and buildings defaced with posters. It was directed that the clean-up operations should be done by the concerned parties and the candidates at their expense, failing which they were to be proceeded against under the law.

꙰

It was usual for electioneers to use loudspeakers to broadcast their messages at full volume. This caused noise pollution and disturbance to the public. The student community in particular was seriously disturbed—their studies were badly hampered when the loudspeakers blared throughout the day and late into the night. The aged, the infirm and the sick, whether in institutions, hospitals or at home, all had to endure severe discomfort.

On 13 January 1994, an order was passed with the purpose of regulating the use of loudspeakers during electioneering. The general idea was that the use of moving loudspeakers was to be permitted only between 8.00 a.m. and 7.00 p.m. For completely static speakers to be used beyond these timings for public meetings or for processions, prior written permission would have to be obtained from the government authorities concerned.

During elections, almost all ministers misuse government facilities, like cars and government planes. Clearly, when members of the ruling party use such government facilities, the elections are not fair anymore because it puts the party in power at a definite advantage. I, therefore, issued instructions to prevent this practice. The order stated that the use of such vehicles, belonging to any of these authorities, by anyone, including ministers, even though their election campaign may be attempted or purported to be in combination with so-called official work in that capacity as ministers, will be a grave violation of the model code of conduct. The only exception will be the case of the PM who is governed by security instructions, which will, of course, override all other considerations.

It did have a subduing effect, but people were not too eager to give up their privileges. Santosh Mohan Dev, union minister of steel, used an aircraft belonging to the Steel Authority of India Ltd and Tata Iron and Steel Co. for his electioneering. The two companies—one public and the other private—recovered the cost of aircraft usage under the directive of the ECI. Action was also taken on the violation of these directives. In another instance, counting in four Mizoram assembly constituencies was stopped after it was found that the Assam CM's car was used in electioneering.

In the interest of free and fair polls, an order was passed banning ministers' visits to poll areas. It clearly stated that no minister—from the Centre or state—shall undertake any official visit of any constituency from which elections had been announced by the commission during the period commencing with the announcement of these elections, up to the end of the poll process. I also passed orders to the effect that no minister would summon any election-related officer of the constituency or the state in which any elections have been announced to a place outside the constituency for any official discussions during the election period.

The only exception would be when a minister or CM summoned any election-related official for work in connection with the failure of law and order or a natural calamity, both of which requires such ministers or the CM to be personally present for supervision of relief operations.

LIMIT OF ELECTION EXPENSES

The reforms related to the usage of loudspeakers, wall posters, misuse of vehicles and other such matters need to be seen as a package; implementing each of the related orders cannot be seen in isolation. These had an organic link with implementing the model code of conduct and ensuring compliance on the ceiling on election expenditure. The model code and the ceiling were the primary drivers of the reform process. In the matter of ceiling on expenses, two important orders were passed in January 1994.

Ceiling on expenses was a feature introduced into the statutes by the founding fathers of the nation themselves. This was taken care of when they passed the Representation of the People Act, 1951, according to which there would be a ceiling on the expenses incurred by a candidate during elections.

According to the statutes, this ceiling was to be revised from time to time by the central government, keeping in view inflation and the requirements of campaigning. The earlier revision had happened sometime in the early 1980s.

In early 1994, as the law stood, the maximum amount that a candidate could spend towards candidature in the constituency, right from the filing of nominations until results were declared, was ₹1.5 lakh. This was a joke because in some constituencies, with electorates of over 10 lakh, it would mean that the candidate could not even spend 15 paise per voter. I did not hesitate to express that the amount was ridiculously low. But then, that was the law, and so I would do everything in my power to enforce it.

Things were not all that simple. The ceiling itself appeared to be a dummy ceiling. The *Gupta vs Chawla Case* of 1974 dealt with the same matter.[59] The Congress candidate had won from his constituency and huge amounts of money were spent in the process, far above the set limit. The returns, however, indicated that the contestant himself had spent within the limits; it was the party that had taken up the major portion of the expenses. This was the position taken by the defence when the petitioner claimed that the candidate had spent too much.

Citing the reason that the ceiling was imposed by the founding fathers for valid reasons, and finding this circumventing of the law to be inappropriate, the court upheld the petitioner and the election of the Congress candidate was disallowed.

The executive response to this Supreme Court verdict was to amend the law. It happened during Indira Gandhi's time in 1974–75, after which the law said that the expenses incurred by friends and well-wishers or by the party towards poll expenses would not be counted as expenses made by the candidate.

This effectively removed the whole idea of a ceiling on expenses. The candidate had to spend within the limit, but his friends and well-wishers or the party could spend as much as they wanted. It was pointless having a law for a ceiling on expenses. Two Supreme Court rulings that came during my tenure were critical of this amendment. They pointed out that it was pointless having the law and that it allowed for

---

[59]Bhagwati, P., 'Kanwar Lal Gupta vs Amar Nath Chawla & Ors on 3 October, 1974', India Kanoon, https://bit.ly/3HMQ1ZT. Accessed on 10 February 2023.

unknown sources to fund elections and vitiate the political atmosphere in the country.

The challenge was that the law, as it stood, said that there was no problem with others spending for a candidate. But the intention of the law was to restrict the expenses. The reason was that contesting elections should be an even playing field for the poor and the rich, and money should not have a decisive say in the selection of candidates.

The commission picked up a clause in the Indian Penal Code (IPC)—Section 171(H), which prohibited expenses of more than ₹10 by 'anybody'—a term that included political parties too—on behalf of the candidate without the candidate's consent. If the candidate gave his consent for such expenses, those expenses would be included in his election expenses for which the ceiling, under Section 77 of the Representation of the People Act, was ₹1.5 lakh.

That was enough. The ECI decided that the law, as it stood, would be strictly enforced. On 28 April 1994, at a meeting with representatives of political parties in Pune, I announced that I would use the provision in the IPC if anybody tried to circumvent the law.

Among the first things I did immediately after the polls that year was to order an investigation into the statements of poll expenses, which each contender was supposed to file before the commission, giving details of the expenditure incurred during the campaign.

In addition, district electoral officers (DEOs) were asked to draw a sample of 33 per cent of candidates in their areas and investigate how much each candidate had spent on posters, transport and other electioneering items. The aim was to compare the DEOs' reports with the poll expenditure statements of the sampled candidates. In other words, this was the time when I started firmly implementing the ceiling on poll expenses.

Work was started on the pro forma that was to be used for submitting returns. Modifications were made in a similar order issued by the commission on 18 September 1981. The new pro forma consisted of two parts: the first was for maintaining day-to-day accounts and the second was for showing the total expenditure with the required details under various heads.

The candidates would have to submit their returns on the prescribed pro forma and also file an affidavit on oath, clearly stating that all election expenditures on listed items had been 'completely and unexceptionally' included in the returns.

Part one of the pro forma included some heads like date of expenditure, nature of expenditure, amount of expenditure, name and address of the payee, serial number of vouchers and bills in case of an outstanding amount. The candidates would have to submit vouchers for all expenses. In case an exception was made, the candidate would have to certify in an affidavit that it was impracticable to obtain vouchers.

Part two of the pro forma was more precise. It took into account the cost of nomination forms and expenditure on security, covering an exhaustive list: remuneration given to election agents, polling agents, counting agents, cost of refreshments given to workers and miscellaneous agents that had not been included in the exhaustive list. The list had 31 items in all.

The DEO, before accepting the account of a candidate, was to conduct an inquiry as was deemed necessary to verify the accounts. The DEO then had to certify to the commission at the time of forwarding the account that the statement of accounts of the candidate concerned was in the manner prescribed and that this had been independently verified by him through an appropriate inquiry.

The ECI also reserved its right to check the authenticity of the accounts at its own level despite the exhaustive procedure.

All the candidates who had contested the recent assembly elections in the five states were directed to submit the accounts to the DEOs within a month in this new format. It was made clear that the commission intended to properly verify the authenticity of the returns filed and would hold candidates personally responsible for any lapse or misinterpretation.

Use of the IPC and the pro forma requiring certification from the DEOs were a potent combination to put brakes on election expenses. But that itself was not enough. The candidates were used to lavish spending. The displays of wealth and positions would intimidate the voters. The idea of a ceiling on expenses could work only if candidates' and parties' habits of spending a great deal were restrained. A set of orders needed to be passed to ensure that the use of monetary resources in elections was curtailed. The restriction on the use of loudspeakers was one way of pushing down the expenses; there were other ways too.

Another order of a similar nature that was passed in January 1994 had to do with restrictions on the movement of cars and other vehicles in a convoy. It was ordered that, except in the case of specific security instructions, no convoy of more than three vehicles should be allowed to move in the state where elections are to take place, even if they belonged to ministers. The order made clear that the commission would be forced to take the extreme step of cancelling the polls if the instructions were not complied with thoroughly.

All the candidates were asked by the commission to register their vehicles with the concerned authorities, and they were expected to display the permits issued by the election authorities on the windscreens of their vehicles. Only vehicles with valid permits would be allowed to be used on the polling day. No exception would be made in this regard, irrespective of the status of the candidate. It was informed that a violation of the order would be dealt with under the Motor Vehicles Act and the Representation of the People Act, 1951.

The ECI's efforts did not end with passing the order. The instructions had to be followed up. For example, a little later, on 8 May 1994, when elections were due in a constituency in Andhra Pradesh, the same directive was emphasized upon again—register vehicles and display the passes on the respective windscreens of the vehicles. It became a procedure.

EFFECTIVENESS OF THE CODE

People responded variously to the developments. While the then CM of Maharashtra Sharad Pawar lauded the efforts, albeit with certain reservations, he also expressed that the government had been put into a straitjacket. He cited, as an example, his inability to publicize 19 of the 20 decisions taken at the cabinet meeting on that day in view of the elections to two seats in Maharashtra.

Pawar mentioned that, for the first time in his political career, he was seeing low-expense electioneering even in Lok Sabha constituencies—Ahmednagar and Baramati—and '...it is a good thing. But other stipulations, like the one which the prohibits government from making routine announcements, need to be discussed with the EC by all state governments.'[60]

As far as the actual elections were concerned, from the commission's and the nation's perspective, the elections did not produce an all-rosy picture despite the best efforts. Certain constituencies in Bihar and Uttar Pradesh were also to have by-elections in that phase of polling. Vaishali was reported to be a test zone. An article titled 'CEC Phobia Works Wonders' in *The Statesman* explains how the high and mighty had sobered down, marked their tour programmes as secret, paid their dues at government guest houses; how well over 1,600 persons, including the district magistrate and returning officer, had deposited their licensed arms; how the police had seized 16 country-made guns and were adhering to the rules framed by the commission. In fact, the report mentions that the CM of Bihar, who was once my main critic, now made it a point to say that he was following the rules at the elections. As many as 524 booths from this constituency had been declared sensitive.[61]

The outcome of the implementation of the code was satisfactory. Lalu Prasad Yadav, CM of Bihar, was eventually disappointed with the poll results. Another headline on 21 May said that major parties were flouting electoral norms in Ghazipur in Uttar Pradesh. This report was in respect of poll expenditure (candidates accusing each other of expenses amounting to ₹50 lakh–1 crore) of the unfettered use of loudspeakers, of six ministers being put up in the constituency at government cost and, therefore, violating the model code of conduct.[62]

These instances give a sample of the kind of work the ECI was doing at that time. Implementing the model code, I was aware that

[60]'EC Directives Have Crippled Govt: Pawar', *The Hindu*, 13 May 1994.
[61]'CEC Phobia Works Wonders', *The Statesman*, 16 May 1994.
[62]Gupta, Sharad, 'Campaigning at Its Peak in Ghazipur, Major Parties Flouting EC Norms', *The Indian Express*, 21 May 1994.

many feathers would be ruffled. While my detractors continued to use their creative energies to discredit my efforts as the work of a maverick, I kept on tackling the emerging situations firmly. Soon enough, the lawmakers started thinking about much needed electoral reforms on a serious note.

ATTEMPTING TO CHANGE THE CONSTITUTION TO CHECK THE CEC

In the beginning of May 1994, there was news of serious attempts in Parliament to float some bills in connection with elections. On 5 May, it was reported that the Centre was planning to clip my 'wings', but was running out of time since the budget session was to end in 10 days and even the draft bill was not ready.[63] There was a further need to develop a consensus since a two-thirds majority was required and they were not ready yet. The next day, it was reported that the government withdrew the proposed Bill just an hour before it was to be circulated. The reason given was that the government had developed 'cold feet'. According to a report in *The Indian Express*, the Bill fell far short of the expectations of the Opposition parties.[64]

The day after that, a discussion reportedly happened in which the Minister of Parliamentary Affairs, V.C. Shukla, was said to have assured the Opposition that the bills would be introduced and the budget session of Parliament would most probably be extended for the purpose.

Finally, two bills were proposed. One was related to electoral reforms and the other was a constitutional amendment bill aimed at making the three commissioners equal. Reports had it that the idea was to make the process of removal of the three commissioners identical.

The Opposition parties were particularly opposed to the proposed method of appointment of the commissioners. While the ruling party wanted that the commissioner should be appointed by the President, the Opposition said that the appointment should be made by a board

---

[63]'Centre Not to Clip Seshan's Wings—Now', News Time, 5 May 1994.
[64]'Govt Withdraws Proposed Bill on Poll Reforms', *The Indian Express*, 6 May 1994.

consisting of senior constitutional functionaries, like the Chief Justice of the Supreme Court, the Speaker of the Lok Sabha and the leader of the Opposition. Similarly, there were disagreements on several reforms specifically related to delimitation and reservation of constituencies.

In this phase, support for the ECI came from an unexpected quarter. Former PM Chandra Shekhar wondered how the government would tackle three commissioners, when it was finding it difficult to manage one Seshan.

The problem the government faced was that it needed to take the Opposition along with it. Even though it did not have a simple majority in the Rajya Sabha, it could have pushed through an electoral reform bill. But it wanted to do more. It wanted a constitutional amendment, and for whatever reason, it clubbed the two bills into a package. Therefore, the government was negotiating with the Opposition parties for a two-thirds majority in both Houses.

The government worked under the compulsion that several of its ministers had to be protected vis-á-vis the action I had taken in respect of the residency status. It had other positions that it did not wish to concede. It was, therefore, obliged to take up the amendment to the Representation of the People Act, 1951, but faced an uphill task to convince the Opposition of the need to push the package.

Finally, on 10 May, the government circulated the proposed bills at a multiparty meeting. The constitution amendment bills had two main purposes. The first was to hold the three election commissioners as equals, and the second was to announce the commencement of a delimitation exercise based on the 1991 census. The other Bill had 20-odd amendments to the Representation of the People Act, 1951. The intention was to introduce a spectrum of changes. The important one, of course, was about changing the eligibility criteria for the Rajya Sabha.

A significant part of the amendment was the proposal for not allowing parties with religious terms in their names to be registered and for providing for deregistration of political parties by high courts on the basis of the behaviour of parties, that is if they promote or attempt to promote, on grounds of religion, disharmony or feelings of enmity, hatred or ill will between different religious groups.

The CPI (M) agreed with the idea of the equal status of the three commissioners but did not agree on the issue of representation in the Rajya Sabha. They took the line that the change would undermine the structure of the Constitution. The BJP and the Telugu Desam Party firmly rejected both proposals. The BJP was against diluting the power of the ECI in any way. On 14 May, the BJP expressed that the result would be chaos in the ECI if the amendment was to come through. On my part, I said that if the government would go ahead with its proposal, I would challenge it in the courts.

As it turned out, the government did run into trouble in the Rajya Sabha and eventually failed to even move the bills in the session. The Speaker said that according to rules, a notice of seven days was to be given to the Lok Sabha secretariat and the bills had to be circulated to the members two days in advance of the actual introduction. When the government was ready with the drafts, it did not have sufficient time for inducting the bills in the scheduled session. The Speaker was willing to relax the procedural requirements, provided there was unanimity in the House. But since the BJP opposed the move and asked for more time, the idea to move the Bill was dropped.

The government then came up with a proposal of a special session of Parliament to take place from 13 June, and this was eventually agreed upon.

THE POLITICIANS' TUSSLE WITH PUBLIC SENTIMENT

The BJP, the biggest opposition party, called for poll reforms but worked on its own strategy. It was opposed to several things I had taken up, and there was an internal churning within the party on the matter of how I should be handled. There was opposition to steps I took in respect of the members of the Rajya Sabha. It did not take kindly to the fact that certain women were exempted from being photographed on account of their observing the tradition of wearing veils. There was also the question of amending the symbols order, which, apparently, they did not like. They were apprehensive that action could be taken against them for appealing on the basis of religion. Apart from these points, the BJP was more or less in agreement with what I was doing.

In May, even Vajpayee came out in support of what I was doing. The BJP, besides saying that I should not be disturbed, also said that reforms were necessary in the field of elections and from time to time suggested to the government that electoral reforms should be taken up. But each time, they repeated that anti-Seshan measures should not be taken. They were also particularly wary of the move by the government to make an amendment by which the high courts would have the power to deregister parties based on their appeal to voters on the basis of religion.

Interestingly, the term 'anti-Seshan' had come into usage some time earlier and had stuck around. The Bill was unofficially nicknamed so. There were comments later in the press that this was probably the first time in the world that a bill was named after a person in this manner.

Because of the opposition to the electoral reforms Bill, the government was always nervous. Besides the Congress, a few parties were supportive. Even CPI (M) started seeing merit in my arguments. The CPI (M) was opposed to the measures and so was the BJP. Further, a group of six luminaries consisting of Nikhil Chakravarthy, Rajni Kothari, V.R. Krishna Iyer, Kuldip Nayar, Devi Singh Tewatia and Upendra Baxi came up with an appeal that the proposed amendments would undermine the ECI, and anything which undermines the ECI amounted to taking away the right to vote of the poor and the oppressed in a society.

Meanwhile, opposition to the provisions of the amendments grew. The odds were stacked against the ruling party in Parliament. In the Rajya Sabha, the total seats were 245, and along with the Left and the Janata Dal, the government needed 14 more to hit the two-thirds mark. But it was not easy. The Janata Dal was wavering; George Fernandes, MP from Muzaffarpur, and many of his colleagues from Bihar were opposed to the bills. The government was wary of the lack of unanimity among Janata Dal's MPs. On the day before the introduction of the Representation of the People (Amendment) Bill in Parliament, the government was in a tight spot. The Lok Sabha Speaker Shivraj Patil's meeting with leaders of various political parties came a cropper.

THE SPECIAL SESSION OF PARLIAMENT (NICKNAMED AS SESHAN SESSION)

If a new bill being put up in Parliament deals with some matter which is already in consideration in Parliament in another bill, then the earlier bill needs to be withdrawn. The 71st Amendment Bill, which was passed by the Rajya Sabha, was with the Lok Sabha for over two years and had to be withdrawn to make space for the new bill and that could be done by a simple majority.

This withdrawing was an exercise that had to be carried forward on a division. The BJP was strongly opposed to it. George Fernandes was the only one from Janata Dal who voted against the withdrawal; the rest abstained. Similarly, there was a division in the Upper House, but the withdrawal sailed through and even the CPI supported it. And after the withdrawal, when it was time for introducing the new bill, owing to the mounting opposition, the government decided to drop the introduction of the new bill.

Whatever the pretentions behind the good intentions of the government were, it was not rocket science to decipher that the amendment bills were proposed to perpetuate all the ills that had been associated with the Indian electoral system until then. The combined forces of sanity won over expediency. When the press asked me for a reaction, I said, 'I am happy that wisdom has dawned on them.' I added, 'I will continue to do my job as I have been doing.'

Kushwant Singh wrote in an article in *The Telegraph* that the most important factor was the people's total disenchantment with the politics and politicians of the country. In his view, the mood was to replace them and that they found a chivalrous knight in shining armor in India's own St George who was trying to rescue the comely woman, Mother India. He added, 'The roly poly, Humpty Dumpty, comic figure of Seshan may not easily fit with the image of a handsome cavalier coming to the nation's rescue but that is exactly how most people see Seshan. They rejoiced when the electoral reform Bills designed to deprive Seshan of his horse, lance and shield had to be withdrawn.'[65]

Eventually, on 27 July, *The Observer* reported that the PM backed my electoral reforms at a Congress parliamentary meet.

An important point that came out in the discussion over introducing a new bill to amend the Constitution on the matter of the three commissioners was that it would, by implication, mean that the government found the new bill necessary, despite its earlier one in which the three commissioners had supposedly been equated. And demand for equation, on the basis of the earlier Bill was therefore seen, even by them, as flawed. Further, by implication, the law in this regard signed by the President in January 1994 was feared by the government to be ultra vires of the Constitution.

$\mathcal{SD}$

---

[65]Singh, Kushwant, 'Election Turned Elected Commissioner', *The Telegraph*, 29 June 1994.

SIXTEEN

CONSOLIDATING THE REFORMS

One of the banes of the political system was the manner in which political parties were run. Many of the symbol-related cases revealed how parties were not being run according to the rules they had framed for themselves. A standardized system could not be imposed on them, as it would amount to interfering with the ideologies and principles on which the parties were built. Benevolent as it may sound, such authority could be easily misused. However, the parties could be asked to function in accordance with the rules they had drafted for themselves.

A DIRECTIVE TO IMPROVE THE FUNCTIONING OF POLITICAL PARTIES

The opportunity came when I was hearing a symbols case by the end of 1994. Pattali Makkal Katchi was a relatively new party in Tamil Nadu at that time and was founded by Dr S. Ramadoss. It had an elephant as its party symbol back then. A dispute relating to it came up before the commission. After due process, I had to rule in favour of the founder and his team. In that order passed by the CEC on 2 May 1994, I had to make a comment, on the way both contesting sides were functioning:

After hearing the oral submissions and perusing all the documents brought on record by both the contending groups, I cannot help expressing my amazement at the way the party had been functioning... Howsoever much the Commission may not like to go into the internal functioning of the political parties, it nevertheless expects them to function in accordance with their respective constitutions which are binding on them.

I said that ad hocism seemed to be the order of the day. Pointing to the parties that did not hold organizational elections as their constitutions demanded, I added:

These party functionaries at the highest levels, who themselves are holding their offices on such borrowed life, perpetuate the lower bodies by granting them ad-hoc extensions because of the postponed organisational elections. Very often, these bodies are dissolved at the whims and fancies of those who have a sway at the highest levels if these bodies are not following their dictates.[66]

It is important to understand that the political parties are registered with the commission, and during this process, they also have to declare their constitution along with the procedures set to run their respective parties. With this, the ECI always has a reference point to check whether the party is being run according to their declared procedures in their respective constitution. I must say that the ECI order asking parties to function as per their constitution was, by and large, well received, and many political parties started the process of internal democracy.

DEALING WITH THE LOW CEILINGS ON ELECTION EXPENSES

We saw earlier how the ceiling on election expenses was very low and how the commission still went about enforcing those limits. Everyone, including politicians, felt the need to raise the ceiling. The power to do this rested with Parliament, and so I wrote to the PM on 29 September 1994, requesting him to get the ceiling revised.

---

[66]The author has a copy of the order in his private collections.

In my communication, I began with the fact that the amendments made in 1974–75 to Section 77 of the Representation of the People Act, 1951, had made the provisions regarding the ceiling on election expenses totally farcical and meaningless. The law, as it stood, had been criticized by the Supreme Court in two judgements—such a situation was a cause for concern, as it led to corruption and great danger. In the list of reforms recommended by the commission, one of the modifications suggested was that the law imposing a ceiling on expenses, as it existed then, should be tightened or scrapped altogether. I had called for legislation to audit party funds, apply punitive measures for unauthorized spending in elections, check the tendency of not maintaining election expenditure accounts by the contestant, and for not filing returns properly. I said that these should be taken up expeditiously if the role of money power in elections is to be checked. But then, I also added that the commission is doing whatever is possible within the parameters of the existing law to put an effective check on the use of money. After listing all the steps taken, I pointed out that a tangible effect was discernible in the last round of elections.

I pointed out that, with the enforcement of these measures, the expenses had been checked, but there was an urgent need for revision of the ceiling that had been fixed at least a decade ago.

In the course of my arguments, I pointed out four reasons why the ceiling had to be raised. The first was the most obvious—inflation. By keeping the base year at 1981–82, when the wholesale index price was taken to be at 100, the figure at 1984, when the ceiling was fixed, was 110. Ten years later, in September 1994, it stood at 271, which meant that there was almost a threefold increase in prices.

The next reason was that the minimum age for voting was lowered to 18 years in the intervening period, and therefore the number of electors had increased by a considerable number.

The third reason was that the population was increasing and the transition in the demographic profile meant that the number of electors was increasing in each constituency.

The final reason was that over 10 years, electronics and other high-tech methods of campaigning had come into vogue in a big way, and it was important to allow extra expenditure to cover these new expenses.

Based on these reasons, I concluded that a fourfold increase in the figure since 1984 would be appropriate. Based on this assumption, the criterion was laid out: In each parliamentary constituency of a population greater than 10 lakh persons, the ceiling would be ₹600,000, while for assembly constituencies of population greater than 1.5 lakh, the ceiling would be ₹200,000. For smaller constituencies, the ceiling would be appropriately scaled down. This, I said, was the bare minimum that the government should do.

On 20 October, while addressing a press conference in Bangalore, I reiterated the stand of the commission on the issue of limit on expenses. The aim was to give wide publicity to the change in the policy that had been implemented in the by-elections so that the candidates are informed and know what to expect. I said, among other things, that any money spent by sponsors with the consent of the candidate would be treated as expenditure by the candidate. If the expenditure was made by anyone without the candidate's approval, the spender would be prosecuted under Section 171(H) of the IPC. I added that, though, under the provisions, a person making unauthorized expenditure would be fined ₹500, depending on the circumstances, the commission may even postpone the elections.

I also pointed out that each candidate's expenses would be verified every day and monitored by the commission and that the income tax commissioners would be empowered to check their records if warranted.

One other thing I did in the second half of 1994 was to talk to those responsible for giving the money. In an address to the All India Association of Industries in Bombay, I pointed out that it was the industry of corporates that was corrupting the system and expressed that eliminating money power was fundamental to electoral reform. Rich businesspersons pumped money into the political system for their vested interests, all at the cost of democracy. Though a precedent for corporate funding in elections had been set in company law, nothing worthwhile had been done on ground.

Even in this forum, I did not fail to inform them about the election expenditure observers and explained how the officers from Income Tax Department would keep a close eye on the expenses.

The government, meanwhile, began to make progress on the matter. It first bounced the idea of raising the ceiling off the Opposition parties to build a consensus. The Opposition also took its time. But on 21 October, the poll expenses limit was finally raised. Parliament eventually okayed it on 19 November 1994.

On my part, I continued to keep the situation under tight control. On 13 November, when the expenditure election observers were being deployed, each was given nearly 2 kg of published literature and guidelines. I told them that if they felt that the expenditure incurred was so ostentatious and so out of proportion as to put him in a distinctively advantageous position compared to other candidates, a special interim report must be sent to the commission by the quickest means of communication. I said that there was enough indication that the ECI would have no option but to postpone the elections if such a complaint was received. 'Even at the stage of polling, if you feel that free and fair elections had not been held, reach out to me... I will stop the counting of votes,' I told them.

A close observer of the Indian democracy will confirm that a substantial way to improve the quality of public life in the country would be to make changes in the election laws. The Supreme Court did not mince words in saying that the electoral laws were not good enough. Besides, there were recommendations from others besides the ECI on how to alter the laws to make the election process transparent and free of money power. For reasons best known to them, or simply because the leaders were not 'tall' enough, such measures were not initiated. If, with the little power I had, I could restrict the use of money to such an extent and drive out whoever used money illegally, legislators could definitely have done much more—but they did not. All that the government finally did was that it raised the limit to around three times the earlier amount instead of four times. Within two years, in 1996, there were calls for further raise to the limit.

AND THE CEILING WAS IMPLEMENTED WITH FIRM ACTION

When ever complaints were received or when information of infringement of the ceiling on expenses came to the commission, action was taken. For example, by 16 November 1994, it came to light that a few independent candidates from Karnataka and Andhra Pradesh had failed to present their daily accounts for inspection by the election expenditure observers. The commission asked for a consolidated list of the defaulting candidates from each constituency in the two states along with an explanation from district election officers, giving reasons for their failure to ensure compliance with the commission's orders on the subject.

Eventually, the state electoral authorities in Karnataka instructed the returning officers to file FIRs against candidates who had not submitted daily accounts of poll expenses in spite of notices being sent to them. Accordingly, by the end of November 1994, FIRs were filed in accordance with the existing rules of the ECI on the matter.

In Uttar Pradesh, four candidates, two from the BJP and one each from the Congress and Samajwadi Party (SP), were given show cause notices under Section 10A of the Representation of the People Act, 1950. This Section deals with the disqualification of a person for a period of three years from the date of the order if he fails to furnish the account of election expenses in the manner required by the Act without good reason or justification. They were sent show case notices and asked to explain as to why they should not be disqualified under that Section of the Act. The documents these persons had first submitted gave prima facie reason to suspect that some vital facts and figures had not been revealed. An inquiry ordered by the commission revealed that many had incurred expenditure for furthering the election prospects of the candidates. This happened on 27 December 1994.

A writ petition had been filed on 14 November 1994 in the High Court of Karnataka against my directives, asking candidates to keep accounts of the day-to-day expenditures incurred by them for electioneering. The petitioner was the state Janata Dal general secretary. He was against the August 1993 and August 1994 orders that made it mandatory for the candidates to keep day-to-day accounts. He also wanted my orders suspended until the court took a final decision on the matter.

A few days later, on 24 November, the court ruled upholding the two orders. It observed that the ECI had the power and authority to issue orders for the superintendence and conduct of elections.

Looking at it from the standpoint of the commission, all that could be said was that there was this concept of free and fair elections, and everything had to be done to implement it. There was an expressed aim that the election expenses had to be curbed and kept under a certain ceiling to achieve this, and I was merely implementing that. The industries that supplied service and materials for the fanfare in elections did suffer collateral damage. But ultimately, it is the motive that matters.

A SERIES OF REFINED ORDERS FOR THE YEAR-END ELECTION

In November 1994, elections were due in Karnataka, Andhra Pradesh, Sikkim and Goa. A few more states were to follow and this phase of elections was meant to go on till April–May 1995. And the first of the string of orders came out at the end of August. Let me take them up one by one:

Discipline in polling areas

The first order dealt with discipline, particularly regarding entry into polling areas. Previous experience had shown that there were instances when MPs or members of state legislatures had entered polling stations and counting centres without authority. Sometimes, they would also be accompanied by a number of supporters.

This was in violation of the law, over and above the consideration that it led to overcrowding inside the polling stations, which tended to overwhelm the personnel and lead to vitiating the poll scene.

In this case, the laws were already in place. In the commission's order dated 31 August, Rules 32 and 53 from the Conduct of Elections Rules, 1961, were quoted as a reminder. These rules clearly laid down as to who were authorized entry into the polling booths and counting centres. In case there was a violation, the political party to which such persons belonged would be held answerable.

Moderated use of loudspeakers

On 1 September, there was another order on the use of loudspeakers, where the time limits were set between six in the morning and 10 at night, both being subject to local laws. Some flexibility resulted from the modifications ordered by the courts.

Videography, printing of pamphlets, use of money power

On 2 September, three more orders were passed. The first was intended to take the use of videography to the next level. The second was on the printing of pamphlets. The third was an order on the use of money power.

For videography, detailed instructions were given regarding how the filming should be carried out and how the returning officer would play a crucial role in it.

As for the printing of pamphlets, a law already existed. It was Section 127A of the Representation of the People Act, 1951. The sum and substance of this Section was that the published material must carry the name and address of the printer on its face. The printer should proceed with the job only after obtaining a declaration as to the identity of the publisher, suitably attested by two persons. Then a copy of the printed material, along with the declaration, was to be sent to either the chief electoral officer or the district magistrate as applicable. This Section also provides for imprisonment of up to six months or a fine of up to ₹2,000 or both for contravening the provisions of the Section.

There were more instances of these laws being breached than being followed. Printers rarely sent printed documents to the authorities and did not care to add their names and addresses on the face of the material. To cap it all, no timely action was taken against them by the authorities.

Keeping all these in mind, the commission, in passing the required directions in the order, expressed that the desire or purpose, of the

Section being incorporated in the laws, was to help monitor the contents and expenses. The order said, and I quote:

> 2. The above restriction on the printing of election pamphlets, posters, etc., have been imposed under the law with a view to establishing the identity of the publishers and printers of such documents, so that if any such document contains a matter or material which is illegal, offending or objectionable like appeal on the ground of religion, race, caste, community or language or character assassination of an opponent, etc., necessary punitive or preventive action may be taken against the persons concerned. These restrictions also serve the purpose of placing a check on the incurring of unauthorised election expenditure by political parties, candidates and their supporters on the printing and publication of election pamphlets, posters, etc.[67]

Making a case for the implementation of the laws, the order went on to describe the procedure that was to be followed henceforth to implement these laws. The district magistrates were to write to the printing presses within three days of the announcement of elections, pointing out to them the requirements of Section 127A of the Representation of the People Act, 1951. The communication would also ask for the printing presses to send four copies of the printed material within three days of its printing. Impressing on them in clear terms that any violation of the provisions of Section 127A and the above instructions of the commission would be very seriously viewed and stern action, which may include in appropriate cases even the revocation of the license of the printing press under the relevant laws of the state, would be taken.

The printers were expected to forward two filled pro formas prescribed by the commission. One would be a declaration of the name and address signed by the publisher and attested by two persons and include further authenticated by the printer. The other would contain information regarding the number of copies of the document printed

---

[67] The author has a copy of the letter in his private collections.

and the price charged for the printing job. This had to be done for each poster or pamphlet printed. On the receipt of these pamphlets, the district magistrates or the chief electoral officers, as applicable, would examine whether the laws had been complied with and display a copy of the same in their office.

The order ended with a caution to the political parties, candidates and others concerned that stringent action would be taken in case of violation of the law and a reminder to all concerned officers was given that severe disciplinary action, apart from penal action, may be called for against them for breach of official duty. What this order effectively did was to bring the statute that already existed into the realm of implementation. Responsibilities were fixed and provisions were made for the law to take its course to its logical conclusion. Hopefully, another judgement should not be compelled to lament the non-implementation of the law in this matter.

The third order passed on 2 September was mostly directed at the paraphernalia that candidates used to create a visual feast during elections—with hoardings, cutouts, posters, and so on. Clearly, all this came from money power, and there was an expressed intention in electoral laws of keeping the expenses down during elections. This matter was very much under the parameters of the ceiling on expenses.

What can be seen here is that election laws, criminal laws and local laws were all used as a package to arrive at a formula to effectively gain control over the 'ostentatious display of money power'.

A careful look at the directives listed above also shows how important it was for the ECI to have control over deputed local government officials, as was promised in the vision of the founding fathers. Not to forget that the eventual control authorized by the interim order of the Supreme Court on 10 August 1993 went a long way in enabling me to implement the desirable changes. I can assure you the measures did meet with reasonable success.

Fielding of dummy candidates

The ECI issued orders to check the tendency of political parties of fielding multiple dummy candidates merely to circumvent the limits on the use of vehicles. The ingenious solution was to get a dummy to stand for elections, and then appropriate the dummy candidate's quota of vehicles for the party candidate. This had to be checked systematically. The measures included withdrawing the authorized vehicles from a candidate if he or she withdrew from the race.

Regulating sale of liquor during election

Another order pertained to the prohibition of the sale of liquor. The high courts of Karnataka and Kolkata had ruled differently on the issue of dry days. The commission thought it feasible to delegate the responsibility to the state authorities. So, the 10 states going to polls (including those going to polls in early 1995) were directed to decide on the dry days as applicable to themselves.

Use of party symbol in another state

On 3 October 1994, a concession was granted to political parties recognized at the state level. If they wished to participate in elections in another state and wished to use their own symbol, they could apply to the ECI within three days of notification of the polls.

Mixing of ballots

An order regarding the mixing of ballots had been sent to the four states that had just elected their assemblies. This order was sent as a copy to all other states on 29 December 1994. It was instructed that the same method of counting be incorporated into the procedures of those states. The small alteration or addition to the order had to do with the mixing of ballots even when counting for a single constituency took place in more than one hall. The order consisted of specific details of how the process should be carried out, so that no one could detect how a certain locality or area in a constituency had voted, which could happen if all the boxes of a certain locality landed up in one room for counting. It was a small technical point to serve the purpose of secrecy of ballot.

Regulating the setting up of booths

An order was passed on 10 January 1995 regarding the setting up of booths to provide unofficial identity slips to voters on the date of polling. These slips would have the voters' serial numbers, which would help them save time spent on searching for the voter's serial number inside a polling booth. The original drafters of the rules and procedures took this into consideration and provisions were made for it. The idea was that booths manned by volunteers supporting candidates would be allowed at a reasonable distance from the polling booths to provide such assistance. This provision was duly incorporated into the handbook for presiding officers and the handbook for candidates by the drafters. However, these rules were being interpreted as a matter of right of the candidates and their supporters to set up booths close to the polling stations. It was an excuse for a large crowd of supporters to gather around such tables and interfere with the process of free and fair polls. It, therefore, became necessary for the booths to be properly regulated. In the order of 10 January 1995, clarifications were issued. Even if there were two polling booths in a particular building, there would be only one booth per candidate. The booth would have a table and two chairs and either an umbrella or a tarpaulin roof to protect the volunteers from the sun and rain. No enclosure using *kanaths* (enclosure made using cloth) was to be set up. Candidates were to submit in writing to the returning officer as to where they proposed to set up such booths and obtain written permission from the concerned local government authorities for the same.

The voter slips were supposed to contain only the name of the voter and their serial number. The booths had to be used for nothing other than issuing unofficial identity slips to electors. Forming of crowds were not allowed, and no one who had already voted was to be present at the booth. This could be confirmed from the indelible ink mark on the left forefinger. The persons manning the booths were not to cause obstructions, in any way, to the voters proceeding for voting.

Finally, one order had to be specifically issued to deal with the matter of voter identity cards. It focussed on the elections that were to follow the next year. We will see more of this when we deal with voter ID cards in the next chapter.

And some other orders

An important order had to do with the defacement of property. We have already seen how the implementation was improved to clean up the process further for the assembly elections.

There was another order concerning the training of police officers to handle election-related problems.

The media picked up all these electoral reforms in bits and pieces and helped in disseminating the information.[68]

A list of dos and don'ts for political parties

Earlier, in October 1994, at the start of the election process for the four states, a circular was distributed among all political parties. It was a digest of all the orders in the simplified format of 24 dos and 21 don'ts. These covered the entire spectrum of instructions. For clarifications, people could read the detailed orders.

The model code of conduct continued to be in the news during this period. In this connection, an order was faxed across to the chief electoral officers of the four states to clarify that as the polls were staggered, the parties had to follow the model code until all the four states completed the election process.

POSITIVE REACTION FROM MEDIA, CIVIL SOCIETY AND CITIZENS

By December 1994, with the elections of 1993 and all of 1994 behind us, the general perception was that the process of election had improved. Consequent recognition was accorded to the commission's work.

The Rotary Club, Belur, honoured me with the recognition as the 'Man of the Year' on 3 December 1994. That was followed by the

---

[68]'EC Leaving No Stone Unturned to Ensure Free-Fair Polls', *The Indian Express*, 8 September 1994.

Sunday selecting me as 'Man of the Year 1994'. The *Sunday* said,

> There was the nation's conscience-keeper warning political parties to keep election expenses under control or else face his terrible wrath.
>
> There was the tireless crusader who remained unwavering in his decision to issue identity cards to all voters.
>
> And finally, there was the musafir who travelled the length and breadth of the country, telling his tale and educating the masses about the great election system they seemed to know so little of.
>
> Could anybody else have been the man of the year?[69]

The *India Today* carried an article titled 'Trail-blazers Who Made an Impact in Year 1994' in its 15 January 1995 edition.[70] It was a review of the year 1994 and, in listing me along with persons like Supreme Court Chief Justice M.N. Venkatachaliah, Sushmita Sen, Aishwarya Rai and others, it reflected that the work we had done at the ECI would sustain.[71]

☙

[69]'Man of the Year: Hate Him or Admire Him, but TN Seshan Is the One Person Who Made Most News in 1994', *Sunday*, 25 December 1994.

[70]Charkravarti, Sudeep, 'Trail-Blazers Who Made an Impact in Year 1994', *India Today*, 15 January 1995, https://bit.ly/3jUgk84. Accessed on 10 January 2023.

[71]Ibid.

SEVENTEEN

VOTER ID CARDS:
A PITCHED BATTLE FOR ITS ISSUANCE

I was telling you up to now what was happening by the end of 1994 and the beginning of 1995. During this time, the voter ID cards issue took centre stage. To understand this, let me go back a little in time in order to tell you how the issue evolved.

It was as early as 1992 when I had put in a formal request to the government to issue voter ID cards. The request was met with a dead silence from the government. I indicated to the government that I was authorized by Section 61(b) and (c) of the Representation of the People Act, 1951, and Rule 28 of the Registration of Electors Rules, 1960, to ask for the provision of voter ID cards for a constituency. These rules, together with Rule 35(3) of the Conduct of Election Rules, 1961, authorized me to make these voter ID cards mandatory for a constituency. I could insist on the same for any constituency, which in my view needed the issuing of voter ID cards. So, I issued this order for all constituencies.

A LEGITIMATE ORDER WITH A GENEROUS TIME FRAME

On 28 August 1993, I issued an order making voter ID cards compulsory for all elections that were to happen after 1 January 1995. The order, sent to Centre and state government, read:

8. The legislation as already enacted by the parliament and the rules as already framed by the Government of India in pursuance of the laws provided for the issue of identity cards to electors.

9. The commission has, therefore, decided that electoral identity cards shall be issued to all electors in all parliamentary constituencies throughout India as soon as possible.

10. As the issue of the identity cards to more than 540 million electors throughout the length and breadth of the country will take time, adequate time has to be given for the implementation of the scheme.[72]

It is no rocket science to conclude that the issuing of voter ID cards would have improved the quality of elections by leaps and bounds. At the commission, we had no doubts that it could make a substantial difference, and thus, I pressed for it. It was also made clear that the name of the voter being on the electoral rolls would be the primary requirement, and only having a card would not do.

Expenditure on the exercise was to be shared between the state and central governments as per the existing pattern for election materials, which was fifty-fifty.

The overall time for implementation was enough (September 1993 to January 1995), and the amount required to be spent on voter ID cards was not unreasonably large. It would definitely be much less than what the candidates spent to get themselves elected.

STRATEGY AND EFFORTS TO ENFORCE THE ORDER

It is possible that some states would refuse to comply with the commission's order. In case of defiance of the order, or implicitly of the Constitution, by a state government, there is no 'punitive' action recommended against such a state in the statutes—save one: if it is established in a particular case that there is a breakdown of the constitutional machinery, there is the ultimate punishment—dismissal

---

[72]The author has a copy of the order in his private collections.

of the state government. But it would be too severe a punishment to be applied in a situation like this. Another possibility was for the commission to go to the courts to get its order enforced. This would be avoided as a first option. When it was within the CEC's powers to postpone elections in case of a 'valid' reason, there was no need to go to the courts.

I was clear in my mind that once the deadline expired, no elections would be conducted without ID cards. If a state defied my order and refused to issue ID cards, the constitutional governance would be deemed as having broken down. As long as my order was legal and reasonable, and if there was defiance of the constitutional scheme leading to a constitutional crisis, the author of that crisis would be the concerned state government alone. If this happened, President's Rule could be imposed. This could stretch out for a year and, as had happened in the case of Punjab and J&K, it could be extended further. I asked all the chief electoral officers of states to report non-compliance by states and reiterated that it was not the responsibility of the ECI to look for funds, but that of the state governments and the chief electoral officers. I went on to define a series of milestones as indicators of the progress so far.

Exactly a month after the order was passed, on 28 September, a conference of the chief election officers was held and this matter was one amongst those discussed. Several decisions were made. Meanwhile, the situation and the reactions of various governments were monitored. This happened around the time when the two additional commissioners were appointed, and matters remained in flux for some time.

On 15 November 1993, the very day the Supreme Court had passed an interim order giving me control over the affairs of the commission, the advocates general of the states of West Bengal (convener), Punjab, Assam, Karnataka and Madhya Pradesh met in Delhi and came up with a statement opposing my threat of not holding elections from 1995 unless identity cards were issued to voters. They are reported to have expressed in their statement that I had no jurisdiction to issue such an order and that they saw in my efforts and intention to alter the basic structure of the Constitution.

On 15 December 1993, I passed an order detailing the steps that had to be taken by the state governments, so that the work steadily progressed to meet the said deadline. The timeline of the milestones to be achieved was something like this:

- Issuance of comprehensive instructions to the electoral registration officer (ERO) by the chief electoral officer and forwarding a copy of the compendium of instructions to the ECI (31 December 1993)
- Award of contract to the agencies (28 February 1994)
- Completion of photography and lamination (31 August 1994)
- Completion of distribution of cards to electors and consignment of duplicates (30 November 1994)
- Supply of paper to EROs (31 December 1994)

'NO PROGRESS, NO ELECTION' IN WEST BENGAL

The government of West Bengal announced that it would go to court over the commission's order. They took strong objection to the deadline of 1 January 1995. They claimed that my order was impractical and that it would cost ₹160–180 crore. The commission was constantly reviewing the action taken by the state government to prepare voter ID cards. No actions had been taken by the West Bengal government. So, on 28 December 1993, all activities connected with the conduct of elections in West Bengal were stopped. It was made clear that if the order on voter ID cards was not complied with, that is, if the required steps were not systematically taken, it would not be possible for the commission to conduct any elections in West Bengal, for which the state government alone would be 'responsible'. Election of five members to the Rajya Sabha from West Bengal was immediately affected.

The state government challenged my order in the High Court on 13 January 1994.

In the court, the West Bengal government admitted that it agreed in principle with the scheme of voter ID cards. I promptly reinitiated election-related work, including preparation for the election to the Rajya Sabha vacancies from West Bengal.

A GENERAL ACCEPTANCE OF THE ORDER

I had nowhere said that voter ID cards were a panacea for all election-related problems. They were not meant to take care of all the problems anyway. But still, the voter ID cards were a significant step forward, as they represented a strong move to check impersonation. The position of the commission was that it would improve the quality of elections in a significant way. On the day of voting, the extent of impersonation would come down drastically. I knew of an Andhra Pradesh minister whose house had been specified in the address given by 300 people. How on earth could 300 voters be living in one house, unless it is a large hotel? Remember that in one constituency in Andhra Pradesh, the number of enlisted voters was found to be greater than the population of that constituency.

As time went by, it finally became apparent that this scheme did significantly reduce bogus voting.

On 31 December 1993, the Tripura government came up with a statement that they were ready for the voter ID cards and that they morally supported it. But again, it was a CPI (M)-ruled state, and surely, it would not sustain too different a stand from its main base, West Bengal.

Mamata Banerjee, who was then with Congress (I) in West Bengal, hailed the move to issue voter ID cards. In fact, by the end of January 1994, it was reported that she was to take up, as part of her political activities, a 'no-identity-card-no-vote' drive in West Bengal.

After the West Bengal government failed to stop the voter ID card project, a CM meet was called by the union home minister, S.B. Chavan, and the union law minister, H.R. Bharadwaj. The Home Minister indicated in the meeting that the central government would not be averse to sharing the financial burden. It was discussed that the CEC should have consulted the state governments and the Centre before taking this momentous decision. The CMs at the meeting came up with the idea that the cards should first be issued in certain pockets before being extended to all other parts. After some convincing, one by one, the state governments started taking constructive action.

Maharashtra, Haryana and Gujarat started implementing the voter ID cards scheme in right earnest.

RESISTANCE ON THE GROUNDS OF INADEQUATE TIME

One could say that in principle, voter ID cards came to be accepted by the entire country. The matter had been taken to court, and the applicability of the orders was upheld. Despite all this, as the days passed by, the deadline became a point of contention for the government. They believed that despite my insistence that I would not allow any polls after January 1995 if the voters did not possess ID cards, judicial intervention would allow the polls to be conducted without a hitch.

On 29 July 1994, the 10 CMs whose states were to shortly go to the polls met at the PM's residence. They were reported to have assembled there mainly to discuss the point of voter ID cards and the deadline. They had supposedly agreed in principle that voters should be issued ID cards but wanted a phased introduction of the same. The PM is reported to have said that the commitment had been made a long time ago and the process needed to be started.

The PM is reported to have observed that because of the practical difficulties, the scheme should not be implemented in a hurried, but in a phased, manner. Lalu Prasad Yadav, the CM of Bihar, reportedly pointed out that Bihar was not financially strong enough to bear the burden of providing photo identity cards to the voters. The CM of Andhra Pradesh wanted the Centre to bear 75 per cent of the expenses and give the remaining 25 per cent as a loan. The PM was finally said to have promised that he would take up the matter with the ECI.

REDUCING COSTS: HOW TECHNOLOGISTS ROSE TO THE OCCASION

One of the main drawbacks of the programme that detractors harped on was the money required for the cards. Without a doubt, they showed inflated figures for the value of each card—₹60—and put the overall estimate at ₹3,300 crore. On the contrary, using basic precepts of productivity and taking advantage of the scale of operations involved, this could be brought down drastically to realistic levels of less than ₹20 per card and ₹1,100 crore for 550 million voters. 'Find me ₹1,100 crore and I will have voter ID cards for all,' I said.

Anyway, the expense was supposed to be split fifty-fifty between the Centre and the states, and it was difficult to get the latter to cough up the money required.

If the political class was stalling the process of issue of voter ID cards on the grounds of high costs, the indigenous public sector companies were outdoing each other in coming up with new technologies to reduce both the time and cost of production of the cards. The technology developed by the BARC and ECIL was based on digital imaging and totally did away with polaroid film and photographic paper. The private firms dealing in traditional photographic material were doing their bit to stall the use of a digital system.

The cost of production of each voter ID card through the new digital system would depend on the total number of electors. But the approximate cost of production of a voter ID card, along with the duplicate, worked out between ₹15 and ₹18 in the Elector Identity Card Preparation System, or ELIPS 500, which was developed by public sector institutions.

Electronics Corporation of India Limited said each system was priced between ₹6 lakh and ₹7.5 lakh and could be mounted on vehicles and taken to remote areas. The voter ID cards could be made tamper-proof, could be printed on ordinary stationery without the need of photographic film, could be laminated and could incorporate a secret code. In fact, the data collected for the cards could be stored and retrieved for other purposes.

On 12 March 1994, the ECIL said that at the rate of 8,000 voter ID cards per day at each work centre for a parliamentary constituency, it could easily meet the deadline of 31 December 1994 for the issue of ID cards to voters in all states.[73]

---

[73]Krishnan, Murali, and Dinesh C. Sharma, 'Pvt Firms Vie for ID Cards Market', *The Telegraph*, 13 March 1994.

In fact, at that time, the technology developed by ECIL was already in use in the northeastern states for the issue of citizenship cards to residents in border districts.

A few days later, on 21 March, Hindustan Photo Films, again a public sector undertaking, came up with a wonderful arrangement. Press reports indicated that its 'modern' video cameras 'could get a photo in just two seconds and in the next 15 seconds, one could get a printed photograph'. Its claim was that, given a chance, it could produce 18 lakh cards per day.[74]

On 17 April 1994, the Pune-based Centre for Development of Advanced Computing (C-DAC) and the Orissa Computer Application Centre, Bhubaneswar, came up with another cost-effective method to provide photo identity cards. Their system involved sending a couple of people with handheld devices to the polling booths and taking a video and simultaneously entering a code number into the data. The material would then be taken to a 'photo-grabbing' station to create the cards using a simple personal computer for inputting the data.[75]

On 18 April, Bharat Electronics Ltd, Bangalore, announced that it had developed a software to deliver a card for as little as ₹10–11, and it would take just three minutes for printing out one card. [76]

Eventually, the states hired the agency they found most suitable for themselves and we saw progress in several states. When the cards began to materialize, it was a mixed bag and the outcome was surely less than cent per cent accurate; but it was workable nonetheless. In the first week of November, a copy of the ELIPS-produced card was sent across to me and I complimented them for issuing a card that I found to be 'very good, cost effective, trouble-free and efficient'. However, on 24 December, the same company came to see me regarding my censure for some sloppy work done in Maharashtra. I said, 'I can allow a mistake level of 1 in 1,000. But I will not tolerate shoddy work. They will have to perform professionally. Some of the staffers do not even know how to operate the computer.'

---

[74]'Superfast Tech. for I-Cards', *Hindustan Times*, 22 March 1994.
[75]'Cost-Cutting Plan over Poll I-D Cards', *The Independent*, 18 April 1994.
[76]'BEL Develops Software for Cheap I-Cards', *The Times of India*, 19 April 1994.

PUSHING HARD AGAINST THE GOVERNMENT'S DELAY TACTICS

Progress on the cards was nowhere close to the schedule I had initially set up, but there was no giving up. I remained firm in my resolve.

In the beginning of August 1994, I wrote a letter to the President telling him that there was a possibility of the ECI not intimating the governors of six states for holding elections, the states being Maharashtra, Gujarat, Bihar, Orissa, Arunachal Pradesh and Manipur, and that the terms of their state assemblies were ending in the first three or four months of 1995. And as such, these were to be the first states to hold elections using the voter ID cards.

In fact, this letter was a follow-up on a letter that I had written to the President earlier in April that year telling him that I would not issue the notification for holding the election in these six states if they did not meet the deadline of 1 January 1995. I had yet not received a reply from the President, though it was already August. In the first week of August, the PM said that there was a consensus that there would be a phased implementation of the order of the CEC to issue voter ID cards. On my part, I continued insisting that there would be no elections where there were no voter ID cards.

Meanwhile, the central government too made some moves. On 11 August, the law minister, Narashima Rao, stated in Parliament that the government would reimburse half the amount required for the identity cards. That was a positive step.

Two days later, he announced in the Rajya Sabha that the government would introduce a constitutional amendment bill in the monsoon session of Parliament, providing for the delimitation of constituencies. This was supposed to be a checkmate of sorts to my deadline.

The idea was that if the Bill was passed, the delimitation of constituencies would take place on the basis of the 1991 census. It would take a minimum of three years for the process to get over. If that be so, then the voter ID cards would have to be reissued on the basis of the new arrangement and that would be seen as a wasteful exercise. So, the government would have two grounds to fight the case in court: One, that it would be wasteful and the other being the limited resources for issuing voter ID cards immediately.

I continued to reiterate the 'no ID cards, no votes' stand. I said in a press conference that if the six states that were to go to the polls after January 1995 fail to meet the deadline, subject to the decision of the court, I would not hold elections there. I even pointed it out that I might not even notify the holding of elections if there are no voter ID cards. But I also added that it was unlikely that the situation would lead to a constitutional crisis, as the Centre had made it clear in Parliament that it would not allow any constitutional impasse to be created.

On 12 September, a meeting was held with the CMs of the states that were to go to the polls shortly. The PM, home minister and I were present. The CMs of Bihar and Orissa, along with the Gujarat CM, said that it was practically impossible to implement the order on the photo identity card. The Bihar CM vocally opposed the scheme. Even in my presence, he accused me of starting my own political campaign. He questioned my crusade against the system. His point was that for the past 30 years, the country had been conscious of the problem of impersonation during elections. He wanted to know how could I resolve it in just four months.

I tried to convince the CMs about the importance of my order. In this regard, I said that it was very much possible that the deadline could be reached since the country had the technology. In fact, I highlighted and complimented the effort put in by Sharad Pawar, CM of Maharashtra, towards meeting the deadline: 'If he can do it, why not you?'

But they stuck to their guns. The PM decided to hold further consultations with the states concerned. However, a good development that took place meantime was that the Centre and the states finally came around to finalizing that they would share the financial burden (fifty-fifty) in accordance with what was normal for election materials.

After the dust had settled, on 15 September, the ECI reiterated its stand. The voter ID cards would be ready by 30 November, given out by 31 December, and no elections would be held without the cards after 1 January 1995.

The voter ID cards were enormously popular with the people. By around the first week of November, about 90 per cent of the work was completed in Maharashtra, and 50 per cent was covered in both Gujarat and Chandigarh. And as I said earlier, an order on how voting with ID cards was to be done was included in one of the series of ECI orders before the impending elections. Needless to say, some states were nowhere close to meeting the deadline.

So, as we got closer and closer to the 1 January 1995 deadline, one thing that I had to constantly consider was whether I should push on relentlessly for the voter ID cards, come what may, or take a break The legality of my position was beyond dispute. Some states who worked on it earnestly, for example, Maharashtra and Haryana, proved that the time I had given was not at all unreasonable. But as I said, most states were nowhere close to meeting the deadline. So, the question remained: Should I push on relentlessly or avoid confrontation and make everyone happy by postponing the issue of the deadline?

VOTER ID CARD ISSUE CHALLENGED IN THE SUPREME COURT

The elections due in early 1995 were in the process of being notified at the beginning of January. At this time, three people, including an MP, took the matter of my orders in respect of the voter ID cards to the Supreme Court. They asked the court to pass interim orders to stay the execution of all my orders in respect of the identity cards. They also sought directions to publish the required notification in conformity with the schedule for elections announced on 8 December 1994. Finally, they sought directions to hold assembly elections in the state of Bihar before 15 March in accordance with the announced schedule.

On 3 January, the Supreme Court passed an order denying a stay on the issue and simultaneously scheduled a hearing of the case on 16 January. Notices were accordingly issued.

The Orissa government, too, joined the fray. They filed a petition under Article 32 of the Constitution, seeking a declaration that the ECI's stand of no polls without voter ID cards be declared unconstitutional, as it violated Article 14. The Supreme Court decided to hear that petition along with the others.

As for the fact that I had delayed the elections, the Orissa government accused the Congress and said that it was behind the delay. The *Hindustan Times* reported, 'Reacting sharply to the postponement of the elections, Janata Dal state president Ashok Das, in a statement here, charged the Prime Minister with conniving with the Chief Election Commissioner to postpone the elections for the benefit of an "ill-prepared" state Congress.'[77]

The BJP expressed its discontent that I had deferred the polls. It said that my decision to extend the campaign period will defeat the aim of curtailing election expenses. But then, the grapevine was that if the Maharashtra counting happened before Gujarat went to elections, it might not be favourable to the BJP. On 5 January, the BJP demanded that polls be held without voter ID cards.

On 11 January, the Communist Party of India (Marxist-Leninist) CPI (ML) moved the SC on the Bihar ID cards issue. They took a stance that was opposed to the incumbent government. In their expressed attempt to protect the electorate's right to franchise, they claimed that the process of preparation and distribution of voter ID cards was being deliberately stalled with mala fide intent. They wanted the Supreme Court to give directions to the ECI to devise alternate means to ensure the proper identification of eligible voters.

On the part of the ECI, an affidavit was submitted to the Supreme Court on 12 January 1995 in response to the averments made by the three petitioners. It was a joint affidavit on my personal behalf and on behalf of the ECI. It was signed by Secretary S.K. Mendiratta. In the affidavit, we took the stand that voter ID cards would improve elections and that the law permitted the commission to ask for the cards. The affidavit also conveyed that the voter ID cards would make voters conscious of their political rights and inculcate in them a sense of participation in the electoral process by preventing impersonation.

---

[77]'Congress behind Orissa Poll Deferment: JD', *Hindustan Times*, 6 January 1995.

We also pointed out that except for Bihar, Orissa and West Bengal, the state governments were completing the identity card preparation programme within the deadline. Most of all, we pointed out that fixing a deadline is important if we want executive governments to complete a job; which is the 'previous experience'. We also added that those resisting the identity cards scheme were doing so for their selfish interest. Making all these points, the affidavit urged the Supreme Court to dismiss the petition.

As if to confirm what I was saying, an article in *The Times of India*, dated 16 January 1995, suggested that games were being played:

[...] Mr Laloo Prasad would like nothing better than dismissal of his government. He could then avoid responsibility for his government's omissions and commissions, make the dismissal an electoral issue and become a hero in the process... Time and again, during the last five years, Mr Yadav has displayed his ability to marshal resources and the administration to suit his interests [...][78]

At that time, if I were to stick to my guns and say that I shall not conduct elections come what may, the matter would go to court and the outcome could be anything. If the courts allowed my stand, then the voters would be disenfranchised for a period of time, even though it was for the larger good or improvement in the electoral system. But that had to be balanced with the inherent perils of going into an unchartered zone in the constitutional history of the nation. If the court ruled against me, then the entire process of issue of cards would be jeopardized. It was best to avoid such outcomes when there was an alternative.

The deadline of 1 January 1995 was not sacrosanct, apart from the fact that it was a date legitimately fixed by constitutional authority, namely the ECI. A delay by a few months would be deemed alright, provided the governments bind themselves to a deadline. If that were the case, I was willing to relent, provided the states were bound by a court

---

[78]Sengupta, Uttam, 'Provoking Seshan is Only Part of Laloo Prasad's Ploy', *The Times of India*, 16 January 1995.

order to finish their job of issuing voter ID cards in a reasonable time.

On 16 January 1995, according to my brief, my counsel Ramaswamy submitted a written assurance to the Supreme Court that since elections to the Bihar Legislative Assembly had been notified (to take place on 5, 7 and 9 March), the ECI would not withhold the elections on the grounds that photo identity cards had not been supplied to all eligible voters. The condition was that the government of Bihar would give an undertaking to the court that it would complete the exercise of issuing the cards in about nine months' time, that is before 30 September 1995. This was to be without prejudice to the contentions of the writ petitioners (on jurisdiction and power of the ECI to insist on the issuance of the cards to every eligible voter). It was made clear in the assurance that the ECI had no intention of creating any constitutional crisis, since 18 months' time had been given for completion of the exercise.

CLIMB DOWN OR PRUDENCE?

The concession of nine months' time was seen by many as a climb down; most papers reflected it as such. Even if it appeared so, in reality, it was not. Had the states committed to the fact that they would provide the identity cards by 30 September, two things would have happened. The constitutional crisis that was supposedly looming large would have been avoided and simultaneously there would have been enough time until September for the governments to complete the process of issuing their voter cards.

With that time frame and with their word given to the Supreme Court, they would have been constrained by the court's order to issue the cards, besides, of course, the constitutional obligation on account of the CEC's order. That was the thinking behind the move. One should note that the deadline was a necessary part of the process.

The court did not take to this line of thinking. It passed an interim order the next day, 17 January 1995. It was a bench consisting of Chief Justice A.M. Ahmadi, Justice S.P. Barucha and Justice K. Jayachandran Reddy.

It admitted related cases from Orissa and said that all the cases will be heard in tandem with the cases dealing with the main question of the legal power and jurisdiction of the ECI to issue directives on photo identity cards that were earlier transferred to the Supreme Court. The cases were to be heard in another four weeks.

As for the deadline of 30 September, which we had asked for in our affidavit, it directed the counsel for the state of Bihar to 'obtain instructions on that behalf' from the ones who were to produce the ID cards and report in four weeks. In fact, from that affidavit, it was averred that even though the ECI was forceful earlier in insisting for photo identity cards, 'the ECI is mindful of the consequences that may follow should the two states (of Bihar and Orissa) not be allowed to go to the polls for their failure to supply the photo identity cards to "all" eligible electors'.

It criticized the ECI for harsh language and in the same breath, it also pointed out that the two states of Orissa and Bihar lagged far behind in implementing the orders of the ECI.

It said that in order to satisfy the mandate of Article 168 of the Constitution, it was necessary that elections be held in those two states in a manner that the election results are declared before 15 March 1995. It said that ECI will not withhold the elections in Bihar and Orissa on the grounds of having failed to issue voter ID Cards. Accordingly, it stayed the relevant orders of the ECI as applicable to the two states.

On 18 January, the verdict, by itself, was covered by most papers on an as is basis. But they did reflect a wide spectrum of follow-ups when it came to opinions. The *Hindustan Times* published a small write-up titled 'CPI-M Hails SC Order'. An article in *The Hindu* gave the views of political parties: 'Right across the political spectrum, parties welcomed the Supreme Court's order today directing the Election Commission to hold elections... But the emphasis, the nuances in their reactions, were markedly different.'[79]

The Left parties were pleased that 'the Chief Election Commissioner's dictatorial attitude had been rebuffed by the apex

---

[79]'Verdict Welcomed', *The Hindu*, 18 January 1995.

court'.[80] The BJP saw the order as squaring up with its own stand that elections must be held when they are due as laid down in the Constitution and welcomed the end of uncertainty regarding the elections in Bihar. But the BJP was not willing to go so far as to say that the CEC had indeed transgressed his constitutional limits by threatening to not hold elections in those states where the work on voter ID cards had not been completed in time.

And in the centre of the political spectrum, the Congress (I) welcomed the resolution of the immediate problem with the court's order. However, the spokesperson of the party, Madan Bhatia, said that the party would give its reaction the next day (19 January) after reading the court's order thoroughly.

In the camp of the Janata Dal, it was celebration time. The Bihar CM, Lalu Prasad Yadav, had won the battle of wits with the CEC. The Samata Party also welcomed the order, with its leader George Fernandes saying that his party's view was that the people's right to vote cannot be taken away simply because the ECI was unsuccessful in getting the state government to implement its directive on voter ID cards. However, he accused the Bihar government of having deliberately delayed the issuing of identity cards in the hope that elections would indeed be cancelled by the commission.

The order was a setback in the ECI's continuing efforts for improved elections. The ECI had to factor in this new development, too. The day the order was passed, I was on leave in Madras. All I could say was that I had not done anything illegal. Why did I fix the date as 1 January 1995? Was it arbitrary? Not at all. It was part of the process of trying to clean up the loopholes in the election system. Having been in administration for most of my working career, I knew that 18 months was a sufficiently long period for the states to issue the cards; it was a realistic deadline to work towards and some states had attained that target. So, was the deadline sacrosanct and reasonable? To the extent that a constitutional authority was issuing a legitimate order, yes it was. But the competent authority that issued the order also had the

---

[80]'Verdict Welcomed', *The Hindu*, 18 January 1995.

Through the Broken Glass

authority to change the date. But going by the best of administrative practices, in tandem with the extension, having a deadline was vital. We could shift the deadline to 30 September, but we had to have a deadline.

The Supreme Court passed the order, so there was no way for me to have the cards programme implemented immediately. There was no deadline. Effectively, a superior authority had overruled it. So, elections were held without cards in Bihar and Orissa. If you can't enforce a rule in one place, you can't enforce it elsewhere.

There was a section of people who wanted me to put my foot down on holding elections only after the voter ID cards were issued. They felt that I should not have even given the few extra days, which states like Orissa and Bihar got. This view of theirs was an option alright, but I had decided otherwise and the rest is history.

One of the election commissioners, Gill, was reported to have expressed happiness that the Supreme Court had upheld the right of the Indian people to elect the governments on the due date. In his opinion, the ECI's job was to 'push and promote' the electoral process and not 'thwart' it.[81] He is even reported to have regretted that the verdict had come at a high legal cost.

He did not say anything about the interests of free and fair elections, or about the need to successfully issue photo identity cards in time. I would have truly appreciated had he taken the pains to mention that on that occasion, but he did not. He did express some other concerns though, when he said, 'I hope the court will be able to adjudicate on all other constitutional matters involving the commission expeditiously.'[82]

Did my critiques understand the intricacies of what happened? Well even if they did, the press reports the next day did not show it. The papers on 19 January had a field day saying things like 'Seshan's volte-face', 'Seshan relents: angry and no-nonsense to executive and soft and reasonable and accommodating for the Supreme Court.'

---

[81]'EC Member Hails SC I-Card Order', *The Times of India*, 18 January 1995.
[82]Ibid.

The voter ID card programme had to be taken forward in other ways, but largely at the mercy of endless delays.

As it stood at the time of the verdict, the voter ID coverage in certain areas of the country was already at 95 per cent. In other places, the process had just about started. Subsequent players in the ECI and in the governments took the process forward. Years down the line, the voter ID cards eventually became available and compulsory all over the nation. The Aadhar cards recently issued have had a positive impact in furthering this process. So, we as a nation have eventually reached there any way. All in all, as on date, impersonation is not as easy as it was in the past, thanks to the voter ID cards.

EIGHTEEN

ELECTIONS AND PUBLIC RESPONSE OF EARLY 1995

E ven when the issue of voter ID cards case was taken up by the courts in the first two weeks of January, a leading Indian daily authorized a survey by MODE, a leading marketing research organization at that time. The survey was conducted on 11 and 13 January 1995.[83] The results came out around the same time as the Supreme Court's verdict on the ID cards and it showed near 90 per cent approval rates for my work. I am sure the verdict by the Supreme Court would have altered this—but clearly, the general public was looking upon my work with admiration and sympathy. One particular politician was vocally supportive...

A FAN FROM AMONGST THE POLITICIANS!

While there was a chorus of denunciation of me and my stand on the voter ID card issue, I got support from some unexpected quarters. Bal Thackeray, president of the Shiv Sena, in an interview with *The Week* (29 January 1995), just two weeks prior to the Maharashtra elections, expressed that he liked the way I worked. Talking of how he

---

[83]Balakrishnan, K., and Gouri Chatterjee, 'Seshan's Actions Have Mass Support', *The Times of India*, 23 January 1995.

would face the situation were he to be in power, he said that he would have initiated an investigation, and whatever be the stature of the person involved, he would not have spared them. 'I am going to behave like Seshan. I like that man. He has done yeoman service to the country; not for himself... Once the people know that you are a hard nut to crack then they will behave. Now see the election machinery moving...'[84]

The New York Times carried a write-up on me on 10 February 1995, titled 'A Demon Housecleaner to Clean India's House'. The article is interesting as it is a perspective about India from an overseas standpoint. Not that it is entirely accurate, but interesting nonetheless:

> If a poll were taken to find India's most admired personality, a strong candidate would be T N Seshan. And if a poll were taken to find the public figure Indians consider most high-handed, Mr Seshan would be a probable winner again...
>
> His major weakness may be his ego... But he contends that in this too he has matters under control.[85]

SUCCESSFUL CONDUCT OF THE EARLY PHASE OF 1995 ELECTIONS

Since the elections were to proceed without the voter ID cards, the idea was to use the cards where they had been issued and to try to make the best efforts of getting them issued where they had not been. According to notifications, Maharashtra, Orissa, Arunachal Pradesh, Manipur and Bihar would have been finished with their elections by mid-March, and the counting was to take place in the beginning of the third week of March.

Manipur went to polls on 17 and 19 February. While the turnout in the first phase was 80 per cent, it was 85 per cent in the second.

---

[84]Kumar, B. Krishna, 'Interview: Bal Thackeray, We Will Win', *The Week*, 29 January 1995.

[85]Burns, John F., 'New Delhi Journal; A Demon Housecleaner to Clean India's House', *The New York Times*, 10 February 1995, https://nyti.ms/3jXJUtm. Accessed on 11 January 2023.

These figures were unprecedented. Unfortunately, despite all the precautions, two persons were killed in the first phase and as many as six killed and 16 others injured in the second. There were deaths even in the run-up to the elections. A lot of this could be attributed to the insurgency that was prevalent in that state despite as many as 40,000 security personnel being involved in the elections. A group called the Peoples' Liberation Army had distributed leaflets, asking people to stay indoors, as they had planned to attack the security personnel on duty at the poll booths. But voters apparently had other ideas, considering they turned up in large numbers. The violence was in stark contrast to Maharashtra, which was peaceful. Manipur, at that time, was considered as being next only to Kashmir in being a 'disturbed' state. Nothing too spectacular was reported from Orissa. As many reports showed, despite the unavoidable aberrations, the general environment was satisfactorily under control.

Despite all the pre-election drama over identity cards, observance of the model code of conduct and other such issues, the actual elections turned out to be rather peaceful. Further, there was no open defiance of the commission's orders and the writ of the law did hold sufficiently.

Gujarat went to polls on 20 and 25 February. Apart from a few incidents of violence like stabbing and scuffles, polls in both phases were more or less peaceful. The state registered between 60 per cent and 65 per cent polling in the first and second phase, respectively.

The following excerpts from an article give an insight into some aspects of the prevailing environment and change. The *Sunday Observer*, on 12 February, carried an article titled 'Candidates Beware, Big Brother Seshan Is Watching'. It was a description of how a particular candidate and his supporters had wandered into a restaurant in Ahmedabad after a hard day's campaign work and ordered snacks and beverages. Then: '...Seconds later, a bright light lit up the area. The troop looked up and lo—there stood the omnipresent videographer, recording the scene for the benefit of Chief Election Commissioner, TN Seshan. And before you could say "cheese pakoras", the politico and his aides jumped up from their seats and rushed out of the restaurant, their hunger and thirst intact!...'[86]

It concludes that it was so because they really had no idea where the model code began or ended. And that they were afraid that the restaurant bill would add to the candidate's election expenses.

Maharashtra went to polls on 9 and 12 February. The overall turnout was nearly 72 per cent. Overall, the phase was described in various papers as 'incident free'.

The Times of India, in an article dated 11 February 1995, reported that more than 75 per cent of voting had happened in Maharashtra on 9 February and that it was a record: 'This record turnout was reported despite the severe restrictions placed on the campaign by the Chief Election Commissioner TN Seshan. In the last assembly elections held in 1990, there was only 62 per cent turnout.'[87]

DID SHARAD PAWAR THREATEN GOOD WORKERS?

A particularly interesting exchange between Sharad Pawar and the ECI happened in this election. In a *Free Press Journal* article, 15 February 1995, he said, 'Once the new government comes to power, an independent inquiry shall be ordered into the alleged misuse of powers vested in them [government officials engaged in elections] by the Election Commission.'[88]

At first glance, it appeared to be a threat. And the same story was reflected in various papers. Threatening election officials is no mean matter, but there was no point jumping the gun to make a response; you could trust the press to mess it up at times. So, while making it clear that the commission would not take kindly to any threat issued to officials for having done their respective jobs, an effort was made to ascertain the correct picture.

---

[86]Thacker, N.P., 'Candidates Beware, Big Brother Seshan Is Watching', *Sunday Observer*, 12 February 1995.

[87]'Voter Turnout Was Maharashtra's Highest', *The Times of India*, 11 February 1995.

[88]'Election Code Enforcement, Pawar Threatens Bureaucrats', *Free Press Journal*, 15 February 1995.

The ECI wrote to the chief secretary, Sharad Upasani, on 15 February, asking him to submit his report by 17 February. In the report, clarification was sought about the 'the exact language of the statements made by the Chief Minister and any of his cabinet colleagues, the names of those who made each of the statements and the occasion and forum' as well as the 'names and designations of officers against whom the members of the political executive have expressed the reported views relating to implementation of the model code of conduct and standing instructions of the Commission'.

On 16 February, presspersons asked me about the issue. I informed them that I had already written to the Maharashtra government, seeking clarification. I also added that the elections were not over in the state, and the commission could stop the counting of ballots if the government had really victimized the officials engaged in poll duty, as had been reported.

I said the same thing when I addressed a voters' awareness programme in Puri, stating that the ECI would act if a government displayed this attitude towards honest officials who were performing their duty as per the law.

The same day, the Maharashtra CM issued his clarifications through a press statement and it was reported in the papers the next day. A *The Times of India* article on 17 February 1995 reported CM Pawar as having communicated that no such thing was intended; and that he would not hesitate to withdraw anything he said if it even gave such an impression. '[...] Mr Pawar noted that the state administration had conducted the poll in the best possible manner, setting an example in the country... Their work was praiseworthy and the suggestion of victimisation was ridiculous [...]'[89] Likewise, all the ministers were queried by the chief secretary, and they had confirmed that none of them had said anything of that kind.

The article went on to say that certain complaints were made to him during the campaign; seemingly, some officers had indulged in excess. As a result of excessive enthusiasm, they seemed to have done things

---

[89]'I Was Misquoted, Says Sharad Pawar', *The Times of India*, 17 February 1995.

like not allowing people to move from one constituency to another, preventing some rural supporters from entering a city, harassing a newspaper employees because it had predicted victory for a certain candidate, and so on. Pawar is reported to have said that the new government would look into it, sieve out the frivolous complaints and forward the genuine ones to the commission for appropriate action.

An explanation on those lines was received by the commission from the chief secretary and that was the end of the issue. The counting went ahead on schedule.

Arunachal Pradesh went to the polls along with Maharashtra in this period. There were no problems associated with these elections. As I had said, the voter turnout was high in Maharashtra and Arunachal Pradesh did not really figure amongst the states that posed challenges for the ECI in terms of security and electoral disturbances. The counting was scheduled to happen after the completion of polls in Bihar.

These elections showed the improvements that had come to characterize elections. A summary appeared in an article in *The Pioneer* on 26 February 1995. It carried a complaint though, that elections had lost their fizz. But it did point out vital positives that are relevant to the socioeconomic realities of our nation: 'The one thing TN Seshan has proved incontrovertibly is that the country's police and administrative officials are not as incompetent and supine as they are generally perceived to be. A modicum of independence and threat of immediate disciplinary action are sufficient to get the otherwise creaking administrative machinery to function smoothly with incredible results.'[90]

As an example, the article cited the district administration in Ranchi, which even refused permission to the PM for addressing an election rally, effectively postponing it, due to violation of procedural norms. Similarly, it spoke about the much-maligned bureaucrats of Bihar who took action against the Congress candidates for election violations. Then it cited how in Gujarat, Bholabhai Patel was arrested

[90]Ashraf, Ajaz, et al., 'Seshan Phobia: A Report on How and Why Elections Have Lost Their Fizz Today, and What it Means for the Country', *The Pioneer*, 26 February 1995.

by a mere sub-inspector. And how the car belonging to K. Makwana, another minister, was impounded by the district administration. In the author's assessment, such actions would have been considered foolhardy even just about five years earlier. It quoted a candidate Gurmeet Singh who said that because the candidates of major parties were on a shoestring budget enforced by the ECI, he stood a chance of winning. According to him, his rivals were also forced to do door-to-door campaigning. The article also said that people were happy because it was for the first time that these big candidates and voters were in a position to know each other. According to the author, if this reduction in gap between voter and candidate was to continue, it would be a sign that the Indian democracy had truly matured.

Eventually, in that phase of elections, in Maharashtra, the Shiv Sena–BJP alliance got a combined figure that was just under the halfway mark, and eventually formed the government. In Gujarat, the BJP by itself formed government. Orissa went the Congress way. It was considered some consolation for PM Rao who, until then, had many more losses than wins.

CHALLENGES IN THE BIHAR ELECTIONS

Bihar was different when compared to the other states. It stood up to my anticipation that it would be the most difficult test for me.

The CM of Bihar was the one who had challenged me on the voter ID cards issue and obtained a verdict in his favour. He used every bit of the mileage he got from this verdict in his campaign. I was variously demonized and accused of colluding with his opponents. With this and with several cases going against the ECI in the Supreme Court, the task of holding elections in Bihar seemed to have gotten even more difficult.

As elections neared, the security assessment of Bihar by the ECI showed that the situation was rather grim. The ECI needed more time. The evolving situation indicated that the security apparatus had to be beefed up and it would take longer to get the necessary arrangements in place.

Bihar was to originally go to elections on 7 and 9 March. On 1 March, an order was passed, postponing the elections to 11, 15 and 19 March. In the order passed on 1 March, I clearly stated the inadequacies that lead to the postponement. This would mean that the elections in Bihar would happen after the day assigned for counting in the other states. Further, a short spell of President's Rule would be needed as the new government would not be formed before the constitutionally mandated five years of the previous government was over.

The postponement was challenged in the Supreme Court and the two-judge bench ruled in the ECI's favour. So, the elections happened according to the new schedule.

The first phase turned out to be one riddled with many instances of violence. Our internal sources of information and the media reflected that it was so. So, a day later on 13 March, the situation was reviewed again and it was decided that the remaining two phases were to be divided into four phases; however, the elections were to end as originally scheduled.

These latter four phases were relatively peaceful. The elections went on as per the new schedule and Lalu Prasad Yadav became the CM once again.

In the meantime, a lot of action was happening in the Supreme Court.

Through the Broken Glass

NINETEEN

INTENSE BATTLE AT THE APEX OF
THE JUDICAL KARMABHOOMI

In the year 1993, under Chief Justice M.N. Venkatachaliah, the Supreme Court had given me two significant interim orders which, as I have indicated earlier, helped in taking the election reform process forward with considerable force. So, one can say that the ECI flourished under Justice Venkatachaliah's watch. But, under the next Chief Justice Aziz Mushabber Ahmadi's watch, which commenced nearly at the end of my fourth year in office, (around October 1994), things did not go quite in the ECI's favour. In fact, out of six significant decisions in which the ECI was involved, from January to July 1995, five went against it. The only one that went in favour of the commission was the one related to the postponement of the Bihar elections, about which I mentioned in the last chapter. Incidentally, the one that went in favour of the ECI was the only one in which the Chief Justice himself was not on the bench.

The first case was that of the voter ID card issue, the verdict on which had come on 17 January 1995, and about which much has already been written.

Ten days later, on 27 January, it was the High Court of Bombay, which ruled that electors in Maharashtra who did not have voter ID cards, would be allowed to vote, provided their names figured in the electoral rolls and their identity was not disputed. This case, too, was not appealed against in the Supreme Court by the ECI.

Ten days later, on 6 February, the Supreme Court passed a major judgement on the issue of aliens in Delhi. As many as 42,000 names had been earlier deleted from the electoral rolls for various reasons related to insufficient proof of them being residents. The High Court of Delhi had earlier upheld this order as justified. But on 6 February, the Supreme Court turned it down and the names were restored.

Along with this verdict, the three-judge bench, comprising Chief Justice Ahmadi, and Justices N.P. Singh and Sujatha Manohar, also quashed the show cause notices issued to 20,000 residents of Paharganj and Jama Masjid localities of Delhi, which, in turn, had sought to remove their names from the electoral rolls.

The very next day, on 7 February, the Supreme Court passed an order disallowing the use of the services of employees working in nationalized banking and insurance sectors.

Two weeks down the line, on 24 February, a bench headed by Chief Justice Ahmadi declined to grant stay to a restraining order passed by the High Court of Bombay. A Congress candidate had not submitted a letter of authorization from the Congress president. Based on a complaint, the ECI had decided to decline the 'hand' symbol to the candidate. This was stayed by the High Court and the stay was not vacated by the Supreme Court.

On 2 March, there was one case that went in the ECI's favour. It was concerning Bihar. As discussed earlier, the two-judge bench said that the commission's decision of postponement of elections was justified.

While all this was happening, the case of two additional election commissioners was being heard in the Supreme Court. Let us see how the arguments progressed.

THE AFFIDAVIT BY G.V.G. KRISHNAMURTY

On 31 January 1995, the issue came up in the Supreme Court, after a long break. The interim order of the Supreme Court given on 15 November 1993 in respect of the status of the two election commissioners was in effect at that time, and as directed in that verdict, a constitutional bench of five judges took up the matter in 1995. G.V.G. Krishnamurty, one of the appointed election commissioners, submitted an affidavit in the court that day.

Challenging my claim that Article 324 of the Constitution vests all powers of the ECI in the CEC, he said that the Constitution envisaged the ECI as a collective constitutional authority, similar to the council of ministers or judiciary of the Supreme Court. His contention was that in such instances, the power is vested not in any individual authority as in the case of the president of India or the attorney general, but in a collective body that exercises power by the principle of unanimity or majority. He contested the claim that the principle of majority can operate only among equals and not unequals. He said that even the PM or Chief Justice is considered first among equals. Besides this, he also levelled certain allegations about the way I had treated him.

WHAT I SAID IN MY COUNTER AFFIDAVIT

I emphasized that the position of the CEC, under the Constitution, is not primus inter pares, i.e. first among equals, but is intended to be placed in a distinctly higher position. I also said, 'I, in any event, do not admit that the Election Commission is a collective constitutional authority. I also do not admit that the principle of majority can prevail in the scheme of functioning of all such collective constitutional authorities. The position in law is that an election commissioner is not equal to the CEC.'

I said that the principle of majority as the basis for a democratic system, as has been advocated by Krishnamurty in his affidavit, was not universal and, in fact, it was not uniform to all institutions even in this country. I also pointed out that the election commissioners were not intended to be 'a permanent part of the Election Commission of India' and this was clear from the proceedings in the constituent assembly.

I had said that the appointment was not valid in law and was unconstitutional, and that Parliament lacked the legislative competence to amend the 1991 amendment to the Election Commission (Conditions of Service of Election Commissioners and Transaction of Business) Act, 1991 by inserting two Sections (9 and 10) that indicated how business would be done within the ECI.

As for personal charges made against me by Krishnamurty, I denied them. I said that I had neither insulted or humiliated nor physically obstructed Krishnamurty from discharging his official responsibilities. I also denied the charge that an exorbitant legal fee of ₹1 crore was being paid to the lawyers and added that the entire budget of the ECI was only ₹2.5 crore.

THE HEARING

Day one of the hearing

The hearing commenced on 2 February 1995, and it had to be opened by my counsel as it was my petition. The CEC's position was defended by G. Ramaswamy, N.A. Palkhiwala and Kapil Sibal, amongst others.

Reflecting on what I had submitted in my affidavit, Ramaswamy said that even a constitutional amendment could not validate a multi-member ECI, as it violated the basic structure of the Constitution. He pointed out that in the Dhanoa case, the apex court had noticed the difference in conditions of service of the CEC and the election commissioners. He pointed out that the CEC had the constitutional protection while the others did not have it. Further, according to a principle applied in modern democracies, including ours, the CEC's terms of service could not be varied to his disadvantage during his tenure and the Election Commission (Conditions of Service of Election Commissioners and Transaction of Business) Act, 1991 had done that. He also pointed out that the CEC could not be placed on par with the other election commissioners, who could be removed on his recommendation.

An article in *The Pioneer*, dated 3 February, in its report of the proceedings, read: 'Mr Palkhiwala said that as he had just come from Bombay he would address the court after Mr Ramaswamy. "Clients who can afford it can bring any number of distinguished lawyers. While we will certainly hear them, we will not allow them to repeat any argument." Chief Justice Ahmadi said...'[91]

The report also said that citing the example of how courts worked, the Chief Justice wanted to know from my counsel as to what was the difficulty in applying the principle of majority when unanimity could not be achieved.

It is instructive to read the reports of that day (3 February 1995) in the *Business Standard*, *The Telegraph* and *The Sentinel* and one can get a good picture of the happenings of the day.

Day two of the hearing

The next day, *The Pioneer*, in its report, said: 'In an unprecedented treatment of one of the foremost jurists in India, the Supreme Court on Friday disallowed Mr. NA Palkhiwala from addressing the Constitution Bench before his colleague G Ramaswamy had concluded his arguments in support of Chief Election Commissioner TN Seshan's petition.'[92]

Palkhiwala said on that day that he wished to draw the attention of the judges to the 'lowest nadir of rampant corruption' because of which the two additional members were appointed in a 'wholly mala fide manner'. He expressed that Sections 9 and 10 of the Amendment Act were bad and that we need not waste judicial time over it.

But Chief Justice Ahmadi asked Palkhiwala to bear in mind that the other side had to be heard as well and that it was not possible to proceed in a compartmentalized manner.

When Palkhiwala persisted, he was told that he was given a chance to open the arguments on the first day and that he had preferred to come after Ramaswamy. The bench asked him to wait for his turn while remarking that he seemed to be in a hurry to leave, after which they asked Ramaswamy to resume.

My counsel submitted that Article 324 of the Constitution placed the CEC on a higher footing than the two election commissioners. He quoted Dr B.R. Ambedkar, stating that the 'Election Commission should be irremovable by the executive by a mere fiat. We have therefore

---

[91]"Multi-Member EC Violative of Constitution: Seshan', *The Pioneer*, 3 February 1995.
[92]"Palkhiwala Not Allowed to Address Bench', *The Pioneer*, 4 February 1995.

given the Chief Election Commissioner the same status as a Supreme Court judge so far as his removability is concerned...'[93]

Ramaswamy also pointed out that in the constituent assembly debates, Dr Ambedkar had said, 'We, of course, do not propose to give the same status to other members of the Commission.'[94]

Therefore, he said that the intentions of appointing and the manner of appointing—as if on the sly, suddenly out of the blue, without giving the CEC any indication and in the CEC's absence—were mala fide. It showed that one of the first acts of the newly appointed commissioner, Krishnamurty, was to countermand the CEC's instruction to engage a senior counsel (Ramaswamy) for a case concerning postponement of the Delhi elections.

The Assam Tribune on 4 February reported about the details about the judges' criticism of the two election commissioners and the CEC. The article read, 'There is nothing to choose between both the sides [Chief Election Commissioner and Election Commissioners] as they have been behaving in an equally undignified manner not befitting their high constitutional office.'[95]

This could have very well been a take on the fact that I had, in my original appeal, described what had happened on 11 October 1993 in that particular meeting. I, of course, had made every effort to avoid opening my mouth. I presented this as an indication to show mala fides in the intention of the authors of the amendment in the law that brought in the two gentlemen. But in the expressed opinion of the judges on that day, it appeared to them that both contesting parties, including me, were trying to exhibit our knowledge in the use of the English language by the use of adjectives and expletives. They thought that both parties were equally responsible for using 'non-court, unparliamentary language' in their pleadings.

---

[93]Dhamija, Dr Ashok, 'Security of Tenure to Two Election Commissioners at Par with Chief Election Commissioner', Tilak Marg, 24 July 2020, https://bit.ly/3k0Cd5E. Accessed on 12 January 2023.
[94]Ibid.
[95]'SC Dismayed over Conduct of CEC, EC Members', *The Assam Tribune*, 4 February 1995.

Day three of the hearing

The hearing resumed after a three-day break, and Ramaswamy concluded by saying that the Act was arbitrary and with mala fide intentions. Thereafter, Palkhiwala presented his arguments.

The Indian Express reported that the bench wanted the counsel to answer two important questions: 'If the constitution envisages a multi-member Election Commission, how does it conduct its business? How should a situation where the Chief Election Commissioner is placed above the Election Commissioners be reconciled with the provision in the relevant Act that decisions are to be taken on the basis of a majority?'[96]

They said the court wanted legal arguments on how the Constitution envisaged a multi-member commission to function and whether the procedure for business had to be evolved by law or by the commission itself.

The crux of Palkhiwala's argument was that if the Constitution said that the CEC was responsible and he is answerable (to the Indian system, like the Supreme Court judge), and if Parliament passed an order saying that these two election commissioners will join the CEC, and then if it also says that the majority decision would matter, and then effectively the order ties up the hands of the CEC, the CEC could recommend the removal of the two election commissioners. While the two continued staying in office, the new scheme made it possible for them to reduce the CEC to a mere figurehead, effectively making him answerable for what 'they' would do. As such, it puts paid to the intentions of the Constitution itself by kind of overriding it. He said that Parliament had no power to pass any law putting the CEC and the commissioners on the same footing. 'The Chief Election Commissioner's views must prevail,' he said, likening the multi-member commission to the union cabinet where the PM can override the majority view, a feature well established in the Constitution.

Palkhiwala said that even if it were to be assumed that the

---

[96]'SC Refuses to Defer Verdict on Seshan's Plea', *The Indian Express*, 8 February 1995.

enlargement of the commission was valid, Sections 9 and 10 were invalid, as they were beyond the competence of Parliament. In his view, Parliament had no power to pass any law on how 'the business of the Election Commission shall be transacted'. Therefore, he said that Sections 9 and 10 of (Conditions of Service) Amendment Act, 1994, were invalid and void.

He added that it is not for the court to go into how they function, and that it is best to leave the conduct of business of the commission to the commission itself. He pointed out that only if wrong decisions were taken, the Supreme Court had the right to correct it.

The Chief Justice told Palkhiwala 'not to proceed on the assumption that all he is doing is good'. He frowned at my withdrawing of the commission's cases 'every time a case has been put to test'. He cited the PIC case as an example, that I had withdrawn it when it was challenged in court.

Mr Palkhiwala said that I had tried to do the right things but may be in the wrong in certain cases. He presented that my intentions were above board. Asking for the present interim orders to continue, he also requested the judges to defer the verdict until I retired in December 1996. The Supreme Court refused to accept Palkhiwala's suggestion. The Chief Justice countered that it was a petition that the CEC himself had filed, so how could he not take it up?

The bench said that they were all concerned with cleanliness in the election process and that the counsel should not give the impression that his arguments had to be accepted, or else the court would be perpetuating the filth.

The Telegraph highlighted that I was threatening with resignation. It said, '[...] Mr. Seshan's counsel, Mr. Nani A Palkhiwala, told the bench that "removal of the Chief Election Commissioner's powers amounted to a removal from office and resignation is one way out for a self-respecting man".'[97]

The proceedings in the court, especially the intervention of the judges on that day, indicated ominous signs. Let me explain. Consider

---

[97]'Seshan Threatens to Resign', *The Telegraph*, 8 February 1995.

the remark made by the Chief Justice on my propensity to withdraw when put to test. It was as if I was knowingly doing wrong and that just before things went to 'test', I would withdraw.

First of all, when my counsel said that the court could always correct me if I went wrong, he meant that decisions made by the ECI were subject to judicial review, except for such instances where the election in question was in process. In this case, the intentions of the ECI to implement the law, as it has interpreted it in all righteousness, and in accordance with precedence, need not be doubted. The judiciary may later give a different interpretation of the law and therefore strike down an order of the ECI as the case may be. This is different from the case where the CEC may have not applied his mind and/or he may have given a decision with mala fide intentions. If this be the case and if it were taken up in the courts, how would the CEC react? Perhaps, as if the CEC was caught in the act. And therefore, he would concede, saying that he had indeed given the wrong decision (I am deliberately exaggerating here). My counsel clearly meant the former case of judicial review; however, the judge surely did not interpret it as judicial review.

Then again, the judge took the example of the voter ID issue and said I had withdrawn. Again, in this case, did I withdraw knowing that I had done wrong and out of fear that I would fail the test of legality?

In the voter ID case, I withdrew a legitimate order not because it was wrong or because it would not stand the test of law, rather I was indicating a way to bypass an impending constitutional crisis by withdrawing my 'legitimate' order and imposing an extension of time with a new deadline. The order would not have failed a test of law. So, an implicit accusation that I withdrew in this case as I was caught on the wrong foot in law was, again, not apt.

Considering both points, it was evident that the judge was not reading the situation correctly at that time, as far as my intention was concerned; once the intentions are questioned, it has the distinct possibility of colouring the outcome of the case we are contesting.

By now, the readers must have sensed, from the reactions of the judges, as to what view they had about me. The questions that arose in my mind were: Would this influence the judges to pass a harsh verdict against me? Would thoughts about my personality influence their decision on a constitutional question? One could only hope.

Day four of the hearing

The next day went relatively easy on the commission, but there was some 'advice' that the three commissioners can sit together and amicably work out how they intend to function together. If they can allocate work between the two election commissioners and the CEC, if they can do it themselves and inform the court, then the court need not have to lay down norms governing the business of the ECI. 'There is no harm in trying it. After all this has not been tried by them so far' is what they said.

Attorney General Milon K. Banerjee told the court that the interim order, giving the CEC overall and complete control of the ECI work, came in the way. To that, the Chief Justice pointed out that the constraint of working under such an order would not be necessary if the three of them work out something. He suggested that I invite the other two gentlemen over for tea in order to resolve issues. Palkhiwala submitted that if the concept of equality was given up, then all things would recede in the background. And referring to the court's suggestions, Palkhiwala submitted that it was of great importance and once the present elections are over, then the CEC will consider the court's advice.

Jurist Ram Jethmalani, counsel for Mr Cho Ramaswamy, editor of *Thuglak*, also made representations on that day. Cho Ramaswamy had also filed a petition against the appointment of the two election commissioners on his own, in public interest. So, the cases were clubbed together.

The press members who covered the proceedings did a fair job and a look at the press reports spanning around three weeks in this period throw good light on how the case was fought. The hearings continued for a few more days till 17 February, when the final arguments were made.

Final day of the hearing

On 17 February, the final day of hearing, Ramaswamy concluded the arguments by saying the other election commissioners were only to assist the CEC and hence could not be equated in position and powers.

He argued that the CEC had different responsibilities and powers, all of which placed him above others, and he, as the chairman of the multi-member body held supreme control. Pointing to the hierarchy in the ECI, Ramaswamy said the other election commissioners were above the regional commissioners and the CEC was above both the election commissioners and regional commissioners. He emphasized that the CEC had 'veto' powers in the commission and even if one presumed that 'all are equal' in a multi-member body, the CEC, as chairman, could 'veto the decisions of the majority'.

He argued that the three commissioners were not equal and did not wield the same powers. 'Even if so (that is, even if the election commissioners enjoyed equal status with the CEC and had the same powers), the voice of the Chief Election Commissioner shall prevail finally.'

Mr Ramaswamy contended that if the CEC was made only a 'clerical chairman' of the commission, that would be inconsistent with the scheme and background of the Constitution. 'The apex court would be writing a new Constitution,' he said, if it held that the CEC and other election commissioners were equal and the CEC was the chairman of the multi-member commission only to chair meetings.

'The history of jurisprudence,' Ramaswamy said, 'has that a chairman in a commission like the ECI is not just a clerical chairman' to fix dates for meetings and preside over them.

On that day, Ramaswamy also made it a point to say that the ECI was like a tribunal and that its actions would always be subject to judicial review and that the CEC was not on par with a Supreme Court judge. He admitted that only the procedure of removal of the CEC was equated to that of a Supreme Court judge, that is, the CEC could only be impeached and not removed at the 'will' of the executive.

A report in *The Assam Tribune*, detailing the happenings of the final day, read: '...Earlier the court rejected a plea by Ramaswamy for summoning records regarding the appointment of the two ECs MS Gill and GVS Krishnamurty to substantiate his claim that there was no material to warrant their induction into the commission and that their imposition was with the mala fide intention of the government to whittle down his powers.'[98]

The reason the court gave for the denial is that the present case relates to the constitutional interpretation of the powers of the CEC in relation to the election commissioners and as such, it was not necessary. This was a setback for me because my counsels' main contention was that there were no grounds for the appointment of the two election commissioners. And where there is no material justifying the appointment, then it would mean that the appointment was made for 'extraneous collateral purposes of ending the independent functioning of the commission...'

Finally, the Supreme Court reserved judgement after it was informed that there was no breakthrough between the two sides in evolving rules of business for smooth functioning of the commission for the ongoing assembly elections.

The Supreme Court, on its part, asked for the date when the current elections would come to an end. By that, it gave an indication as to when the decision would most likely be given.

With that, the hearing came to an end and it took several months before the verdict was finally given.

TAKING STOCK

Losing many court cases was perhaps a string of coincidences, or was there a method in the madness? Some might say that it was a reflection of the extent to which I was taking wrong decisions. But nobody would like losing a series of cases, as had happened over a period of just over a month. The series of losses were a cause for

---

[98]'SC Reserves Judgment on CEC's Power', *The Assam Tribune*, 17 February 1995.

concern amongst most of my well-wishers. It also brought different kinds of responses from those who had a sense of what was happening. Some said I deserved it, some were unconcerned. But a section of people felt sad at the developments and some were dismal. They felt let down because they assumed that I had thrown in the towel on the voter ID cards case. There were others who expressed that they had lost faith in the judiciary.

For example, *The Economic Times*, on 11 February, reflected the adverse sentiment towards the commission's work. It said that political parties and the Centre were shedding their pliant attitude towards the CEC. And that there was a new willingness among the parties to stand up to the CEC.[99]

The article said that the downslide began on January 17 with the Supreme Court's directions. It said that I was only human and with feet of clay. It went on to add that the court ruling seemed to have emboldened the political forces except for the BJP, which, in the author's view, did not like being on the wrong side of the CEC.

It said that my withdrawal of the voter ID cards issue seemed like a tactic instead of a moral stand and therefore the crusading sheen had lost some of its lustre.

It pointed out: 'After this vital court decision, there have been a stream of verdicts and observations going against the Election Commission and Mr Seshan, the most recent being the court's "advice" to him on January [February] 8 to work with his Election Commissioners.'

The article said that the advice came a few days after the Supreme Court condemned the behaviour of the three commissioners as 'undignified' and that a few days later, it said the CEC did not have 'untrammelled' powers to call for the services of non-government officers (banking/insurance, etc.).

The article went on to say that the Supreme Court being held in high esteem among the people has led to my chastisement being widely accepted.

---

[99]Zaheer, Kamil, 'Supreme Court Shows Seshan Too Has Feet of Clay', *The Economic Times*, 11 February 1995.

But that was one side of the story. I was also receiving moral support from outside the court. Even while the court case was being heard, people were going out of their way to appreciate my work and all that I stood for. *The Times of India* reported on 13 February 1995 that I had been awarded the Sulabh Award on the occasion of the silver jubilee of its founding day.[100] Dr Bindeshwar Pathak, founder of the Sulabh Sanitation movement, announcing the award, said: 'Mr Seshan symbolises the yearning of the people for a cleaner public life and strong democratic set-up, a dispensation which alone can ensure growth and fair play in society. His personal initiative in bringing about structural reforms in the system is laudable and praiseworthy.'[101]

Pathak said on that occasion that the elections that were happening at that time were a great departure from the past. It would only be right if photo identity cards are issued to voters; but even in their absence, there has been an improvement in the situation now when contestants show greater restraint and discipline in hurling charge and counter-charges against their rivals. The change is most conspicuous in the states where elections are being held now. For the first time, people are able to vote peacefully and make their choice without fear from rival candidates, who now do door-to-door canvassing, taking democracy to the grassroots.

He added, 'What Seshan has done may be dismissed as trivial or unimportant by the urban intelligentsia. But go to any village in Bihar and see the scope and dimension of change. Earlier, hoodlums used to warn the poor not to be seen anywhere near polling booths.'

It is rather disappointing that the Honourable Supreme Court in its judgement of 17 January 1995 deemed it fit to stay the CEC's directive of 'No I-cards, no elections' which enjoyed the tacit but near-unanimous support of the people of India. The judgement is almost tantamount to not taking the cognizance of the gigantic magnitude of the malaise of corruption in elections, particularly in a state like Bihar. And the daily, *The Times of India*, thought nothing of publishing this critique.

---

[100]'Sulabh Award for Seshan', *The Times of India*, 13 February 1995.
[101]'Seshan Took Democracy to Grassroots', *The Times of India*, 13 February 1995.

TWENTY

THE TWO-COMMISSIONERS VERDICT

With the major elections of the year 1995 being over by 29 March, and the hearing on the two commissioners case having concluded, I went on a leave to USA.

The situation, as far as the powers of the election commissioners were concerned, remained at status quo. The stay by the Supreme Court given in the interim verdict of 15 November 1993 in respect to the two election commissioners case was still in force. Given the situation, when I was going abroad on leave, I did exactly as I had done in the past.

The deputy election commissioner would 'take care' of matters. Signing of papers was not a concern, as there was provision in the law that my secretaries and deputy could sign in my place. Most of all, they could contact me any time through telephone and fax. There was no legal provision for an 'acting' CEC. This issue, if you remember, had cropped up when Rama Devi was appointed as the acting CEC in my predecessor's absence. I had taken up the matter way back in 1991 that this was not lawful. The position had still not changed in 1995. So, my deputy would 'take care', even when no charge was handed over to him. It was a well-oiled system and it worked perfectly fine.

Some four days after I departed for USA, Krishnamurty, and few days later, Dr Gill, filed affidavits in the Supreme Court making a hue and cry claiming that I had handed over the charge to a junior officer and that it was an affront. The media apparently took to this version and went hammer and tongs against my 'arbitrary' act. They had many things to say about my ego and haughtiness. And even before this storm could die down, in the middle of my vacation, the Supreme Court passed its order in the case of the two commissioners.

The gist of it was that the commissioners were indeed equal and Bagga was asked to 'hand over charge' to Gill.

Almost all newspapers carried the story the next day in bold headlines. Some newspapers speculated that I would probably resign; others mainly reported that I was incommunicado. Some of them wrote nasty things, chiefly saying that I was too arbitrary, abrasive and whimsical. While the main contention of these articles was that the ECI's decisions would be tempered with reason henceforth, one particular article even suggested that elections would improve.

OVERVIEW OF THE ACTUAL VERDICT

The verdict was typed out across a 55-page document in the usual way, but a peculiar thing about its physical appearance was that pages 49, 54 and 55 were apparently typed in a different machine than the rest of the document. Next, the arguments presented in the verdict were arranged in a logical order, but the paragraphs were not numbered. The contents in the pages can be roughly summarized as follows:

Relevant Page No.	Content
Page 1	The relevant case numbers and parties involved
Pages 2–8	A narration of happenings: the government issued the ordinance (of 2 October 1993), what changes it brought, appointment of the two election commissioners, objection raised by the CEC and others, the interim order, joining in of some advocate generals, ordinance becoming a law, matter being referred to constitutional bench

Pages 8–9	The actual Article 324 of the Indian Constitution
Pages 10–13	The basis on which the ordinance was being opposed by the CEC and others, and on what basis the opposition was being resisted by the two election commissioners, the government and others
Pages 13–15	'The purpose of the commission' and the 'basic scheme of the composition of the commission' as summarized by the judges from Article 324
Pages 16–39	Deciphering the relative position of the CEC and election commissioners within the commission and the validity of Clauses 9 and 10 of the ordinance (transaction of commission work), finally stating that the ECI was comparable to other commissions, like the UPSC, where members have equal decision-making powers and the CEC was a chairman
Pages 39–49	The question of mala fides; charges levelled by the CEC and the counter-charges by others; if the government thought that a multi-member commission was desirable, the government was certainly not wrong
Pages 49–51	Legislature could definitely make laws in support of the provisions of the Constitution and in case the ordinance has only verbalized a solution which the commission itself would take if it was one with equal members.
Pages 51–53	Remarks about the changes in warrant of precedence involving the CEC and the Attorney General; order to the government to consult with the court when changes affecting the position of judges come into question

Pages 53–54	Raking up the exchanges of 11 October would be akin to washing dirty linen in public, showing the CEC and Shri Krishnamurty in poor light; advised that all must eschew their egos and work in a spirit of camaraderie
Pages 54–55	Ordinance (now law) stands, petitions dismissed, interim order vacated, Bagga hands over charge to Gill till CEC resumes duty
Page 55	Judges sign (CJI, J.S. Verma, N.P. Singh, S.P. Bharucha, M.K. Mukherjee) July 14 1995

THE INTERPRETATION THAT RESULTED IN THE EQUIVALENCE OF THE CEC AND THE ELECTION COMMISSIONERS

If one looks closely, it becomes evident that the arguments in pages 16–39 decided the case in favour of a multi-member commission, with the CEC and the other commissioners having equal vote within the commission. Breaking it up further, this is how the judges went about with the arguments:

Relevant Page No.	Content
Pages 16–18	The CEC and election commissioners made the commission while regional commissioners supported it; election and regional commissioners can be removed only on the recommendation of the CEC; this provision was to ensure that election and regional commissioners were insulated from the executive and may have 'independence of functioning'; their independence cannot be impinged by the CEC himself and he cannot recommend their removal without 'valid reasons which are conducive to the efficient functioning of the Election Commission.'

Pages 18–24	The judges drew from the sub-clauses of Article 324 and also referred to the verdict in the Dhanoa case to say that the idea that a multi-member commission was unworkable must be rejected. The quoted portion of the Dhanoa verdict also pointed out that 'two heads are better than one' and that caution must exist when an institution such as the CEC's has 'excessive uncontrolled power'. They said that the Constitution clearly provides for a multi-member commission. They added that the intended office bearers were high-ranking dignitaries, therefore, faith was placed on them, by the framers of the Constitution, to make it work.
Pages 24–29	They pointed out that because election commissioners are part of the commission and regional commissioners are meant to assist, the former rank higher. As for the relative positions of the CEC and the election commissioners, the judges referred to five points, which the petitioners claimed, indicating that the CEC was higher in status. They concluded through arguments that the service conditions, removability and permanence of the CEC were present for other reasons like 'independence of functioning of election commissioners and regional commissioners' and for continuity of the commission, and cannot be read to indicate that the CEC is superior.
Pages 29–33	To address another issue regarding the chairmanship of the CEC, the judges pointed out that the commission and the CEC are not synonymous. And in the case of a multi-member commission, all the members become part of it and the CEC is only the chairman. Then referring to a dictionary and legal-dictionaries of the world, the judges concluded that the CEC is only first amongst equals and that his role is to 'preside over meetings, preserve order, conduct of business of the day,' etc., 'for smooth transaction of business'.

Pages 33–34	The judges pointed out that the functions of the ECI are 'essentially administrative', but there were certain adjudicative and legislative functions as well. They then argued that if the election commissioners are part of the commission, 'it stands to reason that they must be part of the decision-making', otherwise, the CEC's superiority would render the election commissioners 'non-functional or ornamental'. This, in their view, was not the intention of Article 324 and as such, the contention that the election commissioners are mere advisors must be rejected.
Page 34	Protection extended to the CEC as regards the conditions of service is not the same as extended to the election commissioners; but this, the judges said, was not a sufficient condition to say that the final word was with the CEC, as it would reduce the election commissioners to mere advisors.
Pages 35–37	The judges pointed out that Article 324 did not say how the business in the multi-member commission was to be transacted. To fill this gap and seeing the bitter experiences of the past (when there were two additional commissioners), the ordinance sought to include two Sections (9 and 10) to state how business is to be transacted. They went on to conclude that a claim that these two clauses destroyed the two safeguards for the CEC (irremovability and adverse variation of service conditions) 'does not cut ice'. The claim that the two election commissioners will join hands to render the CEC non-functional was 'unwarranted'. Truly speaking, they said it was about inadequate leadership on the part of the CEC in a multi-member commission. The claim for protection of the two safeguards, they said, was another way of saying that the CEC should have the final word, which, in turn, would render the election commissioners ornamental.

Pages 37–38	i. The claim that Sections 9 and 10 have a valid nexus with the two safeguards was a repetition of the argument that a multi-member commission could not function and that the 'Constitution makers have erred in providing for it'.
	ii. It was the same as seeking exclusive decision-making powers and was 'not conducive to democratic principles'.
	iii. The argument that the added provisions constitute a fraud on the Constitution, in as much as they are designed and calculated to defeat the very purpose of having an ECI (to hold elections independent of the government in power), makes no sense at all.
	iv. 'And to say that the CEC would have to suffer the humiliation of being overridden by two civil servants is to ignore the fact that the present CEC was himself a civil servant before his appointment as the CEC.'
Pages 38–39	Comparing with other public institutions and multi-member bodies, like the UPSC, national commission for SC/ST and parliamentary committees, the judges said that 'it is difficult to accept the broad contention that a multi-member commission is unworkable'. The office bearers must 'cooperate, appreciate and respect each other's point of view'.

JUDGES' REMARKS ABOUT THE QUESTION OF MALA FIDES

Pages 39–42	The judges mentioned the details of my writ petition where I had enumerated the actions taken by me that the central government did not like, and my contention that this resulted in the ordinance and the appointment of the election commissioners. The judges also mentioned the incidents after the election commissioners joined, but only in passing without giving details.
Pages 42–44	The judges mentioned the central government's counter that the ordinance and the appointments were the outcome of a process that was ongoing in which various committees and public forums demanded for a multi-member commission; the ordinance was issued in public interest.
Page 44	The judges mentioned the counter affidavits filed by the election commissioners and a detailing of five charges made by Krishnamurty about how I was trying to throw my weight around on various matters vis-à-vis the judiciary and judges.
Page 45	The judges mentioned the Attorney General, pointing out that the government was within its right to appoint election commissioners, and it was not a justifiable matter. 'It cannot be said that failure to consult the CEC before the appointing the two election commissioners vitiates the appointment'.
Pages 45–46	Petitioner of SLP No. 16940 of 1993's views on my work, including that 'far from advancing the cause of free and fair elections, resulted in hardships to the people as well as the system.' And concluding with the remark that 'the style of functioning of the present CEC itself is sufficient reason to constitute a multi-member commission' so that the check and balance works to 'ensure proper decision-making'.

Pages 46–48	By enumerating various examples, the judges took to the view of the government that the appointment of election commissioners was part of an ongoing process. In conclusion, they said, 'It cannot, therefore, be said that the idea was suddenly pulled out of a bag. If such a nexus is to weigh, the CEC would continue to act against the ruling party to keep the move for a multi-member Commission at bay.' The judges denied there was any malice or that the 'persons were being appointed with the sole object of eroding the independence of the CEC'.
Page 48	They also 'incidentally' mentioned that: i. My decisions had evoked a mixed response. ii. I had revoked decisions when they were unsustainable in court. iii. The Supreme Court had to caution me 'to exercise restraint on more than one occasion', as my utterances were abrasive. iv. All this gave the impression that the CEC was keen to project his own image. v. That I had very often been in the newspapers and magazines and on television cannot be denied.
Page 48	'In this backdrop, if the government thought that a multi-member body was desirable, the government certainly was not wrong and its action cannot be described as mala fide. Subsequent events would suggest that the government was wholly justified in creating a multi-member commission.'
Page 49	Elaborating on the 'subsequent events', the judges said that: i. The CEC has been seen in a commercial on TV and in newspaper advertisements.

| | ii. The CEC has addressed the press and 'is reported' to have said that he would utilize the balance of his tenure to form a political party to fight corruption and the like. |
| | iii. The judges said that serious doubts may arise regarding the CEC's decisions 'if it is suspected' that he has political ambitions and concluded that 'it would appear' that the CEC was 'totally oblivious to a sense of decorum and discretion' that the high office required. |

DID THE VERDICT TURN THE MALA FIDES TABLE ON ME?

The judges more or less said that there was no merit in my arguments that the intention of appointing the election commissioners was not above board. To show proof, I had heavily relied on the happenings of 11 October 1993 when the two election commissioners and I had met. But the judges said that Gill did not concur with my version of what transpired between Krishnamurty and me. And the judges said that they deliberately did not go into the happenings of that day, as it would unnecessarily show both Krishnamurty and me in poor light.

The judgement also highlighted some of the things I had done, or I was accused of having done. Some statements were from those contesting my position and others were by the judges themselves, but nowhere did the judges pass assertive judgments on my personality— very gracious of them. For example, they said 'it would appear' that I was totally oblivious of a sense of decorum. They did not say, 'The CEC was oblivious of a sense of decorum'. If at all, the only implied assertions were that I did not carry the other election commissioners along (lack of leadership skills) and that the exchange between Krishnamurty and me was not worth mentioning, as it was not how 'high officials' behaved. It is like saying that I had behaved in an undignified fashion or something like that.

There were also some 'facts' that the judges pointed out, which were mostly generalizations and were barely incident specific. These were in pages 48 and 49, and we can only speculate what incidents the judges were referring to. For example, the judges said that I withdrew cases when they were found unsustainable in the courts of law; we earlier saw how this was a generalization that carried only half the truth.

The other issue was about my abrasive utterances about the judiciary; maybe they were referring to an incident connected to a talk I gave in Orissa. The press had misreported that I had cast aspersions on the judiciary. When the judges read it, they expressed their displeasure to my counsel. The judges withdrew their criticism when they found a recording of the speech with no such remark about them. But this withdrawal was not reported as forcefully as the actual criticism was. Besides this, I do not remember any significant incident where I was pulled up by the judges for saying something abrasive about them or the judiciary except, maybe, some comments made by the judges during the arguments in this very case. In fact, if you refer to the times just after the order of 2 August 1993, I had received direct praise. On 8 August 1993, *The Indian Express* had reported: 'Venkatachaliah declared that while using the figure of speech "flexing his muscles" for Seshan he had "spoken with great concern and sympathy for the plight of the Election Commission".'[102]

As for me appearing in a TV commercial, well, it had to do with promoting 'vegetarianism'. The other had to do with the TVS Scooty advertisement that appeared in print media. In this instance, I had been invited to witness the launch and was photographed standing next to the new scooter. The owner took the opportunity and flashed it across the print media—what could I do about that? As for lectures and interviews, I enjoyed unprecedented popularity, which came to me on its own. I did not break any law and was putting my time to good use. As long as the commission's work was not compromised, and as long as I was not breaking any laws, I did not see why I could not use my time in that manner. But the judges apparently were not sympathetic to this point of view. 'Bureaucrats are not to be seen or heard...'—that is the line of thinking in which all that I

---

[102]'Seshan Lauded for His Stand by CJ', *The Indian Express*, 8 August 1993.

did could be seen in poor light. But would that apply to a CEC who is a constitutional authority?

THE CONSTITUTIONAL SIGNIFICANCE OF THE VERDICT

At the heart of the points made in favour of the multi-member commission, which the judges said was envisioned by the Constitution, seems to be the argument that if the election commissioners are part of the commission unlike the regional commissioners, and if they are senior to the latter, then 'it stands to reason' that they, as part of the commission, must have a say in the decision-making. Or else, their presence in the commission would be 'ornamental'. This argument, 'or else the election commissioner's presence would be ornamental', has been used to kill most of the counter-arguments.

They read from the clauses and sub clauses in Article 324 of the Constitution and came to the conclusion. Ultimately, they insisted that the ECI should be seen as similar to various bodies, like the UPSC for instance. The designation of the CEC as 'chairman' and the technical definition of 'chairman' in dictionaries, both legal and otherwise, in their view, confirmed this.

Much debate is possible on the forwarded arguments and the paradigm of the forwarded arguments leading to this conclusion, but that need not be dug into. Instead, we shall take an objective look at certain implications of things said in the verdict.

An important assertion in the verdict was that the ECI is predominantly an advisory body and not an executive authority. This they said by disagreeing with the judges in the Dhanoa case who had said the opposite: '...the Election Commission which is not merely an advisory body but an executive one...' For example, the Chief Justice of the Supreme Court takes care of the administrative matters of the judicial system in the Supreme Court and the concerned staff of the Supreme Court. The CEC, in parallel, also takes care of the administration of the ECI and its staff. But in addition, the CEC also administers the entire election process when it happens, and that involves officials in the millions, all of them tasked to take on an important executive task—elections. So, are the CJI and the CEC comparable on administrative matters? And yet the verdict calls the CEC an advisory body and not an executive one.

NEW CHECKS AND BALANCES THAT EMPOWER
THE GOVERNMENT

Another significant outcome of the verdict relates to an additional balance that the judges culled out, which in their view is embedded in the provisions of Article 324 of the Constitution. Checks and balances are provided in the system to ensure that if there are mala fides, other agencies in the set-up act as counter-measures to check arbitrary misuse of power. So, what are the checks and balances that come into play in respect to the ECI?

So, if the PM represents the entire executive on one hand, on the other hand, we have the CEC who becomes the executive for the sake of elections. Consider both having good intention and bearing. In such an instance, there is no need for a check, and the two of them will do good for the nation. If some fault occurs, then people can surely appeal to the courts (only after the elections are over) and right the wrongs.

Then, consider both the PM and the CEC having mala fide intentions. In this case, let's say the nation is doomed, but all hope is not lost because the citizens could still appeal to the judiciary.

The question of checks and balances truly come into play when there are instances of mala fide on either side.

1. **PM acting mala fide and the CEC being righteous:** In this case, the built-in check for balancing is that the CEC cannot be disturbed in his functioning unless the PM can take on a difficult process similar to removing a Supreme Court judge. So, the CEC is protected in the system as much as a Supreme Court Judge is. An autonomous CEC would thus be able to conduct elections without interference from the PM. Then again, the courts are always there to check faults on both sides.

2. **A righteous PM and an irresponsible CEC:** In this case, the first option of judicial review of the commission's decisions is

the primary check on the behaviour of an errant CEC. The second option articulated in the Constitution is of the removal of the CEC, as in the case of the Supreme Court judges.

Now with the coming of the verdict, a third check came to be identified. According to admissions by the judges, though they have said that they mentioned it 'incidentally', in pages 48 and 49 of the verdict, they say, after pointing out to some of my inequities, 'In this backdrop, if the government thought that a multi-member body was desirable, the government certainly was not wrong.' They added, 'Subsequent events would suggest that the government was wholly justified in creating a multi-member commission.' They then go on to mention some of the other things I had done. A reading of this is a clear admission that the shift from a single member to a multi-member commission is admissible if the aim is to check the behaviour of an errant CEC.

This looks alright to the extent that it checks an errant CEC, but what it also does is that in the earlier case of an errant PM and a righteous CEC, it gives additional power to the PM to cow the CEC down. Had it been the case of two additional election commissioners who are righteous, because of the protection they get from the CEC (they cannot be removed unless the CEC recommends so), they would have acted independently. But if the additional election commissioners have mala fide intentions, and are in cahoots with the PM, then it makes the PM/executive more powerful in the matter of elections than he/they originally was/were.

The question arises as to whether the makers of the Constitution had envisioned this additional check, of adding two more commissioners, so that the CEC can be checked when he is errant. The answer is that even though it was not expressed explicitly, the judgement declared that it was implied in the way the clauses of Article 324 were constructed. In the checks and balances consideration, the PM actually had (and we had not known before this verdict) greater powers, in that, if the PM wished, he could add the kind of election commissioners (mala fide or righteous) he wished to appoint into the commission and have his way.

It was, by all means, an epoch-making judgement. While there were many knee-jerk reactions to it, as I have recounted, there were others that went into the nitty-gritties and reacted after reading between the lines. Here, I have enlisted a set of insights that the print media came up with.

The Economic Times on 17 July 1995 termed it an 'unfortunate verdict': 'Unfortunately, the verdict strengthens the hands of the executive at the cost of the Election Commission. We have frequently expressed concern over the excessive centralisation of power in the hands of the executive, and its subsequent abuse. The court verdict makes the situation worse [...]'[103]

The author further expressed that the ECI can now be cowed down into submission by the executive by cynically appointing political hacks to the ECI, just like governors are appointed.

The *Blitz*, on 22 July 1995, carried a no-holds-barred article by Vir Sanghvi. The point he made was that I have massive public support and that is why the politicians could not use Parliament and the impeachment process to get at me. But he said that the Supreme Court is a different ball game because it does not face voters.[104] 'It is composed of precisely those kind of government servants who loathe Seshan's vanity, despise his rhetoric, and believe that he is a chamcha-turned-megalomaniac...the parallel to Seshan's behaviour would be if the Chief Justice of the Supreme Court told his fellow judges that they were donkeys and that he alone could protect the Constitution.'

Vir Sanghvi added that unlike the government servants who think that I am an 'obnoxious publicity hound', the rest of India does not agree. He said that I remain a public hero. He then went on to speculate about the upcoming elections and suggested a surprise candidate—me! But then in the same breath, he explained why it may not be possible. In his view, I have kicked the politicians around long enough, which is why they would not want me to get on the top seat.

---

[103]'Unfortunate Verdict', *The Economic Times*, 17 July 1995.
[104]Sanghvi, Vir, 'Humpty Dumpty Has a Great Fall', *Blitz*, 22 July 1995.

But then, the author anticipated a hung Parliament in the next elections, and in such a case, he was of the view that parties may have to think twice. If the parties concluded that Seshan could make a difference in winning 30 to 40 urban seats, would they still want to keep me out?

Then there were a series of editorials which, though remained guarded on a matter relating to the Supreme Court, did not mince words when they pointed out facts. One such hard-hitting and critical analysis appeared in the *India Today* on 15 August 1995. It said that there are two main criticisms: the first being that the commission had become more vulnerable to the government than it originally was; and second, that the verdict is less bothered about the substance of the petition than my style of functioning.[105]

The article finally ended with a claim that the judges should have perhaps considered more.

Among the known legal luminaries of the time, Fali S. Nariman said, 'The institution is constitutionally less independent after the judgment.' Eminent lawyer Rajeev Dhavan said, 'The judgment has created the possibility that when the government is unhappy, it can pack or unpack the Election Commission.' Advocate Prashant Bhushan said, 'The Court has undoubtedly been influenced by his abrasive personality and the need to cut him to size. That is why it is said that hard cases make bad law.' C.S. Vaidyanathan, a senior advocate said, 'All the so-called unanswered questions arise from the basic proposition that the CEC's decisions alone must prevail. Once that was rejected by the court, the other arguments do not survive for consideration.'[106]

An interesting insight follows from what Vaidyanathan said. 'As far as the applicant (Seshan) goes', he said, 'it looked as if the decision came first and the explanations were given based on that'. It's like solving a maths theorem by first starting with the answer and working back wards, rejecting some arguments presented as proof because the

---

[105]'Judgement: Main Criticisms', *India Today*, 15 August 1995, https://bit.ly/3Gwb3Lu. Accessed on 13 January 2023.
[106]Ibid.

proof would otherwise imply a different result for the theorem. How so? We have seen how in pages 33 and 34, the judges concluded that 'if the ECs are part of the commission, it stands to reason that they must be part of the decision-making', otherwise the CEC's superiority would render the election commissioner's 'non-functional or ornamental'. Therefore, by implication, the decisions of the CEC are not final and binding.

And I was arguing in the reverse direction. I was offering proofs to show why the CEC's decision should be upheld, but the judges, for the given reason, had concluded that the CEC, having decisive powers, would render the others ornamental. And since the CEC's decision could not be upheld, the conclusion was that the proofs I was offering could not be right. Effectively, all my arguments and proofs were being countered by the reasons offered in pages 33 and 34, as to why the other election commissioners cannot be 'ornamental'.

A PETITION TO THE SUPREME COURT TO REVIEW THE CASE

My reading of the law said that the commissioners cannot be the CEC's equals, but the verdict said no! Even the string of arguments given in the verdict indicated that it was obviously done deliberately, to clip my powers. The question on my mind subsequently was whether I should apply for a review petition. I completed the rest of my stay in USA and returned as originally scheduled. Meantime, I had my personal effects cleared from my office and had some consultations with my friends, some of them being advocates and family. I finally arrived at a conclusion that I would file a review petition.

So, I went to court. I put forth my point raising the bona fides of the appointments of the two additional election commissioners.

On 19 August, I filed the review petition which ran into 112 pages. In it, I contended that the Hindi translation of 'chairman' used by the court was *adhyaksha*. I pointed out that adhyaksha is different from *sabhapati*, which is used for the chairman of the Rajya Sabha. Thereby, I said that an adhyaksha denoted the head of a body while sabhapati meant the head of a meeting. The argument apparently did not cut ice. The court, however, held that the difference was on account of the fact that adhyaksha was the chairman of an *ayog* (commission), while sabhapati is the chairman of a sabha. 'We think the use of these different expressions in the context of the two provisions has no bearing on the relation between the CEC and the ECs', the judges said, adding that they saw no reason to review their judgement.

The very fact that I filed a review petition is enough indication that I did not feel that justice had been delivered. However, the court rather thought that the government was right. Thus, my review petition was rejected, and I had to live with the judgement—the commissioners were my equals. Effectively, another constitutional authority that was superior had turned me down. And with this verdict, new rules came into play.

THE FINAL JUDGEMENT

There is a point though. It is rather obvious that the interpretation of the order of the court indicated that my personal actions 'possibly' had 'bad' in it. A question arises as to how much this 'judgement', if one may call it that, really matters to me as an individual. Or rather, what consequence does the verdict have when one assessed, in absolute terms, the work that happened when I was in office?

There is a higher law that judges us humans in the realm of dharma. In this context, I would like to think of what Jesus Christ has said: 'Man will be judged by his actions.'

Both my *karmabhoomi* (field of action) and my *kartavya* (duty) was with the commission. I was answerable for my actions—what I did or did not do—in the commission. Did I stand up for what was righteous? Did I stand up for what was dharmic?

The courts are the karmabhoomi and the kartavya of the judges and lawyers. As dharma judges me by my 'actions', they too will be judged by all they did in the context of their 'professional roles', including the verdict, which is their 'action', and not mine. And as the Lord says in the Bhagavad Gita, everyone receives the fruit of his actions.

I rest with the thought that I have stood up for what was good for the nation, for the citizens and what is dharmic. My conscience is clear; whatever I did, it was to the best of my abilities. Maybe someone else in my place could have done better, but I did give my best. I acted in the way I believed was right and if I made a mistake, may the Great Lord forgive me. Ultimately, I am answerable to dharma and my conscience more than to anyone else.

I had a lot of friends and well-wishers who put in a word of support for me at that point. Many advised me the course for my future actions. There were a lot of sympathizers who did what they could to encourage me. And while I was still agonizing and pondering over the developments, I happened to meet His Holiness, the Pontiff of the Sringeri Math Sri Bharathi Teertha Mahaswami. What he said made a decisive impact. He used the same words that Lord Rama's mother had used while talking to her son, who was about to leave for exile. As she was bidding farewell, she had said, 'The dharma that you protect will protect you.' This was the message given by His Holinesses to me.

My karmabhoomi had a new set-up. The commission now had three equal members, and this three-member commission had its tasks cut out for itself with the massive general elections coming up the next year.

TWENTY ONE

THE PRIVATE PERSON–PUBLIC
PERSONA CONUNDRUM

As we saw in the last chapter, the judges were kind enough to limit their critique to the 'perceptions' that were 'possible' based on what I had done, but others were not so generous. There were many who directly baited me; but yes, there were also many who praised me.

I could only thank the Divine for not letting me land into trouble directly. For instance, I have told you the story of when I was accused of practising black magic with those stolen flowers. Fortunately, on that particular day, I was not even in Delhi, but in Chennai. So that report was nailed. On another occasion, I was accused of taking favours from a rich industrialist, since I had asked him for a lift in his private aircraft from somewhere in Kerala to Chennai. Fortunately, I had paid by cheque and I had a copy of the same to prove my innocence. There were many other instances like that...

And at the root of all this 'cooking up' was the fact that I was on the receiving end of politicians' ire. And given the politicians' propensity and talent to play to the galleries, I was good bash-up material for them, just as I was good copy material for the journalists. For example, before the Bihar elections in 1995, the CM there was reported to have said in his speeches that the CEC was part of some kind of Brahmin conspiracy against the backward classes. But after the same elections, the very same CM was all praise for how well I did my job. When one looks at what was said about me before and after the elections, it becomes clear that I was drawn into the plot, before elections, as part of the 'spin' that this particular politician used in his own bid for getting elected. So, I might have not conspired after all.

You can be rest assured that apart from the good fortune of wonderful miracles that have happened in my life, I am quite a regular guy. I often say that Palakkad Brahmins come in four types: cooks, crooks, musicians or bureaucrats, and that I was all four of them.

MY ATTITUDE TOWARDS MY CO-WORKERS' WORK

I was generally impatient with inaction, inefficiency and laziness. Even at 63, when I was on the verge of retirement, if I had asked for something to be done on a particular day, I would not be happy for it to be done the next day, unless there was a genuine reason. The same applied to me, too. I never went to sleep even one day with a piece of paper left unattended on my table.

Before giving me the job of cabinet secretary, Rajiv Gandhi had said, 'Mr Seshan, my ministers are all afraid of you. Will you promise to be softer?' I had said, 'No, Sir. I promise that I will not change. And if it doesn't suit you, don't give me the job.'

I have never wanted to hurt people unnecessarily. But if unavoidable, I have never cringed. Whenever I have spoken the truth, I have paid the price.

There is regret. If after speaking harshly to a person, only the harshness remains and the desired outcome is not achieved, what's the point of the harshness?

Once I wrote a balance sheet about myself. I put to myself the question of the single characteristic in me that I would like to change. The answer was my impatient temperament. What was fundamental to me was character, honesty and integrity. My father was totally self-made. He had turned out to be a successful lawyer. He had inherited values from his father, and I had inherited them from him: integrity, efficiency and the shortness of temper (that is not fair).

I have no qualms in admitting that I can be brutally blunt. This probably added to my image of abrasiveness. Finally, being human, there certainly must have been instances of error in judgement years down the line. Looking at those errors through prejudiced eyes would make things look really bad.

MY KARMABHOOMI AND MY MOTIVATION

Around the time when I was through with a major portion of the reform process, a certain K.P. Srivastava from Varanasi wrote a letter to *The Times of India,* in which he said: '[...] Mr TN Seshan is going about his business with Arjuna-like concentration. He has one goal: free, fair and clean elections. No wonder, therefore, that the people of Karnataka have hailed him as the "second ironman after Sardar Patel".'[107]

He also highlighted a range of realities associated with my area of work in the commission—my karmabhoomi so as to say. The letter reflected the contrasting perceptions of the same work: while some called me Hitler, others sang my praises. He talked about the odds I was up against, namely the people in power. He described the scope for action, which was limited to the powers possessed by the CEC in the commission. Then he went on to say that now there was hope that patriotic and honest candidates with no money or muscle power could win elections and be our future rulers. He credited me with creating this possibility. Surely, the nation has not come to a final decision on this yet, but the probability definitely went up. So, that was a fair summary of my karmabhoomi.

MY SPIRITUALITY

As I have said earlier, my spirituality is less about temple-going and worshipping rituals and more of a 24-hour spiritualism. It has to do with the way I live and approach life.

---

[107]Srivastava, K.P., 'Hail Seshan: Letter to the Editor', *The Times of India,* 7 December 1994.

There are three routes to how one can approach religion: One is *karma marg* (the path to action), the second is *bhakti marg* (the path to devotion) and the third is *gyan marg* (the path to knowledge). For me, it is all about the last one. I am religious in the sense that I have an intellectual appreciation of spirituality; it is not sentimental or demonstrative. Going to a temple is not something I make a point of.

The gold bracelet and chain that I wear was given to me by Shri Satya Sai Baba as a form of protection. I neither believed nor disbelieved in Sai Baba. My attitude to most spiritual leaders is that of suspended disbelief. Who am I to believe or disbelieve? They have the ability to attract thousands of people, so they must have something to offer.

I was not and will not be judgemental. I am not a *muni* (sage), but there has been a constant attempt to reach that level. If someone has tried to harm me, then is it necessary to take revenge? The answer is 'no'. God is seated above; He will take care of it. This is the way I see it.

As for the importance I give to spiritual authority, the fact that I gave up the UN job on the Paramacharya's advice and paid ₹96,000 for a plane ride to reach the saint's funeral in time says a lot. That money was a princely sum at that time (approximately ₹1,000,000 of today by gold standards), definitely so for a salaried person like myself. But it was not as important as missing the last rites of the saint.

WHY THE SUDDEN VISIBILITY AFTER BECOMING CEC?

Accusing me of harbouring ulterior motives, some people used to ask why my fiery attitude became visible only after I was appointed as the CEC. My answer was that however high ranking a bureaucrat may be, even of the level of cabinet secretary, he or she is only a civil servant. My suggestions were overruled by my superiors. But my conscience is clear. If I was silent in those earlier phases, it is because bonded labour does not speak.

At the ECI, things were different. I was only restricted by the Constitution and the statutes enacted by Parliament. I was definitely answerable to the courts and Parliament under the constitutional scheme. But otherwise, I had a free hand to work within these constraints. I was authorized to respond appropriately to the challenges faced by the commission—within those laws and rules—and I had to report to no one else.

Not many people really understood what I was doing. The effects were visible though, and even the common person perceived the changes. But there has always been a need for a certain degree of involvement with the issues facing the commission to understand what was happening within.

It would be good if one would familiarize oneself with the challenges I was facing as the CEC and the motives that were driving me. In other words, the person would need to understand what goals were set in the booklet of reforms that I had presented to the central government and what the fire in my belly was. Then all the apparent whimsicality would disappear and my actions would look logical.

The best I can say is that it would be fair to decide whether a person was rule-bound or not only after hearing what the person has to say on each matter. I stand by my assertion, that each of my decisions, regardless of how they were perceived, had sound reasoning as per the law. Whether people agreed with me or differed on the logic behind my decisions is another matter. But I cannot be charged for prima facie malicious intent—not a chance.

IS SESHAN'S DISPOSITION THAT OF A DICTATOR?

I have faced this criticism on a few occasions. Like all praises, this criticism was part of what came on my plate. Even now, I do not need a certificate of merit, most certainly not from those who have had axes to grind or nests to feather.

A distinct proof of dictatorship is that a person does not value the rule of law. A dictator does what he pleases—dictates! Was that the case with me?

I can say that I have lived by the dictum that 'it is criminal to underutilize one's powers that could advance a noble purpose'. I have pushed against the bounds of law as far as it was possible. But I can say with conviction that as a person with immense responsibilities as the CEC, I never broke the bounds of law—not when I postponed elections, not when I suspended elections, not when I amended the symbols order, and not when I set a deadline for the voter ID cards. After the court drew boundaries, wherever it drew them, there was no question of my overstepping those boundaries. Therefore, the charge that I was a dictator simply cannot hold water.

Being a dictator goes against my highest motivations. My inner strength arises from spirituality. I have my personal dharma to fulfil, and I had the dharma of my duty. Maintaining the rule of law was part and parcel of that dharma. Would I go against the very source of my strength?

WOULD THE TERM MEGALOMANIA APPLY?

A term occasionally used to describe me was megalomaniac. I wonder whether people really opened the dictionary to see what that word meant and checked whether it was applicable in my case. When it comes to knowledge, one should be clear that democracy does not work in certain things. If a million people say a foolish thing, it is still a foolish thing.

When it comes to a person who did relatively well in academics at school, topped the IPS exam and came second in the IAS exam, how would you describe him? Someone who eventually became union cabinet secretary; someone who, along with his team, was successful in achieving so much in the ECI; who is known by name to a huge section of the Indian society for mainly positive outcomes; in whose name, fan clubs have appeared as if he were a film star, how would you refer to such a person?

I never claimed that I was a saint and totally devoid of ego. But delusions of personal greatness are an impediment in one's way; this is a lesson from the Bhagavad Gita, and I was more than aware of it. What flaws I have are not those that numbed me into inefficiency. In fact, I had to battle great emotions when people were trying to foist on me a leadership role. I had to do great soul-searching to come to an answer, and the answer was that the nation deserved better than

Seshan. But if I was given the responsibility, I would not have shirked from it. I would have done my duty to the best of my ability.

Was I contemptuous of the positions that were offered to me: of an ambassador, a governor or an MP? No, I was not. I was certain that either I was not cut out for it, that it did not offer a challenge for me or that I was sceptical of the impact of being in that position. In any case, I did eventually contest for an MP's post, so there was no ego or grandeur in scoffing at it. Most of the times, when these positions were offered, there were undertones of wanting to get me out of the way—out of the ECI—that is why I responded the way I did. Was that a sign of greatness and madness? Or was it a sign of pragmatic (and soul-searching) assessment of the situation?

THE DAMAGE PERCEPTIONS CAN DO VIS-À-VIS OBJECTIVITY

I would like to say something about perceptions. I have told you that reporters very often said that I was 'good copy material' and 'cartoon material', too. It is important to note that whenever they came to see me, a predisposed attitude would automatically (voluntarily or involuntarily) come into play. To explain this, there is nothing better than to quote from the horse's mouth—a journalist. I would like to recount a piece from a write-up by a foreign journalist in June 1996. The reporter was on a mission to write about what had happened in Kashmir.[108]

He recalled an incident of pelting of stones in which a group of 200 or 300 persons had rushed into the street, shouting slogans and throwing stones. The security forces had responded by lobbing teargas shells and firing in the air. And the protesters had suddenly disappeared, but not before the presspersons present there clicked their photos. Then the presspersons scurried back to their hotel rooms with photos to show and stories to tell.

Then he went on to say that probably the stories were already half written in their minds and the field trip was a kind of confirmation of the plot that was preloaded in their minds.

---

[108]'Viewing Poll with a Jaundiced Eye', *Hindustan Times*, 9 June 1996.

Now, is it not true that most press reporters who go anywhere would have at least a small tendency to do the same? Of course, they would internally battle with it. Would the person coming to interview me come with an objective mind or with a coloured perception that would make him pick up on only those things that fit my preconceived image? It may be deliberate sensationalization to satisfy the editor or an involuntary and unintended act, but nonetheless, the damage is done.

The important question here is: Is truth not a casualty in this type of reporting?

The press showered me with both praise and criticism, and eventually, I accepted both with the same amount of equanimity. Both criticism and praise have to be taken with a pinch of salt. The comments about me were a result of the 'reality' as perceived through the respective reporters and editors, and also through the filter of character and leaning of the newspapers. The search for truth is the search for objectivity in these reports.

Speaking of critics, I admit I have my faults, but these were not necessarily represented correctly. It was evident that critics would have done what I had done had they been motivated by self-gratification or whatever else they were accusing me of. They accused me of love of ego, of self-gratification or of whimsical behaviour, and expected me to not behave in certain ways. But I am sorry, you have given me a job and power, which by God's will, I wield it completely—and rightly too—in pursuit of what is my duty. If one can see that I was motivated by my primary aim of free and fair elections, fair enough. If not, it's their problem.

THE EVOLVING PUBLIC ACCEPTANCE AND ENCOURAGEMENT

I started receiving positive responses from proactive 'citizens' who wrote to me, most of the times, with no other motive than concern for the motherland. The first of such letters came in as early as 1991 after a Doordarshan interview, which had happened immediately after I had postponed elections in Punjab. I had received many congratulatory messages on that occasion, praising me for my stand, for my thinking and for my responses. From there on, the flow of appreciation letters steadily picked up. There was a constant stream of letters that now form some 100 odd volumes.

The public support only grew stronger with the attempts of my impeachment, with my spats with the government over control over poll staff, with the implementation of the reforms, the work stoppage order of 2 August, the appointment of the two additional election commissioners, the peaceful completion of the elections of November 1993, and other such successes. By early 1994, people were even forming fan clubs. Many of these were in Andhra Pradesh, and the press reported such things from time to time. The beauty of these initiatives lay in the fact that neither did I have anything to do with them nor could I give them anything in return. They were all self-driven expressions of the participants' desire to do something good for the nation. Each such initiative deserved appreciation and respect on its own mite. Finding that the work I was doing offered hope for the country's redemption, my well-wishers did not hold back from expressing a wish that I take up a position of leadership in the country. I can quote from scores of letters that spoke of such anticipation. Needless to say, such expectation can promote great soul-searching. Questions as to whether I should actively pursue such an option and how I should do it naturally burdened my mind. Should I plunge into politics? Am I cut out for it? Do I have a right to take it up?

DO I PLUNGE INTO POLITICS?

At that time, I did have the desire to take a larger role. But as a student of international history, I could not find an example of even one non-political, moral leadership anywhere, let alone in India.

Was I looking for office—for a position, its perks, its privileges? I had been offered the ambassadorship and the governorship of a state of my choice in as early as 1991 and had said no. In fact, I had told the PM that I was not looking for a job but was looking for work. If I were asked to contest elections or asked whether I would stand for public office, the answer would be an unequivocal 'no.'

One thing was clear. Handling the assignment I had been given at that time, I had no duty other than as a CEC and as a citizen of the nation. If there was a question of taking up any kind of political activity, it could happen only when I was no longer the CEC. I was yet to address the question of entering politics that came from others and from within myself as well.

Do I take a plunge into politics? To be fair, I cannot say that I had one single answer to it. Over a period of time, as my popularity increased, this question came up in the public arena and became a matter of debate in the public space.

In an interview with a leading journalist, I said that I was prepared to take up the heaviest possible responsibility and would certainly take the plunge if the situation in the country were to deteriorate. But I categorically ruled out standing for any public office even though I was being asked by politicians from different political parties to 'come forward and take up leadership'.

Between the desire to take up leadership and the desire to hold myself back, I said the balance was absolutely even. I always thought that the decision was going to be serendipitous.

I was agonizing over what role to play. Could I join one of the existing political parties? No. Would I do something extra-constitutional? No. But I did not know what the available options were.

My greatest agony was that whatever changes I had made in the electoral process could be undone once I left the office of the CEC. Whenever I had tried to get the government to make systemic changes, I had met a stone wall. I almost thought this was done by the PM and his party deliberately. An indifferent successor could, in collusion with a non-benign PM, take elections back to not only the joke they were but even worse than they had been.

The hopeful factor amidst the despair was that people across the nation were rising to stand up to the misuse of authority and corruption. There was the collector of Gorakhpur who forced the food minister, Kalpnath Rai to end his election meeting because he went on speaking beyond the deadline. The collector of Satna in Madhya Pradesh blew the whistle when the governor's staff car was flying all around the constituency where his son was contesting and the election was finally scrapped. Officials were taking on politicians and finding the courage to say 'but this is not right.'

I ended the interview by saying that people across the board from different political parties told me that I should take a leadership role. I was aware that if I kept people waiting too long, whatever momentum had been generated would dissipate.

Even as I continued to give talks to audiences across the country, there was one occasion when I was invited to Haryana by the organizers to give a talk at Meham Chaubisi to a large crowd. Meham Chaubisi is considered to be a nerve centre of politics in Haryana. It was there that on 25 September 1857, the poor villagers of the area braved bullets to announce their love of freedom and equality. The event to which I was invited was oragnized to commemorate the martyrdom of 167 people who were killed during the incident. In the just levelled stadium, there was a *chabutra* built in their memory. An apex body called the *sarvakhap panchayat* honoured me with honorary membership and gave me a *pagri* (turban) and a stick as symbols of justice, honesty and fair play. These symbols signified my new status among them.

On that occasion, I clearly stated that I had no ambitions and that I did not intend to enter politics. All I wanted to do was carry out electoral reforms.

I pointed out that people had come to be disillusioned as politicians had destroyed the polity by playing caste and language politics. I said, 'Ours is an ancient civilization. Exploitation of caste, religious and regional divisions by politicians has to be stopped.' I mentioned that a man was not a Brahman by birth but by the purity of his thoughts.

Speaking of the reforms that were underway, I emphasized on my latest agenda to depute tax sleuths to monitor poll expenses of candidates in the coming elections. It is here that I also expressed the possibility of excusing teachers from poll duties in the future.

In February 1995, I was giving a talk at the B.J.B Autonomous College at Bhubaneswar as the chief guest at their annual day function. I said that I was also 'partisan'. 'I belong to my wife's party. She is my sole authority and I am her only supporter. The party goes on.'

So, you can see that even at this stage, the question of entering politics was churning in my mind. In 18 months, from the end of 1993, I had addressed close to 300 different gatherings. The audiences varied in kind. At one end were the tribal women of Rajasthan and at the other, the American Alumni Association in Mumbai. About 100 or 120 of the meetings were university gatherings.

Political leaders would come to me and ask me to take up leadership. These leaders were from different political parties. The desire to go ahead and the desire to hold back were evenly matched. My wife used to say I was mad because I would sit in the drawing room at three in the morning and ponder what to do.

TACKLING CORRUPTION

If there was one area that made me most angry and worried, it was corruption. You could not get an electricity connection repaired or pay the electricity bill without paying an extra five rupees. I can go on and on. Corruption in India was generated by corruption in elections. From my vantage point, I could see the rot. It was possibly this that made me think on the lines of an organization that would strike at corruption.

I was aware that there were small and big people in the country trying to do something to solve the problem in their own ways. My theory was that if I got enough dots, one day they would connect to form a network. In that sense, there were enough places at which movements against corruption were starting.

At that time, the one remedy that I was willing to shout about from the rooftops was an awakened public or Jan Chetna Jagran; that could connect the dots. What if all the people, all the workers could say, 'This is wrong, Mr Minister, you cannot come for an election meeting in a government car.' I was telling voters to go and sit in front of the minister's car.

The question of whether I would do something in public life or not was again put up to me in May 1995, just after the Bihar elections were completed. This time, it was Vir Sanghvi interviewing me for

The Sunday. His reading was that, though I had said that I was yet undecided on the issue, there was no doubt that I was headed for the political arena.

The discussion was taken up by the Deshbhakt Trust, which was taking shape at that time (mid-1995). It was an NGO. I was not an office bearer in it, but my wife was.

Somebody had given me money. I did not want to mix that with my private earnings. So, in order to park the ₹5 lakh somewhere, I had started the trust. I had drafted it, and it covered anything and everything one could think of. It was the most amazingly comprehensive thing that anybody could think of. Did that make me politically ambitious in the sense of becoming an MLA or MP? The answer was 'no'.

As for its main purpose, the thinking was still emerging. However, there was a general idea that we would be targeting corruption. 'Shoot corruption' was the term I used. I said that it would include people from all walks of life, except for politicians because that would give a feeling that I was using a trust as a camouflage to get into politics.

I pointed out that if I were to decide to join politics, I would not hide it and would announce it from Vijay Chowk. I would not remain in the CEC's job for even a minute after making the decision.

When Sanghvi suggested that the day when I would make the announcement at Vijay Chowk was drawing nearer, I said there was no doubt that I had reached a level of popularity from where it was impossible for me to run away. Because of the public request, I added, I was not going to shut out that option. But then the question was: how do I go about it? How do I get ₹200 crore to field 200 candidates? I was more than sure that the four major parties would be willing to take me into their fold. I narrowed down to three alternatives amongst the political parties and said, 'Whichever one I join, people like you will make fun of me.'

Then Sanghvi wanted to know that whether I would take up an offer if a party were to give me leadership and the freedom to choose candidates. To the query, I replied, 'There would be temptation to join politics...a temptation that would be too great to resist.' If the party would let me have a say in the character of the candidates, it would be extremely difficult not to yield to the temptation.

Then he asked me squarely, 'Are you going to take the plunge?' I considered the situation. I was left with over a year and a half at the CEC's office, and that meant that I had to hold some elections, including the Lok Sabha elections of 1996. Next, the government was not likely to pass any electoral reform legislation. Finally, there was the pending judgement in the Supreme Court.

I went on to tell Sanghvi how, in a conversation with the PM, we had arrived at a point where I told him, 'Anything that is within your power to give is ipso facto unacceptable'. So, that ruled out all public and semi-public offices. I found the offer of a vice-chancellor's post offered to me by a Congress MP rather funny when I had already rejected the chancellor's post. The option left was to do voluntary service or retire, and both were fine by me.

Sanghvi then suggested about the president or PM's posts. I said I would accept no less, not even the home minister's post. To him, that sounded arrogant. I replied that I had not applied for either yet and added that if the public of the country would chase me, then I would run for office. But then I added that this country deserved better than Seshan—that is what I thought.

I DID NOTHING MORE THAN MY JOB

So, you see, I have highlighted some of the 'publicity'-related things as it happened in those days. You would be able to sense what I felt. You must have figured out why I might have responded the way I did. Did I have the ambition to join politics or was I keen on finding a solution to the problems confronting the nation—which of the two was it? I would honestly say it was the latter. Would I use my position as the CEC to further my ambitions and would I do anything that is inconsistent with my role as the CEC? I never intended on doing any of the two things.

The popularity grew on its own, the members of the media came to me on their own (except for official reasons when the commission had to disseminate some information); the invitations to speak at various forums came in so thick and fast at one time that I was trying to dodge. The media took a lot of interest in caricaturing me in their work. I spoke my mind with them and many a time, the media themselves were a target for my expressed displeasure and criticism. When invited, where it was not improper and where I had the time, I went. And of course, I also did walk off from one or two meetings when my presence there was being misused for other reasons.

In any case, I don't think I overstepped the law ever. I never let down my guard when on duty. In my private and in my public life, I have always wished and done the best I could for the nation and for what is right. What the critics thought about all this was up to them.

∽

TWENTY TWO

THE FINAL EXAM AND A KIND RECOGNITION

With the new interpretation of the law coming into effect as regards the election commissioners, the rules were modified in the middle of the game, or as the saying goes 'the goalposts were shifted'. My duty now was to ensure that, even in this new set-up, things must work out in such a way that the primary aim of the commission—free and fair elections—was followed. There were three of us responsible for that now and I had to play my part.

On my arrival to India from USA in the end of July 1995, I immediately left for Pune for a few days. Gill was supposed to have relinquished charge the moment I touched down at Delhi. In the previous arrangement, it would have made no difference, since I was always in control. No decision would have been taken by my juniors without consulting me or having my implied consent. With the Supreme Court's handing over charge to Gill, it was now possible that decisions were made without my consent. The two commissioners had taken some decisions in my absence, one of which was an office order relating to how decisions would be taken by the three-member team. It was revisited early in the next year and on 16 February 1996, a final order was issued. This order clearly laid down the rules as to how the files would be seen by the three of us. The order had four main points:

1   Files requiring direction of the ECI will move from deputy election commissioner concerned via the CEC, to one election commissioner (Gill), and then to another (Krishnamurty) and back to the CEC.

2. Where any one of the commission members/CEC has amended or modified what has been stated earlier in the file, the file will go back for perusal of the other one or two members before being finalized and seen finally by the CEC. If there are no changes, after the CEC has seen the file, it will be marked to the concerned deputy directly from CEC, unless, for specific reasons, it is marked to some other person.

3. In cases of urgency, the routing may be short circuited, with the reasons recorded in writing.

4. This issues with the approval of the commission.

This order laid down that files could be seen in the comforts of our respective offices and at the same time, we could ensure that each had his say. Finally, the commission was running smoothly.

A great effort was made to make me leave. It took an enormous amount of patience for me to stay in my post. I learned to live with it. Not that these two friends of mine were causing any difficulty of any kind whatsoever. It was just that earlier, I could arrive at a decision in two minutes and now we had to go through a process of consultation and consensus.

Where the arrangement functioned as a tribunal, differences emerged. In one very important case, the commissioners turned down my verdict through majority vote. By a coincidence, it happened to be a case where the PM was involved. The verdict of the case is in public domain and anyone can access both points of view. I believed I had done the right thing. I suppose my two other friends also thought the same.

THE FINAL TEST

The big event of 1996 was the general elections to the Lok Sabha. Things had come full circle. I had started my work as the CEC with the elections of 1991, and now it was time to wind up—almost. It was a culmination of a process of reforms that we had started working on since the end of the previous Lok Sabha general elections.

A system for elections was in operation before I came into the scene. The ideas were already there, but the implementation was not up to the mark. A lot of changes happened in the early part of my tenure and the new initiatives were brought up to speed in consecutive elections. All these were further refined as per the requirement in the 1996 elections. The changes manifested in a series of orders issued by the commission towards preparing the ground for the impending election. In the final analysis, though no major new initiatives were taken in the three-member phase of the ECI, the reform process did not slacken. It rather got stabilized. Some fine-tuning was done, but the approach remained more or less the same insofar as the general instructions for elections were concerned. Let's take a look at the factors on which the commission had focussed its energies in the reform process.

On 7 February 1996, it was decided that the commission would request the appropriate agencies of the government, like the income tax and revenue intelligence authorities, to keep a close watch on the various developments and to use all available legal powers to ensure that purity of the elections was not damaged. Wherever and whenever necessary, the commission itself would move the courts of law.

On 23 February, an order was passed to all the chief electoral officers of the states and union territories and to the chief secretaries in respect to the model code of conduct. They were asked to monitor what the government was doing in terms of handing out doles before the elections, though, of course, the elections were still not announced.

On 7 March, there was a meeting between the home secretary of the central government and the ECI in which all three of us were present. It was part of a continuing dialogue with the government, but on that occasion, the preference for timing, security issues and other such matters were discussed.

On 13 March, the ECI issued an order relating to the restrictions on the possession of arms during elections. There was a recent development in the Patna High Court on this account. Anyway, the order included a ban on issue of license, mopping up operations by the police, review and assessment of all license holders, deposition of arms one week prior to the elections (keeping in mind exceptions for certain groups that are tradition bound), fool proof arrangements for custody of arms, prohibitory orders, vigil on transport of arms and ammunition by vehicles and trucks, and other such issues.

On 19 March, elections were announced and scheduled between 27 April and 21 May in four phases, and the notification were to be issued on 27 March. This was done after discussions and consultations with all political parties, state governments and union territories' administrators. Weather, economics, academics and other such conditions were taken into account. The present Lok Sabha's term was to end in early July, and so were those of certain state assemblies.

On 20 March, the actual dates on which the various constituencies were to go to the polls were announced. On that day, a letter was written to the chief electoral officers and chief secretaries regarding the voter ID cards. In principle, due to the slow progress made in issuing the cards, the ECI could not insist on their use. However, because a considerable expenditure was made on the preparation of the voter ID cards, it was decided that they would be used as an additional aid in helping the polling officials verify voters' identity. The presiding officers were to be given a miniature copy of the cards as and when they would be ready.

Instructions were also issued that absence of identity cards would not necessarily mean an inability to vote, provided the voter's name appeared in the voters' list. As for the returning officers, they were instructed to follow the proper civil procedure code while issuing notifications to voters to get themselves photographed or to prove their identities. As for deleting names from the voters' list, instructions were given to follow proper procedure and precautions. An exercise would have to be carried out to identify the names of those who had died or migrated or shifted from the constituency in which their names appeared in the electoral rolls.

On the evening of 25 March, the commission received a letter from the government suggesting various changes to the schedule of polls. It wanted the polls on 27 April to be reconsidered on account of several representations received; a long campaign period should be avoided; the date, 21 April, the for Kashmir elections was not appropriate; a separate notification should be issued for Kashmir and that the elections for J&K should be held in three phases instead of two.

The President was to issue notifications on 27 March, so there was hardly any time. An urgent meeting was held that evening, which went on up to 11.00 p.m. and an order was passed and dispatched then and there. In that meeting, the home secretary gave a presentation for close to an hour and a half. But it was decided that the status quo would be maintained partly due to exigencies and partly due to the irrelevance of the request. However, in respect of J&K, the point was taken into consideration and a three-phase election was approved.

On 27 March, an order related to television broadcasting was issued. In it, specific dos and don'ts were listed: do cover campaign speeches; do cover flags, posters, etc.; do discuss party manifestos; don't telecast inflammatory speeches; don't project just one candidate of a constituency. At the end, it was said that a recording of all the telecast material should be maintained for future reference. In case of any dispute, the commission's decision would be final.

On the same day, an order was issued regarding the provision of facilities to mediapersons for the coverage of the election. It was an updated version of the orders passed earlier, incorporating all the learning that had taken place over the years.

On 29 March, control rooms were established and details about time and contact numbers were circulated. The idea was that until mid-April, there would only be a day-long shift, but after that date, the rooms would be manned around the clock.

One day before the poll on 26 April, the *Deccan Chronicle* in its caricature series, Counter Point, showed a politician emerging in the moonlight with a suitcase loaded with money. The man is shown leaving his home, saying to his wife, 'Canvassing with placards is over, dear. We are now going for the final round of campaign!'

On 27 April, a curious order had to be passed regarding finger ink, which identified that a person has voted. Besides Lok Sabha elections, Bihar and UP were also to have elections for their legislative councils and the polling for this was to be held separately in certain cases. This confusion was caused by elections from the graduates and teachers constituency. The question was where to put the indelible ink. The answer was: left forefinger for Lok Sabha; left middle finger for re-poll; left ring finger for graduates and teachers constituency and for graduates' constituency; and left little finger for only teachers' constituency.

On 28 April, a note had to be circulated to call for everyone's attention to the High Court of Andhra Pradesh's order, dated 26 April 1996, that MPs were to be restrained from spending beyond what was specified in the local area development scheme until elections were over. This was, of course, in connection with the model code of conduct.

Another matter related to the model code of conduct happened in the case of two port trusts. In one instance, two persons allegedly belonging to the ruling party at the Centre were appointed to the Chennai Port Trust, and the commission received a complaint. On the commission's direction, the appointments were cancelled. A similar case took place in respect of the Kandla Port Trust (now called Deendayal Port Authority). A plea was made that the constitution of the board was necessary for many pressing reasons. The commission directed that, except for ex-officio trustees and those elected (15 out of 19), the four others appointed by the minister of surface transport, using his statutory powers, may be cancelled. Appointments made after 20 May would stand cancelled.

It is interesting to consider, at this point, a hypothetical situation. Suppose, I were the lone member of the commission and done the same thing in terms of exercising my powers. In such a situation, was it not very likely that some people would have pounced on me, saying that I was being arbitrary, dictatorial, whimsical, among other things? But since there were three of us, there was little scope for their making such comments.

On 4 May, the commission passed an instruction to the election expenditure observers that they would oversee counting of votes. The earlier instruction was the contrary. This was in response to a request by the political parties.

POSTAL BALLOT

An important development in this election was regarding postal ballots. This was one of my pending requests to the central government, especially in regard to the migrant voters from J&K. On 1 May 1996, an ordinance was passed that added a Clause(c) in Section 60 of the Representation of the People Act, 1951. It provided for a class of voters, 'notified' by the ECI, to vote by postal ballot.

The conduct of election rules was also appropriately amended. These were issued by the law ministry on the same day, jotting down specific details about how the postal ballot scheme was to be executed. Within the next two days, the ball was set rolling and instructions were issued for postal ballot. It would definitely create an impact where there had been large-scale migration, irrespective of the reason. The places to which these would apply immediately and the officers who were to act as assistant returning officers were immediately notified. A press release of the developments was issued on 5 May.

At last, service voters, voters on election duty, special voters and electors under preventive detention could vote by postal ballot by applying to the returning officer 10 days before the polls.

The election produced a hung House. The Congress and its allies had just garnered about 140 seats. The United Front managed a tally of 179 seats and elected Deve Gowda as its leader. The BJP and its allies Shiv Sena, Samata Party, Haryana Vikas Party and SAD had a tally of 194. The United Front finally came to power with the external support of the Congress. Gowda became the PM.

So, by mid-June, the political transition happened and a new team started heading government at the Centre. But the old team was very much present in the background, as they were giving external support to the party in power.

Taking stock of how we conducted the 1996 elections, I could say that we would have done better had the voter ID cards been issued.

But other than that, it went well. It is another matter that a lot more people spoke well of the commission's efforts this time compared to previous polls.

AN UNEXPECTED COMPLIMENT AND RECOGNITION

A surprise awaited me in early July 1996. One fine day, some reporter from the Philippines interviewed me in my office. It was like any other interview. A few days later, someone called me up from Philippines at 8.30 a.m. and told me that I had won the Ramon Magsaysay Award. Incidentally, previous winners of the award are requested to suggest names for a particular year's award. These persons are not supposed to tell their nominees about it. To this day, I do not know who recommended my name. They have their internal process of finalizing the name. That year, I was selected for my government services.

The award was announced on 8 July. I called up Jaya, who was away in Madras at the time, to tell her about it. A stream of congratulatory messages, calls and visits immediately followed from people hailing from all walks of life.

The Pioneer reported its impression of my disposition that day, saying that I was obviously in a contemplative mood. They did not find me feverish with excitement or unduly overjoyed, but rather more mellow and congenial: 'Mr Seshan said he was feeling happy, grateful, humble and yet worried on hearing that he had won the award. "Worried that I should live up to the superlatives used in the citation," he said. Quoting from the Bhagavad Gita, Mr Seshan described how he was not unduly elated or flustered but steady in his happiness.'[109]

Almost all papers wrote positively, complimenting and congratulating me, except for one write-up in the *Blitz*, which questioned my fairness as an executive within the commission and quoted several anonymous ECI officials of lower rank who said that I ill-treated people in the commission.

One paper took pride in the fact that India had figured in the international award for government service. The previous year, it was

---

[109]'Mellowed Seshan May Turn to Books after Retirement', *The Pioneer*, 9 July 1996.

Kiran Bedi. Several organizations took the pain to hold functions to congratulate me on receiving the award. My two colleagues were not lagging behind and made it a point to go out of their way and applaud me. There were many others, including the juniors at work, friends and family, who extended their best wishes.

The *Hindustan Times* on 10 July printed an editorial titled 'A Worthy Award'. Some of its excerpts were as follows:

[...] Overt rigging and booth-capturing, for long an essential feature of election in several parts of this country, have manifestly declined [...]

[...] Mr. Seshan, more by bluster than by constitutional authority, was able to reduce ostentatious campaigning by the affluent candidates.

[...] With a spectral model code of conduct with no legal sanction of any sort, Mr Seshan nearly achieved the impossible, namely stopping governments from announcing official projects to be projected as party benevolence to the people [...][110]

There were also reports from Pakistan. The cricket team captain, Imran Khan, was reported to have expressed his appreciation of my work and also expressed a desire that I extend possible help in his country.

There is not much I can remember of the actual ceremony, except that my wife and some friends attended at their own expense. There was a ceremony in which I got a citation, a medal and a cash award. There were some speeches, interviews, a dinner, after which we were back. The actual award event, which took place in the first week of September, was not covered as extensively as the declaration of the award. I guess, by then, it was a two-month-old story. It was overall a simple affair but a new experience nonetheless. It has built a reputation over the years and the award is considered as the Asian Nobel Prize. For me, personally, it was a kind honour and a fine experience.

---

[110]'A Worthy Award', *Hindustan Times*, 10 July 1996.

THE CHALLENGE FACED IN J&K

As I had mentioned earlier, elections were declared for the Lok Sabha in all states, including J&K. Both J&K and Uttar Pradesh were under President's Rule and their assembly elections were not held together with the parliamentary elections. As for Kashmir, it had already been 12 years since it had had an election. Most, if not all, well-wishers hoped that the democratic process would return to the state.

The problem of delimitation was settled, but there were problems in getting voters' lists updated in a proper manner. The situation in Kashmir was far from conducive to fair polls, and not very different from what I had assessed in December 1994. The government, however, sometimes said that it wanted to go ahead with polls, and sometimes it did not want to. In fact, there was a clash of opinions within the Cabinet. The situation on the ground was so bad that it was difficult to get voter lists updated because the threat of violence deterred the staff from doing so. By the end of 1995, when all three commissioners went to take a look at the ground situation, we more or less came to the same conclusion that holding free and fair polls in the situation was not possible.

The Supreme Court took the initiative in the matter of Kashmir, and passed an order on 11 January 1996, asking the Centre and the ECI to arrive at a consensus on the elections. It said that if a decision cannot be taken, then a judicial decision would be taken. The ECI agreed to reconsider the issue. Eventually, an understanding was reached with the government that the Lok Sabha elections could be conducted in Kashmir, but the Kashmir assembly elections could be delayed and held separately along with the Uttar Pradesh assembly elections, which was under President's Rule at that time. That is how the elections came to be held separately.

Eventually, the Kashmir elections were held in four phases during September. The elections went off rather smoothly.

Security forces were used extensively. The other two commissioners toured the state to take a look at the arrangements. It was they who addressed the press most of the time in respect of Kashmir. I was aware of the system in place and was responsible for ensuring that it worked well and that decisions were being taken appropriately. There was the usual trouble. A right-wing militant group that had lost face in the Lok Sabha elections did not participate in the assembly elections and called for a boycott. The first three phases went off without much problem. There was a strike on the day before the fourth phase of polling. But the turnout was good—given the conditions, the 53 per cent voter turnout was commendable. The National Conference came out victorious, and Farooq Abdullah took over as the CM.

The Uttar Pradesh elections took place simultaneously. There were rough spots, but it was all over by early October. The assembly came into existence on 16 October, but since no one could form the government, President's Rule was reimposed. However, on 26 March the following year, the BSP and the BJP came together to form a government. The Uttar Pradesh elections effectively brought the important assignments in my tenure to an end. Beyond that, the decisions that had to be taken were internal.

TWENTY THREE

I TAKE A BOW

The ECI did everything it could within its limits to take the process of development and change forward. The procedures in respect of improving the quality of elections were finally consolidated at reasonably good positions. But then, this was as much as I could do. Some of it was achieved as I could cajole the government into action. But how I wished there were titans amongst the leaders of that day, amongst the leaders in the government.

HAD THERE BEEN TITANS AMONGST LEADERS...

To me, Mahatma Gandhi, Jawaharlal Nehru, J.R.D. Tata, Martin Luther King and Nelson Mandela were leaders. Neither were there any such leaders in India at that time nor do I see any in today's times. Even to watch the greatness of leaders like Gandhiji and Nehru was an extraordinary experience in itself for me.

When the Magsaysay award was announced, on 8 July, I was interviewed by many pressmen. One from *The Pioneer* wanted to know what I was contemplating in respect of my future in politics. I replied that the only kind of politics I would enter would be the one in which I will wipe every tear from every face.

A little later, in a television interview on 22 September 1996, I admitted that I was tempted to seriously consider the job of the president or vice president. But then, I also pointed out that the two jobs would not provide the work I wanted to do. Anyway, those were remote possibilities.

Evaluating whether I was presidential material, I said in the interview, 'I allowed my mind to wander and think about getting into a palace. Even a beggar has the prerogative to dream.'

I added that there was a likelihood of my resignation after the elections in Uttar Pradesh were over by 15 October. I would consult an astrologer to decide the appropriate time. My job was done; my work was over. Between the said date and the day my tenure was to get over in December, there were no elections. I had had a long innings. I said I had several irons in the fire and would pick up one of those.

I had no delusions about myself. I even said in an interview that the maximum a frog could blow himself up to is a toad. A frog cannot become a lion. If someone needed me and gave me a role, it would be good. But if I thought the role was not good enough for me as I was much bigger, I would turn it down.

WHILE BIDDING ADIEU

Sure enough, the time for my stepping down neared. Many papers wrote this way and that, and the usual prejudices also showed. But on an average, there was appreciation for the work done and speculation of what I would do when I leave.

Even when there were just weeks to go, I was being invited across the country for lectures at various forums, and there were official visits to go on.

In October 1996, I went to the Mata Amritanandmayi Ashram in Kollam. It was in connection with her birthday celebrations. On that occasion, I was honoured with the opportunity of inaugurating some houses built under one of her mission's projects and a hospital established near the ashram. I remarked at that time that she was a tower of light to the whole world and expressed the hope that the strength derived from Amma would help people fight evil forces, including politicians.

By the end of October, when I was out on one such tour, some decisions were taken at the commission in my absence. The procedure that was laid down clearly stated that decisions could be taken if a commissioner was on leave but not when one was on tour. There was a mismatch in the interpretation of the procedure, and an unpleasant exchange ensued. I insisted on taking back the decisions that were illegal because the procedure was not followed. It was a matter of principle. I might as well have agreed with the order and ruled exactly in that manner, but this was not the right thing to do. Of the two decisions, one was in respect of the revision of electoral rolls in Assam and the other pertained to the acceptance of Mendiratta's resignation. Mendiratta was one of the secretaries who had been in the commission during my entire tenure and had done an excellent job. It led to a needless exchange, and the environment remained acrimonious. But life goes on, and the time for stepping down was due. There was a mention of the fact that I was on tour during most of the month; Gill joined Krishnamurty in pointing fingers at my travel plans. The position remained at that.

On 1 December, I addressed a press conference, where I answered many questions. The following excerpts reflect what the press wanted to know and what I had to say at that time. On the issue of changing laws to improve elections, I said: 'I would give myself one out of 10 if I were generous.'

When asked about being approached by political parties to join them, I replied, 'I have kept all of them at the level of suspended friendship. Neither have I said yes nor have I said no.'

As the topic of becoming president of India was picked up, I said, 'Why should I not build castles in the air if I think that something good can come out of it?'

Sharing my views on the condition of media today, I said, 'Several institutions in the country have fallen in standards. But the media is the worst in this respect.'

Some asked me about the charge of launching a deliberate anti-politician campaign over the last six years, to which I said, 'Yes, I went out in search of politicians, so be it.'

When asked about the Deshabhakta Trust and whether it would be me employed in some way, I said, 'I don't want staff, a car or telephone. I just want a square metre that I can scrub and clean.'

On 5 December, at the Pink City Press Club at Jaipur, I was asked about my future plans. I said I have a house in Chennai. And my wife has one in Bangalore. I can go to either of the two places after 11 December.

On 8 December, I was at Palghat to deliver a valedictory address at the national seminar on 'Challenges of Management Beyond 2000 AD' organized by the Palghat Management Association. It was my last official function, and I wanted it to be there, as I had started my journey from there.

On that occasion, I spoke little about what I was looking forward to in the future. I said that I did not need a job, but I needed work. Various national parties had asked me to join them, but I stayed equidistant from them.

Needless needling by the establishment happened even in these last few days. After spending 36 years as a civil servant, where money in thousands of crores must have passed under my signature, after six years at the commission, where crores of rupees were dealt with in elections, and several lakhs of rupees were spent just to do up the cabins of the newly appointed election commissioners, would I misappropriate bags?! Someone raked the issue in the press. The author of the piece was eager to put his weapon, the pen, to the concerns of several junior officers who had apparently written five letters since October regarding ₹9,000 worth of bags to put things that were in the home office authorized to a CEC. The article conveniently forgot to mention that a person on transfer has a minimum of one month after he gives up his office, and a retired officer gets three months, to settle his dues. After listing what all actions could be taken against me in connection with my retirement on account of this, he ended the article and the excitement by saying what the juniors said: 'We doubt whether the matter would come to that.'

WHO DO I HAND OVER THE CHARGE TO?

There were two contenders for the post of the CEC, Krishnamurty and Gill—the former senior in age by one year but the latter with longer service and vast administrative experience. Some papers speculated that since the Supreme Court had put Gill in charge of the commission in July 1995, he would be the more likely candidate for the post. On 10 December, most papers suggested that Gill was likely to succeed me. One of them brought out that a vacuum is unlikely in the event of a succession not being announced before the expiry of my tenure. They attributed this to the fact that the Supreme Court had earlier ruled that Gill would look after the affairs of the ECI in my absence.

On 11 December, the newspapers declared that it would be Gill. But until the last moment, I had absolutely no official word from the government as to who would take charge.

'Why did you not go to office on the day of retirement on 11 December?' 'Is it true that you did not go?' These are the questions that some people closely associated with me still ask.

Yes, indeed, on that day, I did not go to office. Everyone knew that I was going to retire on 11 December. In fact, I had started mentioning at different places, six months in advance, '11 December is my last date in office', so that they would not forget the date.

According to government rules, I was supposed to hand over responsibility on 11 December before afternoon. I was waiting at home until 3.30 p.m., expecting the government to announce the name of my successor. But there was no such announcement. There was a time when I was at a loss as to whom I should hand over the responsibility to.

Just to sign a piece of paper and hand it over to the undersecretary, it was not necessary for me go to Nirvachan Sadan in person. It was six months since I had set all my files in order.

Having waited till 3.30 p.m., and before someone could point a finger at me that I had not handed over the job, I wrote my handing over responsibility letter and sent it across to the undersecretary.

Some journalists were apparently waiting for me at Nirvachan

Sadan, expecting that I would come to office. They had to leave disappointed.

The new CEC, M.S. Gill, had been an IAS officer for just as many years as me. He had been working as a secretary in the agriculture department before he came to the commission. He had experience on his side, and he was mature, too. Having all the qualities necessary for this post, I had a feeling that he would do a perfect job.

I neither have any personal ill-feelings towards Gill nor Krishnamurty. The only thing I did not like was the manner in which they were appointed. Krishnamurty would often indulge in loose talk. I never told anyone what he used to say except for the meeting on 11 October. I had narrated that in the case I had filed in the court to establish that the intention of the government in appointing them was not above board. I also mentioned the same incident in *The Regeneration of India*. Be that as it may, there was not enough love lost between us for formal speeches or teary goodbyes.

I was stepping out into a new phase of life, and I could go out in peace, happy that I had done my job.

AND I LOOK ON

At the time of my retirement, the home ministry was kind enough to keep my security intact until further orders. For some time after I retired, so long as the ministry found it fit according to the threat perception, I was given Z-plus protection.

I have since shifted to my house in Madras and have managed to keep myself occupied. In the years since that day when I stepped down from the CEC's post, much has happened: a trip to Washington where I met the President of USA; a trip to Sri Lanka where I met the PM and President, and delivered a talk; developmental work in the Deshbhakta Trust in whose activities I was involved for some time; the presidential elections of 1997 that I contested; the Lok Sabha Elections of 1999; and a host of educational institutions with which I have worked, the Karads' School of Government in Pune being one of them. Today, I continue to be associated with many of these activities. My telephone has not stopped ringing. And I still answer the phone myself.

For the moment, I sign off in gratitude for the opportunities I have had to serve in various positions throughout my career. I must, of course, say a word of thanks to the excellent teams in each of my positions in the nearly 42 years since I entered the IAS in 1955. I may have been the Alsatian—what many called me behind my back—that growled, barked and bit. But in each and every post I served, there was a great team behind me that not only did their individual jobs but also helped me do mine. I am grateful to each and every one of them. Special mention is due to my team during my tenure as the CEC:

DEC Bagga, Secretary Mendiratta, the other administrative officers, the advocates who represented me in the courts, the other staff in my office and the staff in every state's chief electoral officer's office, down the line to those who manned every polling booth. The commission's success rests on them having done their duties conscientiously. I am grateful to each and every officer and staff who assisted me in my various positions and made my work simpler and better.

As I look back on my life and career, all that I can think and say is, 'Life has been great—stormy, but great!'

I look on in wait for titans, in the hope that the youth will march with them to make this nation rise to its ancient greatness. It is still not happening the way it should, but it will, and of that, I have no doubt.

ACKNOWLEDGEMENTS

We finally get to see in print the story of the man and the reforms that have made an invaluable contribution to the largest democracy in the world that is India.

People who have seen him up close say that Mr Seshan has rendered 'yeomen' service to the nation; and all those who have worn a similar set of shoes or have walked in the corridors of power in India acknowledge in their heart of hearts—even if grudgingly—that his contribution to the nation is vital. A hundred horsemen thundering across the countryside moving from one location to another, terrifying voters and capturing polling booths—such things can happen only in banana republics. The reality is that such an incident was actually reported during Mr Seshan's time in one of the places in India. As of today, 2023, we Indians have weaned away our nation from going that way and credit for most of it must be attributed to Mr Seshan. He has shown how through his own example, through his righteous passion, and through promoting the correct behaviour in the officialdom during elections, the simplest of government officers can be transformed into persons of courage and daring, delivering a great future for the nation. It is a great story of how, inch by inch, things were turned around. And we get to read that in this memoir.

I, Nixon Fernando, was fortunate enough to have helped Mr Seshan with the research towards his book. With Mr Seshan having passed on, I take it upon myself to acknowledge some persons involved in this project. But rather than acknowledging people and their efforts on behalf of Mr Seshan, it would be more proper that I propose a vote of thanks on behalf of the readers instead.

Most of all, we are all thankful to Dr Vishwanath Karad and Mr Rahul Karad, eminent and innovative educationists of the MIT World Peace University, Pune, who were, first of all, able to convince the hesitant author, and then even provide the support, including my services, required to finally pen down his memoir. Thanks are due to (Late) Mrs Jayalakshmi Seshan, his wife, who believed that the story must be told and helped in convincing Mr Seshan about it; although she failed to convince her husband to have his memoir published in his lifetime itself.

Thanks are due to friends and former colleagues of Mr Seshan, including Dr D.K. Sankaran, IAS (Retd), Dr Joyce Sankaran, IAS (Retd), Mr D.S. Bagga, former deputy election commissioner, Mr S.K. Mendiratta, former secretary at the election commission, and other lawyer friends who went through the manuscript and helped with the edits, trimming it down and providing initial feedback.

A big thanks to Mr R.K. Mehra and his son, Mr Kapish Mehra, both of whom met Mr Seshan personally around 10 years ago even when Mr Seshan was unsure of having his memoir published, expressing that they would be happy to render their services as publishers. After Mr Seshan's demise, when the manuscript was presented to him, Mr Kapish took it upon himself to have the book published and we are thankful to him for keeping his word.

Thanks are due to the incredible team at Rupa, including Yamini, Sandhya and Sakschi amongst others, who have done an amazing job in scaling down the book to an acceptable size, in rounding off the rough edges, while, in the process, converting the manuscript into an elegant book.

We also extend our gratitude to the Narayaneeyam Trust who preserve and provide access to Mr Seshan's records. This, in turn, helped in bringing completeness to the raw manuscript in the final phases of editing.

Nixon Fernando,
Former Research Assistant to T.N. Seshan

INDEX

Advani, L.K., 101, 104, 112, 116, 137, 150

Andhra Pradesh, 7, 111, 117, 149, 150, 155, 157, 166, 213, 237, 250, 251, 263, 264, 326, 338

Assam, 21, 72, 115, 123, 124, 125, 166, 167, 207, 222, 232, 261, 290, 296, 346

Bagga, D.S., 134, 146, 159, 189, 196, 300, 302

Ballygunj, 157, 158, 164

Banerjee, Mamata, 157, 263

Bangalore, 33, 38, 54, 69, 71, 73, 75, 143, 248, 266, 347

Bhabha Atomic Research Centre, BARC, 67, 265

Bharatiya Janata Party, BJP, 101, 102, 103, 104, 105, 118, 123, 131, 136, 137, 143, 152, 153, 156, 157, 158, 161, 164, 167, 190, 193, 196, 223, 241, 242, 243, 250, 270, 274, 283, 297, 339, 343

Bihar, 108, 111, 112, 113, 117, 118, 122, 136, 149, 150, 156, 157, 159, 160, 161, 163, 164, 166, 167, 225, 238, 242, 264, 267, 268, 269, 270, 271, 272, 273, 274, 275, 278, 282, 283, 284, 285, 286, 298, 318, 329, 338

by-polls, 149, 156

Chavan, S.B., 263

Communist Part of India (Marxist), CPI (M), 131, 136, 157, 158, 159, 161, 165, 190, 241, 242, 263

Congress, 26, 27, 28, 49, 61, 96, 101, 102, 103, 104, 107, 110, 117, 118, 122, 123, 128, 129, 130, 131, 135, 136, 138, 139, 140, 147, 149, 156, 157, 158, 159, 160, 161, 163, 167, 189, 190, 225, 234, 242, 244, 250, 263, 270, 274, 283, 286, 331, 339

Constitution, viii, 16, 118, 130, 133, 152, 153, 164, 168, 171, 173, 174, 176, 177, 178, 179, 180, 181, 184, 185, 193, 194, 195, 199, 218, 220, 224, 225, 239, 241, 244, 260, 261, 269, 273, 274, 287, 288, 289, 291, 295, 301, 303, 305, 310, 311, 312, 313, 321

Dravida Munnetra Kazhagam, DMK, 61, 62, 96, 105

Electronics Corporation of India Ltd, ECIL, 215, 265, 266

Etawah, 118, 121, 145, 146, 147, 148, 149

Fernandes, George, 242, 243, 274

Gandhi, Indira, 61, 62, 64, 68, 69, 70, 73, 77, 82, 84, 115, 234
Gandhi, Rajiv, 34, 73, 74, 75, 77, 81, 84, 85, 86, 91, 92, 98, 113, 115, 139, 150, 215, 319
Gujarat, 72, 150, 264, 267, 268, 269, 270, 279, 283
Gujral, I.K., 118, 119

Haryana, 108, 111, 117, 176, 177, 223, 264, 269, 328, 339
Hegde, Ramakrishna, 93, 140

impeachment, 129, 134, 136, 137, 138, 143, 144, 149, 150, 163, 165, 184, 203, 313, 326
Indian Express, 99, 118, 123, 127, 164, 187, 193, 195, 238, 239, 257, 291, 309

Jammu and Kashmir, J&K, 108, 123, 124, 175, 176, 187, 261, 337, 339, 342
Janata Dal, 99, 106, 118, 124, 131, 134, 135, 137, 143, 149, 157, 160, 161, 164, 165, 193, 242, 243, 250, 270, 274
Jayalalithaa, J., 105
Jethmalani, Ram, 161, 193, 294

Kanchi, 97, 98, 114, 151, 226

Left Front, 111, 134, 138, 144, 150, 158, 163, 164, 165
Lok Sabha, 108, 109, 113, 115, 118, 124, 131, 135, 137, 149, 156, 163, 181, 182, 221, 222, 238, 240, 241, 242, 243, 331, 334, 335, 336, 338, 342, 343, 350

Madhya Pradesh, 21, 101, 102, 116, 117, 229, 261, 327
Madras, 2, 5, 7, 8, 9, 16, 17, 19, 21, 22, 27, 29, 34, 36, 38, 43, 45, 47, 50, 53, 57, 60, 61, 67, 226, 227, 274, 340, 350
Madurai, 10, 25, 26, 27, 31, 40, 43, 44, 45, 46, 47, 48, 49, 50, 51, 52, 53, 56, 62, 81
Maharashtra, vii, 63, 72, 117, 191, 237, 264, 266, 267, 268, 269, 270, 277, 278, 279, 280, 281, 282, 283, 285
Manipur, 267, 278, 279
Mukherjee, Pranab, 116, 130

National Front, 134, 137, 144, 150, 161, 163, 165
Nehru, Jawaharlal, 20, 22, 344

Opposition, 28, 62, 86, 87, 130, 131, 138, 143, 149, 150, 160, 161, 162, 164, 168, 193, 239, 240, 249
Orissa, 116, 135, 157, 266, 267, 268, 269, 270, 271, 273, 275, 278, 279, 283, 309

Palghat, viii, 2, 5, 6, 8, 9, 11, 32, 347
Palkhiwala, N.A., 288, 289, 291, 292, 294
Patil, Shivraj, 163, 165, 242
Patna, 109, 112, 118, 119, 120, 121, 135, 147, 159, 160, 184, 336
Pawar, Sharad, 116, 237, 268, 280, 281
Punjab, 115, 122, 123, 124, 125, 126, 127, 128, 129, 130, 131, 132, 133, 134, 136, 137, 139, 156, 163, 177, 204, 223, 261, 325

Rajya Sabha, 90, 92, 137, 138, 139, 143, 159, 160, 178, 181, 219, 220, 221, 222, 225, 240, 241, 242, 243, 262, 267, 315
Ramaswamy, G., 145, 186, 200, 288

Rao, P.V. Narasimha, 128
Representation of the People Act, 90,
101, 105, 118, 119, 124, 128, 130,
133, 152, 153, 160, 171, 174, 176,
177, 179, 181, 196, 218, 220, 221,
224, 233, 235, 237, 240, 247, 250,
252, 253, 259, 339

Samajwadi Janata Party, SJP, 118, 139,
144
Samajwadi Party, SP, 250
Sarabhai, Vikram, 66, 67, 68
Sethna, Homi, 67
Sharma, Shankar Dayal, 161, 162
Shekhar Chandra, 94, 95, 97, 108, 113,
115, 128, 240
Shiromani Akali Dal, SAD, 123, 127,
339
Shiv Sena, 104, 105, 277, 283, 339
Singh, Arun, 77, 82
Singh, V.P., 91, 92, 93, 94, 95, 106, 118,
136, 140, 149, 164
Singh Yadav, Mulayam, 112, 121
Special Protection Group, SPG, 82, 83,
84, 85, 92
Subramanian, Swamy, 63, 96, 98, 107,
121, 134, 135, 138, 155, 222

symbol, 101, 102, 104, 105, 106, 107,
152, 153, 154, 245, 255, 286

Tamil Nadu, viii, 9, 22, 23, 34, 35, 37,
38, 42, 43, 47, 48, 50, 52, 53, 61, 62,
71, 72, 105, 183, 209, 210, 245
Telugu Desam Party, 139, 149, 157, 241
The Times of India, 104, 112, 190, 266,
271, 275, 277, 280, 281, 298, 320
Trivandrum, 27, 226

United Nations, UN, 150, 151, 321
Uttar Pradesh, 20, 72, 111, 117, 121,
163, 203, 204, 217, 238, 250, 342,
343, 345

Vajpayee, Atal Bihari, 119, 123, 242
Venkataraman, R., 37, 46, 63, 97, 150,
161

West Bengal, 111, 157, 158, 164, 166,
178, 191, 216, 261, 262, 263, 271

Yadav, Laloo Prasad, 118, 119, 271, *see
also* Yadav, Lalu Prasad, 238, 264,
274, 284